SchoolCounselor.com 2.0

A Friendly and Practical Guide
to the World Wide Web

Russell A. Sabella, Ph.D.

Copyright ©2003

Russell A. Sabella, Ph.D.

Library of Congress Control Number 2003103185

ISBN 1-930572-24-7

Publisher—

Educational Media Corporation®
P.O. Box 21311
Minneapolis, MN 55421-0311

(763) 781-0088 or (800) 966-3382

www.**educationalmedia**.com

Production editor—

Don L. Sorenson

Graphic design—

Earl Sorenson

Cover design—

Adquarters, Inc
Ft. Lauderdale, Florida

(954) 525-1901

www.adquarters.com

Russell A. Sabella, Ph.D.

Preface

School counseling is a relatively young profession compared to other mental health or human services related fields. Thanks to many pioneers and dedicated practitioners, the profession has made tremendous progress in developing a systematic approach to assisting students succeed in their personal, social, academic, and career endeavors. Comprehensive developmental guidance and counseling programs have become more clearly defined as are emerging school counselor roles. The arrival of the Internet and the World Wide Web can be both an opportunity and a threat to future progress.

An opportunity exists for embracing this powerful medium for training, program management, support, accountability, service delivery, and much more. Professional school counselors have the opportunity to use the Internet to better inform and interact with important others. The Web can help us teach school administrators, teachers, parents, and community stake holders about the nature of school counseling. Indeed, if educators and others better understood school counseling, they could then better support the sometimes extensive challenges that school counselors face. The Web presents an opportunity to engage our students whom are quite rapidly adopting information technology. There also exists ample opportunity for more creatively, and perhaps more effectively, delivering guidance and counseling knowledge and skills via the Internet. However, since interactivity, by its very nature, requires both senders and receivers, the potential is only realistic when everyone is involved.

Like any powerful tool, the World Wide Web also poses potential threats to school counseling. It presents a dilemma between enhanced availability and outreach (high-tech) and facilitating the core conditions of empathy, genuineness, and unconditional positive regard (high-touch). In the absence of Internet literacy, school counselors may find themselves already left behind in a state of inadequacy, confusion, and incompetence. At the very least, those who avoid learning about technology may not be able to make fully informed decisions about how to invest their time, work, and money. Opting out of technology literacy is to opt out of a rapidly developing information culture.

Although there have been many texts written about the Web, this book is especially designed to help school counselors in a step-by-step fashion. The chapters will introduce you to the Web, help you gain access, effectively navigate, and interact with others around the world. As a starting place, I have included illustrations and examples of resources throughout including over 1,200 counseling Websites. This book will also help you think about and design your own guidance and counseling Web site. Finally, I have included a chapter regarding special issues, ranging from Internet addiction to WebCounseling, about which I believe counselors should be aware.

You will also find helpful the supporting website for this book located at www.schoolcounselor.com. There, you may find summaries and links of chapters, an option to subscribe to a free newsletter, extra resources, a website database, and more.

Traveling the World Wide Web can sometimes be an adventure and other times a daring journey. Our competence in using the Web will in large part determine our experience with this blazing medium. Before you begin, you might imagine that you are on an exotic vacation to multiple destinations. Prepare, have fun, learn a lot, and be amazed.

Please feel free to send me an e-mail about your journey; about how technology has indeed helped you become more effective, efficient, or have more fun in your work; or send feedback/ suggestions to consider for *SchoolCounselor.com 3.0*.

Russell A. Sabella, PhD

March 2003

Acknowledgments

I would like extend my appreciation to the millions of people whom have freely shared their resources over the Web thus contributing to its value. I want to thank my wife and partner in life, Betty, for her continued support and encouragement. Thank you also to my two sons, Joseph and Matthew, for the joy you bring into my life which helps me to stay balanced and have fun.

About the Author

Russell A. Sabella, PhD is a counselor educator in the Counseling Program, College of Education, Florida Gulf Coast University. He specializes in comprehensive developmental guidance and counseling, counseling and technology, sexual harassment risk reduction, solution-focused brief counseling, and peer helper programs and training. He is also President-Elect of the American School Counselor Association. Dr. Sabella conducts technology literacy training for counselors throughout the country. He may be reached via e-mail at sabella@schoolcounselor.com.

Readme.txt

SchoolCounselor.com 2.0 is a major upgrade of the first version. As is the case with software upgrades, I am including a Readme.txt file so that you may learn more about new features, known "bug" repairs, and any other important user information:

- Links throughout the book were analyzed and replaced if necessary.
- Of course, references were updated and added.
- Each chapter was enhanced with updated information and reference to tools where applicable.
- Chapter four was added as there are now many more methods for dealing with web-sites as compared to only a few years ago.
- New and more descriptive graphics have been added to further aid in learning.
- My photo on the back cover has definitely changed, that's all I'll say about that.

Table of Contents

Russell A. Sabella, Ph.D.

Russell A. Sabella, Ph.D.

CHAPTER ONE

Get Ready ...
School Counselors and Technology

The following transcript of an alleged conversation between a computer user and a technical help person was circulated over the Internet not too long ago:

Q - "Computer helpdesk; may I help you?"

A - "Yes, well, I'm having trouble with my word processing program."

Q - "What sort of trouble?"

A - "Well, I was just typing along, and all of a sudden the words went away."

Q - "Went away?"

A - "They disappeared."

Q - "Hmm." So what does your screen look like now?"

A - "Nothing."

Q - "Nothing?"

A - "It's blank; it won't accept anything when I type."

Q - "Are you still inside the program or did you get out?"

A - "How do I tell?"

Q - "Can you see the C:\ prompt on the screen?"

A - "What's a C:\ prompt?"

Q - "Never mind." Can you move the cursor around on the screen?"

A - "There isn't any cursor, I told you, it won't accept anything I type."

Q - "Does your monitor have a power indicator?"

A - "What's a monitor?"

Q - "It's the thing with the screen on it that looks like a TV." Does it have a little light that tells you when it's on?"

A - "I don't know."

Q - "Well, then look on the back of the monitor and find where the power cord goes into it." Can you see that?"

A - "Yes, I think so."

Q - "Great." Follow the cord to the plug, and tell me if it's plugged into the wall."

A - "Yes, it is."

Q - "When you were behind the monitor, did you notice that there were two cables plugged into the back of it, not just one?"

A - "No."

Q - "Well, there are — I need you to look back there again and find the other cable."

A - " Okay, here it is."

Q - "Follow it for me, and tell me if it's plugged securely into the back of your computer."

A - "I can't reach."

Q - "Uh huh." Well, can you see if it is?"

A - "No."

Q - "Even if you, maybe, put your knee on something and lean way over?"

A - "Oh, it's not because I don't have the right angle — it's because it's dark."

Q - "Dark?"

A - "Yes — the office light is off, and the only light I have is coming in form the window."

Q - "Well, turn on the office light then."

A - "I can't."

Q - "No?" Why not?"

A - "Because there's a power outage."

Q - "A power..." A power outage?" Aha, Okay, we've got it licked now. Do you still have the boxes and manuals and packing stuff your computer came in?"

A - "Well, yes, I keep them in the closet."

Q - "Good." Go get them, and unplug your system and pack it up just like it was when you got it." Then take it back to the store you bought it from."

A - "Really?" Is it that bad?"

Q - "Yes, I'm afraid it is."

A - "Well, all right then, I suppose. "What do I tell them?"

Q - "Tell them you're not ready to own a computer yet."

Some stories make us laugh because we relate to them as they are similar to our own experiences. The helpdesk story made me laugh out loud because it made me remember that using computers can be so frightening that we may sometimes lose our ability to perform simple thinking tasks. The story also reminded me that, because computers have become so pervasive, we may erroneously assume that using them only requires common sense. We need only to recall that VCRs have been around much longer and, with the exception of the play and eject buttons, many people still don't know how to use them. Just because home computer purchases now outnumber new television purchases does not mean that people are instantly becoming computer literate. For those of us whom have developed a relationship with computers since their early inception, this assumption is easy to make. To the contrary however, there are numerous people, certainly including counselors, whom are only recently discovering the true power of their computers.

In the early 1980s there was a cry heard by counselors across the nation, "The computers are coming! The computers are coming!" Computers were to open a new professional world to counselors and other educators. It was to be the dawning of a new age of technology, education, and counseling. When first introduced to school counselors, computers were viewed as magnificent, albeit mysterious, machines that promised to expedite routine clerical tasks and offer students innovative learning opportunities. Tools for information retrieval would be at the hand of the counselor, who could examine a student's record in the blink of an eye. Counselors were about to enter the twenty-first century of modern technology and computer-assisted counseling. However, it did not quite work out that way.

The pace of educational technology quickened when desktop personal computers were introduced and became more accessible. This allowed counselors to have computers on their desks and to go beyond the district mainframe. The now commonplace floppy disks, CD-ROMs, other high capacity storage devices, and local area networks allowed them to have a storage system with numerous files that could be instantly called upon. Within the past few years, recent changes in technology have introduced many new computer-based tools that have enormous potential for education and, once again, counselors have taken notice. The new technology tempo picked up even more with the establishment and proliferating popularity of the Internet. The Internet, sometimes called the "Net," is a vast global network that enables computers of all kinds to share services and to correspond directly, as if they were part of one giant machine. It has the capability of changing many of the ways in which people interact, collaborate, communicate, and deliver services (Myrick & Sabella, 1995).

Counselors whom have used computers to assist them in their work have done so in many areas such as:

❖ **conducting computer-assisted supervision** (Casey, Bloom, & Moan, 1994; Christie, 2002; Coursol, & Lewis, 2002; Schnieders, 2002; Froehle, 1984; Myrick & Sabella, 1995; Neukrug, 1991);

❖ **having discussions of counseling issues with other counselors** (Rust, 1995; Sabella, 2000);

❖ **conducting counselor training** (Baggerly, 2002; Cairo & Kanner, 1984; Casey, 1999; Jones & Karper, 2000; McFadden, 2000; Woodford, M. S., Rokutani, L., Gressard, C., & Berg, L. B., 2001);

❖ **conducting support and similar groups** (Delmonico, Daninhirsch, Page, Walsh, L'Amoreaux, & Thompson, 2000; Finn, 1995; Gary, 2001; Tyler, 2000; Weinberg, Uken, Schmale, & Adamek, 1995);

❖ **establishing online communities** (Sabella, & Halverson, in press).

❖ **conducting counselor interventions with children** (D'Andrea, 1995; Glover, 1995; Shulman, Sweeney, & Gerler, 1995; Wong, & Law, 2002);

❖ **creating counseling simulations** (Sharf & Lucas, 1993); and

❖ **advocacy** (Stone & Turba, 1999).

Probably the most extensive use of computers in counseling so far has been in the area of career development (e.g., Chapman & Katz, 1983; Clark, 2000; Haring-Hidore, 1984; Harris, 1972; Harris-Bowlsbey, 2001; Katz & Shatkin, 1983; Kivlighan, Johnston, Hogan, & Mauer, 1994; Lumsden, Garis, Reardon, Unger, & Arkin, S., 2001; Pyle, 1984; Sampson, Norris, Wilde, Slatten, & Reardon, 1998; Sampson, 1998a; and Sampson, 2002). Career counselors need to amass and process a great deal of information about various careers, the career decision-making process, and a diversity of client personal and professional characteristics. Computers do a splendid job of compiling such data and helping individuals select the best fit among working environments, required aptitudes, interests, values, and other human qualities.

Some counselors, however, have avoided or only very recently began using computers in their work. One reason for relatively late entry into computing is that some see computer technology as an evil force to be circumvented at all costs. Such counselors hold computers in contempt because they see them as replacing people in jobs such as telephone operators, professional desktop publishers, and even perhaps teachers. This belief is sometimes true for people in more product oriented professions or those in human service professions that involve simple and repetitive tasks. For counselors however, no technology has ever come close to providing quality and appropriate counseling services. Computers have merely changed the shape of the work force by introducing new vocations and changing the methods for how we accomplish our work tasks.

Some counselors say they can still effectively perform their jobs "the old fashioned way" — keeping index cards instead of a database; using a typewriter rather than a word processor; using overheads in lieu of multimedia presentations; and trekking to the library rather than accessing online text resources. Their reasons for avoiding computer technology may be justified since comparative research on delivery and learning effectiveness is only just beginning. On the other hand, critics of this excuse say that such thinking is shortsighted because the world of technology is the world in which our children live and will be more an integral part of their society than even ours. Avoiding the new high-tech tools increasingly integrated in our profession will continually diminish our abilities to do our work in a timely and effective manner. Eventually, the low-tech school counselor will face ethical issues such as the one which addresses functioning within the boundaries of individual professional competence.

And, yet other counselors might acknowledge the usefulness and need for keeping up with the rapidly changing times although are frozen in the fear generated by an unknown frontier. "I feel intimidated by computers," has been a common comment by counselors, who even after training, frequently revert to more traditional procedures. The customary statements, "My kids know more about computers than I do" and "I'm not a technical person" suggest that although counselors may be interested or even intrigued, they frequently feel awkward and uneasy with computers and their operations (Myrick & Sabella, 1995). I have witnessed such fear in the faces of some of my students, especially those returning to higher education after raising their families for many years. Ironically, it's the same fear that, when attempting to become computer literate, makes the learning curve significantly more steep. Joyce L. Winterton, Ph.D., national education advisor for USA Today couldn't have said it better during a presentation I attended when she quipped that, "*Computers are like horses, if they know you're scared of them, they'll try to throw you off.*"

Although computers and related technologies are rapidly changing, one fact remains constant — counselors who resist the new tools of this and future centuries will find it increasingly more difficult to do so. Consider that the Net, which connected 2,000 computers in 1985, now connects approximately 620 million people (see Global Internet Statistics at http://www.glreach.com/globstats), and is continuing to double in size every year. The number of users could surpass one billion as early as 2005. And, in addition to growing in terms of people accessing the Internet, it is growing in terms of the types of services provided over the network. Satellite and wireless systems are already providing users with "anytime, anywhere" communications. Directory and search services help users locate important resources on the Internet. Electronic mail servers manage and store critical information. Authentication and electronic payment services handle more and more of the Nation's commerce. Building blocks for new applications are being developed such as digital signatures, secure transactions, modeling and simulations software, shared virtual environments for collaboration, tools for discovering and retrieving information, and speech recognition (President's Information Technology Advisory Committee, 1998; USIC & ITTA, 2000).

The Internet provides access to a wealth of information on countless topics contributed by people throughout the world. On the Net, counselors have access to a wide variety of services: electronic mail, file transfer, vast information resources, interest group membership, interactive collaboration, multimedia displays, and more. The reality of the matter is that no aspect of society or economy can function effectively and compete without such tools. Counselors who decide to "opt out" of information technology such as the Internet will essentially be working with students whom will perceive them to live in a world that no longer exists. Whether we like it or not, information technologies are now essential tools for manipulating ideas and images and for communicating/collaborating effectively with others — all central components of a counselor's job.

If not for professional competency, then perhaps more personal reasons for becoming proficient in information technologies might make the case for counselor technological literacy. Within the next two decades, computer networks will have penetrated more deeply into our society than any previous network, including telephone, radio, television, transportation, and electric power distribution networks. Soon we will depend on the information infrastructure for delivery of routine services such as banking and financial transactions, purchases of goods and services, entertainment, communications with friends, family, and businesses, as well as for vital services, such as government and medical services. As users come to depend on the Internet each and every day, and as billions of dollars are transacted using electronic commerce, the information infrastructure becomes more critical to each counselor's and our Nation's well being. A counseling profession literate in information technology will be critical for ensuring that it is prepared to meet the challenges and opportunities of the Information Age (USIC & ITTA, 2000). Therefore, be it by necessity or interest, the time is now for exploring contemporary methods for accomplishing our work using computer and networking technologies such as the Internet.

According to Sabella (2001), counselors who took an early interest and continued to gradually follow technology's progression have probably accumulated relatively high levels of technological literacy at a manageable pace. Veterans to the Net, for instance, may find themselves only having to keep pace with incremental changes, new additions, and creative ways for harnessing the Net's power to more effectively and efficiently do their jobs. For those whom have more recently taken an interest, or force themselves to be exposed to technology because of trends or new standards, becoming technologically literate may be a burdensome venture. The good news, however, is that you can effectively start today. The road to technological literacy does not necessarily have a beginning and an end, but like an intricate system of highways and sideroads, can be accessed from many on-ramps. Today's software is more user-friendly and more highly automated than ever before. Beginning a course of self-study and formal training will better assure more enjoyable travel for the road ahead. Before you know it, you will be traveling along side others whom have laid many more miles behind them on the information superhighway. And sooner, rather than later, you will be staking and claiming your property on this vast electronic terrain.

Benefits of Counselor as Cybernaught

Some use technology because it is the "latest and greatest" without careful consideration for the technology's utility. Such people usually want to achieve new levels of power, efficiency, and perhaps the ability to mesmerize or excite others when demonstrating their newfound capabilities. However, just because a new technology application can do more or perform a task more quickly, does not mean we should all go out and purchase it. New technologies arrive on store shelves every day, and although many are alluring, only a few will truly result in great benefits to a counselor's professional and personal productivity. Every technology must be carefully evaluated for its merit (e.g., see Offer, & Sampson, 1999). As smart consumers of technology, counselors must ask questions such as:

→ How much are the initial costs for purchasing the software or hardware?

→ Will my computer run the software or will I need to upgrade (e.g., add more memory or purchase a new peripheral, therefore adding to the overall cost of the new application)?

→ If I choose to purchase new software or hardware, what will it cost to maintain it in the form of upgrades and especially in the form of human resources, specifically paying someone for upkeep, training, or consultation?

→ How user-friendly is the technology? How much time might it require to adequately learn and apply the new technology? Can I do this on my own or will I need to spend even more money for training?

→ Is the company that provides the technology reputable and stable? Or, will the technology lose long-term support because of a fleeting company?

→ How well will the new technology work with other already adopted computer applications?

➔ How compatible is the new technology to already existing technologies? That is, will others be able to share and collaborate with someone who uses the new technology?

➔ Is the new technology convenient and enjoyable to use?

Ultimately, the main question is, will this technology provide me with a significant Return of Investment (ROI)? That is, will an initial and anticipated investment of financial and human resources provide me with a long-term and desired level of benefit to my work? If the ROI for a technology is significant, then one might more easily make the decision to learn and use it. If the ROI is poor, then one might only spend the time to understand the technology to better make informed decisions about their use. For example, I used to avoid personal information managers, database applications, photo and video editing software, and bibliographic managers. Today, these applications are integral in my work. Currently, however, I avoid software for sharing files over a network, electronic post-it notes, and instant messaging (although it's getting more difficult every day to ignore instant messaging). Through careful consideration, I have determined that these applications are inefficient and too time consuming for my work style and needs. For others, they are essential tools that, without them, would cause undue stress. With changes in available time, work demands, and support, I too may find these latter tools important and useful. Each user must decide for him- or herself the level of utility for each high-tech tool, especially for how it integrates and works with other tools to increase overall productivity and enjoyment.

The Internet is one technology that has a high ROI for virtually all professionals, especially those who deal with products and increasingly for us in the human services sector. The Net has become cheaper to use now than ever before due to continually falling computer prices and the ubiquitousness of Internet access. Business and education have recognized for some time that their employees, faculty, staff, and students need Internet access to effectively function in a more global and information driven world. So for many counselors, Internet access is provided,

at least somewhere in the school, as the cost of "doing business." If not, counselors can now access the Net from many public libraries or community centers until more convenient access is available. At the same time, the Net brings more returns on shrinking investments for an overall exciting picture of its benefits. What are some potential ROI factors when counselors decide to use the Internet? Consider that:

➔ The Internet is highly customizable. Such technology, when used with students, allows counselors to accommodate individual differences in student goals, needs, learning styles, and abilities, while providing improved convenience for both students and counselors on an "any time, any place" basis.

➔ Of all the new technologies, online communications has the strongest potential to break down the barriers and inequities encountered by students of different socioeconomic, racial, linguistic, and ability backgrounds. Networks expand the limits posed by time, pace, and space (location), giving students and counselors more equitable access to expertise, information, and tools. Through such tools as the Internet and the various online databases, access to enormous quantities of information is becoming quite common. As systems become increasingly sophisticated, the Internet will continue to provide a growing capacity to navigate among even greater information resources at an increasingly lower cost. Counselors and their students will progressively interact with advanced media that augment the school-to-work process and promote guidance and counseling standards for all children.

➔ Over the Net, counselors can communicate and collaborate with students, teachers, administrators, parents, other counselors, and community members with continually greater convenience and efficiency. For example, one study conducted with teachers with online access showed that teachers had more positive teacher conferences, more parents visiting the classroom, and more positive communication with parents online, than did teachers without online access (Center for Applied Special Technology,

1996). While you are reading this, thousands of school counselors enjoy the convenience of corresponding and consulting with each other through listservs such as the International Counselor Network (http://listserv.utk.edu/archives/icn.html). Already in progress is the ability to communicate from simple text based messages to sending video messages to others across the net (e.g. see http://promo.yahoo.com/videomail and http://www.imagespro.com/programs/824). This will further enhance professional collaboration, consultation, and open even greater opportunities for working with our students.

→ Schools are paid for by their communities: the taxpayers or tuition-payers. They have a stake in the school, and they want to know what is going on there. Counselors who maintain a website have taken the next step for keeping these important citizens informed and motivated to support their mission and activities. The Internet is becoming a standard feature in American homes, libraries and businesses. As it does so, this form of connection with the community becomes increasingly important to maintain community support for your school counseling program. In essence, through maintaining a guidance and counseling website, you can hold an "anytime, anywhere" open house.

→ A more sophisticated website can be home to more than a tool for information dissemination. When counselors make their sites interactive, it can become a virtual counseling center that helps various stakeholders interact with us and each other, submit data, make requests, and engage in self-guided lessons. For instance, a website can help a group of middle school children learn more about conflict resolution by watching a streaming video of pertinent skills, respond to interactive scenarios, and play a game which supports multicultural sensitivity. Parents might use the site to explain to the counselor a presenting problem and then request a meeting. Similarly, teachers can request consultation.

→ After reviewing your online portfolio, a community member may want to recognize you (and the school) with a grant or award.

→ Professional development opportunities are being made available all year round with the help of the Internet. Instead of attending a workshop or presentation during a specific time and place, a counselor can conveniently engage web-based modules, for continuing education credit, that assist in learning new information, discuss issues, ask questions, and submit homework.

→ Counselors who take part in e-mail communication and Internet interactions can stay better alerted to the many events and situations which affect the profession on a seemingly daily basis. Information about a new legislative bill, counseling resource, grant opportunity, or perhaps professional challenge can be met with appropriate response in a more timely manner. Time in the information age seems to be changing from human years to "dog" years as information can change a situation in a matter of days or even minutes. So, for example when the state of Virginia faced new legislation that would seemingly diminish the potential for children to receive guidance and counseling services (see http://www.counseling.org/ctonline/archives/ct0797/ct0797a7.htm), counselors from all over the world, who otherwise would not have known for days, where instantly informed over e-mail broadcasts. In a public comment period that ended May 17, 1997, more than 5,500 of the 7,514 comments addressing elementary school counseling expressed support for the program. As a result, both houses of the Virginia legislature voted in late February of that year to require that public elementary schools in the state provide school counseling services, restoring a mandate that was eliminated by the Virginia Board of Education in September of 1997.

➔ The Internet has become a convenient and efficient way to obtain a profusion of computer programs and other files that can make our work simpler and more manageable. For instance, a counselor can easily locate, download, and use programs such as contact managers, desktop publishing programs, computer-based career interest inventories, search utilities, graphics, sound files, and much more with a couple of clicks of the mouse. Some of these programs are free and can be used at no charge (if you are willing to accept some advertising or periodic e-mails about other related products). Many of the programs available for download are specific to counselors (e.g., http://home.okstate.edu/homepages.nsf/toc/cnslngsw.html). Relatedly, some organizations are providing many more member services over the Net, usually in the form of secured websites and downloadable files, such as professional development kits, already created multimedia presentations about various topics, brochures, newsletter materials, journals, forms, and entire texts (e.g., see ASCA Resource Center at http://www.schoolcounselor.org).

➔ Online stores have made it quite simple and convenient for counselors to research and securely purchase counseling related materials. Instead of traveling to a store, walking the aisles, and waiting in line, a counselor can literally spend 4-5 minutes to find and purchase anything from counseling related books, play counseling media (e.g., puppets, games, or music), to specialty paper, business cards, food, or extra supplies. And, because the cost of doing business over the Net is usually much less than in a storefront, companies can offer their wares over the Net at a significantly reduced price. Within a couple of days, your order is delivered to you or anyone else you choose. People in general who shop online do so because they say it is a great time saver and convenient because one can shop in multiple "stores," anywhere in the world, and at any time of the day or night.

➔ Counselors can noticeably supplement their small or non-existent budgets by finding and applying for grants which are easily processed on the Net.

➔ Because counselors understand the benefits of leisure, what about the vast opportunities for entertainment over the web? So that a weary counselor can rest and rejuvenate, there are sites that allow users to play games with others around the world, do a crossword, read an online novel, play a song, or even print the pattern for your favorite cross stitch.

➔ By becoming Internet literate, counselors can more skillfully help their clients to become proficient. Inroads have already been made to support the use of the Net for enhanced student performance within traditional curricula (Bialo & Sivin-Kachala, 1996; Indiana's Fourth Grade, 1990; Kulik, 1994). One in particular, The Role of Online Communications in Schools: A National Study (CAST, 1996), demonstrated that students with online access perform better. The study, isolated the impact of online use and measured its effect on student learning in the classroom. The study compared the work of 500 students in fourth-grade and sixth-grade classes in 7 urban school districts (Chicago, Dayton, Detroit, Memphis, Miami, Oakland, and Washington DC) - half with online access and half without. The results showed significantly higher scores on measurements of information management, communication, and presentation of ideas for experimental groups with online access than for control groups with no online access. It offered evidence that using the Internet can help students become independent, critical thinkers, able to find information, organize and evaluate it, and then effectively express their new knowledge and ideas in compelling ways.

In what ways will counselors and students using online resources better be able to achieve the goals of guidance and counseling? At minimum, the Net provides a great deal of resources which help counselors share best practices and ideas. Additionally, others have already discovered uses of the Internet to augment various guidance and counseling goals. For instance, consider the following examples of how the Internet may enhance your school counseling mission:

❏ In late 1996, The Georgia Board of Regents Office of Information and Instructional Technology (OIIT) in collaboration with the Georgia Department of Education (DOE) Office of Technology Services announced that an electronic account will be provided to middle school and high school buildings as part of an on-going project called "Connecting Students and Services." The account is intended for use by middle school and high school counselors only and provides schools with a single point of access to various Internet resources including e-mail addresses. The goal is to enhance the guidance counselor's utilization of resources available on the Internet's World Wide Web (WWW). School counselors are able to access admission's information for institutions in the University System of Georgia through the institution's web pages, exchange information via e-mail, access the "Georgia Career Information System" and do electronic transcript transfers between high school and colleges and universities (see http://www.usg.edu/admin/oc/initiatives/studsum.html).

❏ Similar to traditional pen pals that maintain a relationship via correspondence using letters sent through the mail, KeyPals send electronic mail to establish and maintain a friendly peer relationship. One such site contains the following introduction:

Mighty Media presents the KeyPals Club , a place for young people, teachers and students to locate and correspond with other youth and students around the world. The service provides an incredibly easy-to-use interface and database to quickly locate and contact a student or a class from around the world. Start a project with another class, or just create a new friendship with someone on the other side of the globe (http://www.teaching.com/keypals/).

Counselors might think about the following example of how KeyPals was used as a way to create, implement, and evaluate more expanded peer helper programs using the Internet: One high school teacher wanted to improve student activity, participation, and outlook toward physical education. His alternative class of special education students became "KeyPals" with university kinesiology majors. Through e-mail communication, the students established rapport with older students who value physical activity. A bond developed between the high school and college students, which helped the younger students improve their attitude about positive active participation.

A research study to help determine whether this KeyPal relationship between high school alternative Physical Education (PE) students and university kinesiology majors could positively influence their participation and attitude toward gym class was conducted. Results suggested that attitudes, motivation, and relationships positively influenced the KeyPal relationships. Complaints about participating in PE class had been replaced by enthusiastic participation in basketball and volleyball games with the university KeyPals. Most of the KeyPals demonstrated a sense of belonging and connectedness, perhaps for the first time since their elementary school PE experience. And, most important, the essential ingredient of fun in gym class had reappeared (Fargen, 1996).

→ Another popular example of an online collaboration tool can be found by visiting ePals at http://www.epals.com. On this site, a counselor can post a request for collaboration and connect with others whom, when using the site's searching system, identify the counselor's group as having a common interest or goal. Conducting a search for groups using the keyword "counselor" provided results such as the following:

> → I am a guidance counselor for 6, 7, and 8 graders in an urban district. This experience would allow them to meet other children from different backgrounds.

> → I am an elementary school counselor in Tennessee. I would like to find ePals for my fifth grade students to correspond with in order to expose them to different cultures and ideas.

> → As a high school guidance counselor, I am working with students who are now thinking about what colleges they might want to attend. The 12th graders are already applying to colleges and seeking scholarships. I would like my students to be ePALS with students who are also starting to think about college and to apply for colleges and scholarships. I would welcome students from any part of the United States, but since most of our students attend college in state, students from South Carolina might be the best. My high school is a magnet school for artistically talented students. The school is located about 10 miles from the historic peninsula of Charleston, and the students have access to wonderful cultural and historic opportunities.

→ We are a counseling group of seven middle school students ages 11-14 years known as the "Cyber-Cygnets". We have created a website through which we share our life stories through personal pages and tackle issues related to being an early adolescent. We like to receive e-mail about concerns that kids have. We are currently focusing on violence and violence prevention. We discuss e-mailed issues from other students and respond with the help of a counselor to anyone who writes us. We do not give advice, but share our thoughts and experiences as they relate to the issues presented to us. We try to be a community service through being there for kids. We would like to communicate with any students who are interested in sharing their feelings with us about any topic related to kids today. Our pledge is to be there for others. "No one needs to be alone with a problem." Hope to hear from you!

→ Elementary school average children, all African American. Guidance counselor for the school encouraging them to read more than they usually do.

→ Our school has about 350 students. We are very small and rural. We are about 60 miles from Oklahoma City, our state capital. A large part of our school population is Native American. In this gifted program it is our desire to exchange information about our background with others. We want to explore our world even from little Bowlegs, Oklahoma. At this time our school does not have access to the Internet. However, this is forthcoming. When this happens we would like to fully utilize this ePals. Until that time, should you like to contact us, please do so at the mailing address.

→ Hewlett Packard (HP), a well-known computer and printer company, created what is no known as the International Telementor Program which exists to maximize youth potential (see http://www.telementor.org). Mentors support and encourage students to excel academically, explore unique interests, create solid career and education plans, and develop professional networks. Participants come from public, private, home school, and after school environments.

→ D'Andrea (1995), wrote about how peer helpers can consult the Web and provide teachers with educational resources and information related to people from diverse cultural, ethnic, and racial groups, which might be helpful when planning class discussions and activities. This might include sharing materials that describe the unique traditions, values, foods, clothing, and lifestyles associated with people from various cultures. Also, peer helpers may gather information about the ways in which children are raised in other cultures and the roles they are likely to play within their communities, families, or tribes. This sort of information may be of particular interest to elementary school students who enjoy making comparisons between their own lifestyles and other youngsters from different cultural, ethnic, or racial groups. D'Andrea also suggested methods for using telecommunications such as the Net to promote multicultural awareness among elementary school age students. Students can exchange photos, text, sound (e.g., music), and language from various cultures to gain a better appreciation of self and others.

→ Some counselors have provided websites with links to colleges, financial aid sources, GPA calculators, planning checklists, after school homework centers, and resources for parents to name a few.

→ School counselors can help students with disabilities by learning how computers and the Internet can serve as assistive technologies. For instance, once counselor downloaded a text-to-speech converter (from www.readplease.com) to have children's stories read to a group of children without sight. Another counselor used a website (http://where.com/scott.net/asl/) to help teach the siblings of a hearing impaired child American sign language (ASL). The site has an ASL dictionary, interactive quiz, and text to ASL converter.

→ While surfing the Net, an elementary school counselor became aware of and now uses "HIV and AIDS: What Kids Want to Know" and "Lets Talk About HIV and AIDS," two interactive, multimedia, computer-based training programs for children ages 9-12 and children ages 6-9 (see http://www2.uta.edu/cussn/kidshiv/kidsaids.html). The most innovative part of the software is the use of children who are affected by HIV/AIDS to guide development and narrate the programs. The programs contain voice, sounds, animation, and video to keep children involved in the learning. The use of sound is an important feature in the software. Using children affected by HIV/AIDS as narrators creates a powerful experience while hearing the children talk openly and honestly about HIV/AIDS.

What Exactly Is the Internet?

The Internet is a series of computer networks linked to one another around the world, communicating almost instantaneously with one another. A single network of computers might be all the computers linked to one another within an office or school building. A larger network might be all the computers connected within an entire school district. The Internet is many thousands of these networks communicating with one another — University networks connected to government networks connected to business networks connected to private networks. The networks are linked to one another by telephone, radio, cable lines or via satellite. Networks from other continents are interconnected by the large, intercontinental telephone and fiber optic communication lines that run beneath the ocean floor (Using the Internet for Teachers, Schools, Students: An Introduction, 1997). The Net encompasses various special parts which include electronic mail (e-mail), listservs, discussion groups (Usenet), bulletin boards, chat rooms, telnet, gopher, file transfer protocol, and the World Wide Web (WWW).

The first edition of this book introduced counselors to the various aspects of the Internet while focusing primarily on the World Wide Web — the most popular and powerful part of the Net — as a vital resource for facilitating our work. Only several years later, this is much more difficult to do because the afformentioned parts of the Internet are now much more highly integrated into the Web. Distinctions among them have become blurred if not invisible. What once required different software applications or procedures for e-mail, chat rooms, sharing files, etc. can now be mostly done with only a web browser and a connection to the web. Therefore, this second edition focuses on the web in a much more greatly expanded manner, here, and throughout the following chapters, to include more of the details of each of these parts as it relates to you, the counselor.

Indeed, the World Wide Web of today is much more vast and involved than only a few years ago. As you think about the potential of the Web in your work, you might use the following schema that I have developed which I have found to assist me well in managing all that there is involved. The World Wide Web can help school counselors in four areas:

1. **Information/Resource**: In the form of words, graphics, video, and even three-dimension virtual environments, the Web remains a dynamic and rapidly growing library of information and knowledge.

2. **Communication/Collaboration**: Replete with chat rooms, bulletin boards, virtual classroom environments, video conferencing, online conferences, electronic meeting services, e-mail — the web is now a place where people exchange information and connect.

3. **Interactive tools**: The maturing of web based programming has launched a new and unforseen level of available tools on the net. Interactive tools on the web can help counselors build and create anything ranging from a personalized business card to a set of personalized website links. In addition, interactive tools help counselors to process data such as calculating a GPA or the rate of inflation, convert text to speech, create a graph, or even learn about the interactive effects of some prescription drugs.

4. **Delivery of services**: Most controversial yet growing in popularity is how counselors use the web to meet with clients and deliver comprehensive guidance and counseling services. In essence, the Web has become a medium that potentially diminishes barriers of space (location), pace, and time when delivering our school counseling programs.

Russell A. Sabella, Ph.D.

The World Wide Web

In the beginning, the Web was mostly found useful among academicians, scientists and businesses as a way to share and coordinate information, communicate, and conduct transactions. Only after a few years (circa 1997), the proliferation of Web content in the areas of human resource, psychology, counseling, and mental health has rendered the Web as a valuable resource for counselors. School counselors could be better informed about knowledge and practical techniques via the repertoire of materials in the form of scholarly journals, resource information, program descriptions, and articles to name a few. Today, more sophisticated hardware and software, exponential growth and capability of the Web, together with continually decreasing costs, have made the Web as much of a tool for counselors as most other professionals.

The basic format and structure of web sites have remained consistent — dynamic documents which usually contain links (called hypertext links) to other related documents in the form of selected words or symbols such as graphics and icons. However, instead of pointing to static web pages, today's links may point to a sophisticated set of programming instructions which allow users to run software and interact with dynamic pages generated by warehouses full of data. For instance, a visit to the National Center for Education Statistic School Locator website (http://nces.ed.gov/ccd/schoolsearch) allows the counselor to look up information about any school in the United States, a list of schools in their district, state, or perhaps the entire U.S. school database. Further, the site allows you to generate a spreadsheet of your requested information and then download it to your computer.

How did the Web begin?

The following timeline, partly adopted from Dave Kristula's *The History of the Internet* (http://www.davesite.com/webstation/net-history.shtml), Robert Hobbes' *Hobbes' Internet Timeline* ©2002 v5.6 (http://www.zakon.org/robert/internet/timeline), the World Wide Web Consortium (W3C; http://www.w3.org/History.html), PBS (http://www.pbs.org/internet/timeline/timeline-txt.html), and Henry Hardy's Master's Thesis, *The History of the Net* (http://www.ocean.ic.net/ftp/doc/nethist.html) should help you to appreciate the rapid development of the Web:

➤ **1957**

The USSR launches Sputnik, the first artificial earth satellite. In response, the United States forms the Advanced Research Projects Agency (ARPA) within the Department of Defense (DoD) to establish America's lead in science and technology applicable to the military. There Internet does not yet exist.

➤ **1962**

Paul Baran, of the RAND Corporation (a government agency), was commissioned by the U.S. Air Force to do a study on how it could maintain its command and control over its missiles and bombers, after a nuclear attack. This was to be a military research network that could survive a nuclear strike, decentralized so that if any locations (cities) in the U.S. were attacked, the military could still have control of nuclear arms for a counter-attack. Baran's finished document described several ways to accomplish this. His final proposal was a packet switched network. Packet switching is the breaking down of data into packets that are labeled to indicate the origin and the destination of the information and the forwarding of these packets from one computer to another computer until the information arrives at its final destination computer. This was crucial to the realization of a computer network. If packets are lost at any given point, the message can be resent by the originator.

➤ 1969

A Honeywell minicomputer was chosen as the base on which they would build the switch and would link four nodes or sites: University of California at Los Angeles, Stanford University, University of California at Santa Barbara, and the University of Utah. The network was wired together via 50 Kbps circuits.

➤ 1972

The first e-mail program was created by Ray Tomlinson.

➤ 1973

Development began on the protocol later to be called TCP/IP, it was developed by a group headed by Vinton Cerf from Stanford and Bob Kahn. This new protocol was to allow diverse computer networks to interconnect and communicate with each other.

➤ 1974

The term Internet was coined by Vint Cerf and Bob Kahn in a paper they wrote about transmission control protocol.

➤ 1975

Satellite links cross two oceans (to Hawaii and UK) as the first TCP tests are run over them by Stanford, BBN, and UCL.

➤ 1976

Dr. Robert M. Metcalfe develops Ethernet, which allowed coaxial cable to move data extremely fast. This was a crucial component to the development of local area networks (LANs). Also, SATNET, Atlantic packet Satellite network, was born. This network linked the United States with Europe.

➤ 1977

THEORYNET, created by Larry Landweber at the University of Wisconsin, provides electronic mail to over 100 researchers in computer science.

➤ 1979

USENET (the decentralized news group network) was created by Steve Bellovin, a graduate student at University of North Carolina, and programmers Tom Truscott and Jim Ellis. The creation of BITNET (Because its Time Network), by IBM, introduced the "store and forward" network which was used for e-mail and listservs. Also, the emoticon was born when on April 12, Kevin MacKenzie e-mails a message group with a suggestion of adding some emotion back into the dry text medium of e-mail such as -) for indicating a sentence was tongue-in-cheek.

➤ 1980

While consulting for CERN, Tim Berners-Lee writes a notebook program, "Enquire-Within-Upon-Everything", which allows links to be made between arbitrary nodes. Each node had a title, a type, and a list of bidirectional typed links.

➤ 1983

The University of Wisconsin created the Domain Name System (DNS). This allowed packets to be directed to a domain name, which would be translated by the server database into the corresponding Internet Protocol (IP) number. This made it much easier for people to access other servers, because they no longer had to remember numbers. Also, Mark Andreesen turns 8, only a few more years until he revolutionizes the Web by first developing the Mosaic web browser and eventually founding a company called America Online.

➤ **1984**

The ARPANET was divided into two networks: MILNET and ARPANET. MILNET was to serve the needs of the military and ARPANET to support the advanced research component. The Department of Defense continued to support both networks. Upgrade to CSNET was contracted to MCI. New circuits would be T1 lines, 1.5 Mbps which is twenty-five times faster than the old 56 Kbps lines. IBM would provide advanced routers and Merit would manage the network. The new network was to be called NSFNET (National Science Foundation Network), and old lines were to remain being called CSNET.

➤ **1985**

The National Science Foundation began deploying its new T1 lines, which would be finished by 1988.

➤ **1986**

The Internet Engineering Task Force or IETF was created to serve as a forum for technical coordination.

➤ **1988**

Soon after the completion of the T1 NSFNET backbone, traffic increased so quickly that plans immediately began on upgrading the network again. Research into high speed networking began and would soon result in the concept of the T3, a 45 Mbps line. In the same year, a malicious program called the "Internet Worm" temporarily disables approximately 6,000 of the 60,000 Internet hosts.

➤ **1990**

Tim Berners-Lee (considered the father of the WWW), with CERN in Geneva, implements a hypertext system to provide efficient information access to the members of the international high-energy physics community. Also, the Electronic Frontier Foundation is founded by Mitch Kapor.

➤ **1990**

The World comes on-line (world.std.com), becoming the first commercial provider of Internet dial-up access. Also, the first remotely operated machine to be hooked up to the Internet, the Internet Toaster by John Romkey, makes its debut at Interop.

➤ **1991**

Files become available on the net by File Transfer Protocol or FTP, posted on several electronic bulletin boards. Jean-Francois Groff joins the project.

➤ **1992**

The Internet Society is chartered and the World Wide Web was released by CERN.

➤ **1993**

InterNIC was created by the National Science Foundation. They would provide specific Internet services such as directory and database services (by AT&T), registration services (by Network Solutions Inc.), and information services (by General Atomics/CERFnet). Marc Andreessen and NCSA and the University of Illinois develops a graphical user interface to the WWW, called "Mosaic for X". Also ...

- The United States White House comes on-line;
- Internet Talk Radio begins broadcasting;
- The United Nations and the World Bank come on-line;
- The US National Information Infrastructure Act is passed;
- Businesses and media begin to take serious notice of the Internet;
- By mid October, there are over 200 known HTTP servers;
- Mosaic takes the Internet by storm; and
- the WWW proliferates at a 341,634% annual growth rate of service traffic. Gopher's growth is 997%.

➤ 1994

No major changes were made to the physical network. The most significant thing that happened was the growth. For instance, the load on the first Web server (info.cern.ch) was by this time 1000 fold what it had been three years earlier. Many new networks were added to the NSF backbone. Hundreds of thousands of new hosts were added to the INTERNET during this time period. Significant Net events included Pizza Hut offering pizza ordering on its Web page; advent of First Virtual, the first cyberbank; and the installation of the ATM (Asynchronous Transmission Mode, 145Mbps) backbone on NSFNET. Also,

- Communities begin to connect directly to the Internet.

- US Senate and House provide information servers.

- First flower shop took orders via the Internet.

- First Virtual, the first cyberbank, open up for business.

- Shopping malls arrive on the Internet.

- Mass marketing finds its way to the Internet with mass e-mailings.

  and

- "A Day in the Life of the Internet" begins its publication.

➤ 1995

National Science Foundation announced that as of April 30, 1995 it would no longer allow direct access to the NSF backbone. They contracted with four companies that would be providers of access to the NSF backbone that would then sell connections to groups, organizations, and companies. A $50 annual fee is imposed on domains, excluding .edu and .gov domains which were still funded by the National Science Foundation. Also, traditional online dial-up systems (e.g., CompuServe, America Online, Prodigy) begin to provide Internet access.

➤ 1996

Within 30 years, the Internet has grown from a Cold War concept for controlling the tattered remains of a post-nuclear society to the Information Superhighway. Just as the railroads of the 19th century enabled the Machine Age, and revolutionized the society of the time, the Internet takes us into the Information Age, and profoundly affects the world in which we live. In this year ...

- The controversial US Communications Decency Act (CDA) becomes law in the U.S. to prohibit distribution of indecent materials over the Net. A few months later, a three-judge panel imposes an injunction against its enforcement. The Supreme Court unanimously rules most of it unconstitutional in 1997;

- Internet phones catch the attention of US telecommunication companies who ask the US Congress to ban the technology (which has been around for years);

- The domain name tv.com was sold to CNET for $15,000; and

- The WWW browser war, fought primarily between Netscape and Microsoft, has rushed in a new age in software development, whereby new releases are made quarterly with the help of Internet users eager to test upcoming (beta) versions.

➤ 1997

The American Registry for Internet Numbers (ARIN) is established to handle administration and registration of IP numbers to the geographical areas currently handled by Network Solutions (InterNIC), starting in March 1998. Also ...

- the domain name business.com sold for $150,000;

- 71,618 mailing lists registered at Liszt, a mailing list directory; and

- 101,803 Name Servers are now in the whois database.

➤ 1998

Web size estimates range between 275 and 320 million pages for the first quarter. Also:

- Internet users get to be judges in a performance by 12 world champion ice skaters in March, marking the first time a television sport show's outcome is determined by its viewers;

- Network Solutions registers its 2 millionth domain on May 4th;

- On November 2nd, ABCNews.com accidentally posts test US election returns one day early. They respond by saying that they were simply testing out templates;

- Chinese government puts Lin Hai on trial for "inciting the overthrow of state power" for providing 30,000 e-mail addresses to a US Internet magazine; and

- Speculators agree that this is the banner year for E-commerce and E-business.

➤ 1999

- The U.S. Supreme Court rules that domain names are property that may be garnished;

- A forged Web page made to look like a Bloomberg financial news story raised shares of a small technology company by 31% on April 7th;

- Free computers are all the rage (as long as you sign a long term contract for Net service); and

- The domain name Business.com is sold for $7.5 million.

➤ 2000

- The millennium bug (y2k bug) turns out to have less bite than the average mosquito. A few time-keeping services still operating Radio Shack TRS-80s report the new year as 19100. Consequently, people try to return all the camping gear they thought they'd need during the big blackout, which sets off an economic slowdown;

- A federal judge rules that Microsoft constitutes an unfair monopoly and should be broken up;

- Estimates put the size of the Web at over one billion indexable pages;

- America Online and Time Warner merge. It's the largest media deal in US history;

- Various domain name hijackings took place in late May and early June, including internet.com, bali.com, and web.net;

- After months of legal proceedings, the French court rules Yahoo! must block French users from accessing hate memorabilia in its auction site. Given its inability to provide such a block on the Internet, Yahoo! removes those auctions entirely; and

- Napster.com allows users to swap files, especially music files, across the net challenging intellectual property and copyright laws.

➤ 2001

- The first live distributed musical — The Technophobe & The Madman — over Internet2 networks debuts on February 20th;

- Radio stations broadcasting over the Web go silent over royalty disputes;

- European Council finalizes an international cybercrime treaty on June 22nd and adopts it on November 9th. This is the first treaty addressing criminal offenses committed over the Internet;

- Code Red worm and Sircam virus infiltrate thousands of web servers and e-mail accounts, respectively, causing a spike in Internet bandwidth usage and security breaches; and

- The terrorist attacks of Sept. 11 prompt a swelling of patriotism, personal support, and anti-Taliban sentiment across the Web.

➤ 2002

- Despite the dot.com bust, Internet usage and audience continues to grow. Nielsen/NetRatings reports that the number of people around the globe using the Internet grew 18 percent to about 500 million users. Further, Internet activity in April 2002 compared with April 2001 showed web users going on line 18 times a month, compared with 16 a year earlier. Also in this year ...

  - pop-up advertisements cause a severe ruckus among web surfers which also spurs software to block them; and

  - More U.S. users log on using broadband (51%) than narrowband (Jan 2002 - Nielsen/NetRatings).

NOTE: For interesting and amusing Internet snapshots, consult Win Treese's Internet-related Facts and Figures at http://www.openmarket.com/intindex/index.cfm).

Summary

A single event that many say marked the "coming of age" of the Internet was reported on September 13th, 1998 across television, print, and electronic media. An estimated twelve percent of adult Americans, some 20 million people, used the Internet to gain access to Independent Counsel Ken Starr's report about President Clinton. Twenty million people all logged on to get the same information at the same time. As important, while there was gridlock in some corners, the Internet did not melt down under the demand, as some had predicted.

Information technology will continue to be one of many key factors driving progress in the 21st century — it is quite literally transforming the way we live, learn, work, and play. Advances in computing and communication technology will create a new infrastructure for business, scientific research, and social interaction. That infrastructure will provide us with new tools for conducting our work at home and throughout the world. And, advances in technology will help counselors to acquire knowledge and insight from others to make more informed decisions about all aspects of their programs. The Internet will assist counselors to understand the effects of guidance and counseling on all stakeholders, especially children and their academic success. It will provide a vehicle for professional development and personal growth. Internet technology can make the workplace more rewarding, improve the quality of services to all, and make counselors more responsive and accessible to the needs of a progressively complicated and diverse clientele.

CHAPTER TWO

Get Set ...
On-Ramp to the Web

To begin your interactive adventure on the Web, you must have at least four things: a computer, a connection an Internet Service Provider (ISP), and appropriate software. Similar to purchasing a car, investing in the appropriate hardware and software will depend upon your preferences and needs. For instance, how fast do you want to travel on the information highway? Which options will you require to make your travels more comfortable and enjoyable? And, probably the most important question for most people, how much are you able to invest?

A Computer or Other Appliances

What kind of computer must one have to effectively access the Internet? This question is more simple to answer than if the question focused on the right type of computer for other applications such as desktop publishing or, say, conducting statistical analyses. Because the Internet relies on a more global programming language (hypertext markup language or HTML), just about any computer will do. Both Macintosh and Windows compatible computers work just fine because the software needed for surfing is available for both operating systems or platforms. Incidently, since the first edition of this book, there are now available other ways to access and use the Web which are not quite as popular as using a computer although continue to have promise. For example, as a school counselor, you may find it valuable to soon use the web over a personal digital assistant (PDA; e.g., http://www.visor.com), cellular phone (e.g., see http://www.soho-telecom.com/wireless/) , web enabled telephones (e.g., http://www.bpgroups.com/iphone/) or television (e.g., http://resourcecenter.msn.com/access/MSNTV).

Using a Computer

Getting on the Net may be a large part of your computer experience although it is usually only one application among others such as word processing, information management, desktop publishing, games, and running educational software. So, if you are considering the purchase of a new computer, which one should you choose? There is no correct answer for this question because it truly depends on personal preference. Following are several questions you should ask yourself and your computer retailer when deciding on your purchase:

1. *What is the quality and availability of software for the applications I will most use?* For instance, professional desktop publishers and advertisement agencies typically use Macintosh related hardware and software because publishing and photo editing applications seem to be best achieved with this kind of system. On the other hand, those who engage in mostly word processing, database management, and multimedia might find that the Windows compatible hardware would serve them best.

2. *With whom will I be mostly collaborating and what do they use?* Although there are methods for running both platforms on either a Macintosh or Windows compatible computer, it is usually easiest to run the same software as others with whom you work closely. When using the same or similar operating systems, transferring and sharing files does not pose a problem because compatibility is very close to 100%.

3. *How much should I spend?* Although *cost* is always a factor, competition among computer companies has made price a virtual

non-issue for entry level computing. Companies seem to be driving at the lowest price that their profit margins will allow. And because all computers share many of the same parts which cost the same for all, no one company seems to have an edge over another when it comes to cost. Fortunately for consumers, price wars have now steered the cost ceiling for a complete package (computer, monitor, multimedia peripherals, software package, and a printer) below the $1000 dollar mark for both large and small retailers, direct warehouses, and online stores. This question is also related to question #5 below.

4. *What level of tech-help can I reasonably expect?* The quality and cost of technical help and customer service that come standard with your personal computer seems to be the more important concern among consumers. That is, smart computer shoppers wonder about the average wait time when calling a company's customer service, and the average time and cost from problem presentation to solution.

5. *How much power will I need?* The difference between low-end and high-end hardware is significant and can easily run into thousands of dollars. A general rule in the world of computers is to purchase as much computer as you can get as allowed by your budget. The reason for this is that this year's most revered computer will be shadowed by next year's innovations. The speed at which hardware is developing is indeed amazing. In 2003, my recommendation is to use the following technical specifications as a minimum criteria for purchase:

- ❖ **Processor**: Intel® Pentium® 4 up to 2.0 GHz or Intel® Celeron® up to 2.0 Ghz.
- ❖ **Memory:** no less than 256MB, 520MB recommended
- ❖ **Storage:** 40 GB
- ❖ **Drive Bay:** CD-RW (DVD+RW/+R recommended) and 3.5" 1.44 MB diskette drive

- ❖ **Video Graphics**: Integrated Intel® Extreme 3D Graphics.
- ❖ **Ports**: 3 USB 2.0 ports, one serial port and one parallel port. Some computers have available infrared ports which sometimes can be useful such as for printing to a printer or sharing files with another computer with infrared ports.
- ❖ **Monitors**: 17" or bigger (Flat Panel recommended)
- ❖ **Sound**: any sound card with speakers and microphone
- ❖ **Slots**: at least 3 extra slots for adding peripherals later
- ❖ **Mouse**: Optical USB Mouse
- ❖ Communication device: Integrated 10/100 Ethernet (for high speed access) and 56K DataFax Modem for dial-up.

6. *How expandable is the computer?* That is, how much room is there to add extra hardware or peripherals such as scanners, digital cameras, extra memory, new cards (e.g., video editor), zip drive, CD-ROM writer, or a second printer? Many peripherals use what is called a USB (universal serial bus) connection which, since April 2000, is available in version 2.0 which is very fast transferring data at rates up to 480Mbps.

7. *Will the company customize a computer for my exact needs and charge me only for what I want?* Relatedly, if I ask the company to remove a standard option, either hardware or software, will they give me a price rebate? The top computer companies in the world (e.g., Dell, HP, Gateway, Compaq) typically allow you to customize a computer and purchase it directly online. You might even do some comparison shopping for computer packages and parts at http://froogle.google.com.

A Connection

The transmission rate with which you connect to your Internet service provider will determine how fast you will receive information from the sites you access. At slow rates, modems are measured in terms of baud rates. The slowest rate is 300 baud (about 25 characters/second). At higher speeds, modems are measured in terms of bits per second (bps). The fastest modems run at 57,600 bps, although they can achieve even higher data transfer rates by compressing the data. Obviously, the faster the transmission rate, the faster you can send and receive data. Note, however, that you cannot receive data any faster than it is being sent. If, for example, the device sending data to your computer is sending it at 2,400 bps, you must receive it at 2,400 bps. It does not always pay, therefore, to have a very fast modem. In addition, some telephone lines are unable to transmit data reliably at very high rates (Webopedia, 2003).

When accessing a site, what you are essentially doing is requesting that the site send to your computer all relevant elements that the site contains: text, graphics, video, audio, etc. With all else being equal (such as level of Internet traffic and computer processor speed), the faster the connection, the more quickly you are able to view the site's contents. When added together, the time required to access and view many sites during an online session can have a grave impact on your productivity and viewing pleasure. Additionally, the time required for downloading files such as software from an Internet site to your computer is vastly different depending upon the speed of your connection. The following table represents average download times for a relatively small (100 kilobyte) picture at various connection speeds (also see http://support.summersault.com/bandwidth_chart.html):

Connection Method	Connection Speed	Average Time to Download a 100Kb file
Modem	56.6 kb/s	14 sec
ISDN	64 Kbps to 128 Kbps	6 sec
ADSL/DSL	128 Kbps to 8 Mbps	2 sec
Cable Modem	512 Kbps to 20 Mbps	1 sec
T1 Ethernet	1.544 Mbps	0.27 sec

Cable modems. The fastest growing technology in computer connection involves using a cable modem. Basically, companies that provide you with cable television access use the same connections and a special piece of hardware called a cable modem to provide you with Net access. The speed that a cable modem provides is much greater than that of a telephone modem. The reason for this is that cable modem connections transmit data via fiber optic cable with much greater capacity (or bandwidth). The result is a transmission rate that reaches 2 million BPS. This, combined with the fact that millions of homes are already wired for cable TV, has made the cable modem something of a holy grail for Internet and cable TV companies. However, this relatively new technology is still a luxury for most people since cable companies are slowly upgrading their equipment to provide such a service which may not yet reach those that receive television services from the same companies. For those that do have cable modem access, the cost of a cable modem and the monthly fee for this kind of access significantly exceeds telephone modem access, $45-90 and $15, respectively.

Companies that provide digital satellite systems that beam hundreds of television channels into your home are also getting in to the Internet Service Provider business. In this case, they use satellite connections to beam Internet data to your computer. Similar to cable modem access, digital satellite access is still in its infancy and much less pervasive as compared to telephone connections.

Two other promising and upcoming communication technology hopefuls are ADSL and wireless. Short for asymmetric digital subscriber line, ADSL is a new technology that transforms ordinary phone lines (also known as "twisted copper pairs") into high-speed digital lines for ultra-fast Internet access. ADSL also enables access to corporate networks for telecommuters, as well as exciting new interactive multimedia applications such as multiplayer gaming, video on demand and video catalogs. It is not currently available to the general public except in some areas, but many believe that it will be one of the more popular choices for Internet access over the next few years (Webopedia, 1999; To learn more about ADSL, visit www.adsl.com).

WiFi (Short for wireless fidelity), also known as 802.11b, is the most popular high-speed wireless Web technology. Essentially, data is transmitted over the air similar to your wireless telephone. One wireless access point can reach from 200 feet to an area covering several blocks. It is used mostly in homes and businesses and slowly expanding into public areas, largely due to the efforts of telecommunications companies which have set up pay-as-you-go networks at coffee shops and airport lounges. Many business are providing free wireless access as a way to attract customers (e.g., see http://auscillate.com/wireless/ for a list of free access points in Austin, Texas). To access the web over a wireless access point, all that is needed is a wireless transceiver in your computer. For a laptop, these transceivers come in the form of a credit card sized piece of hardware called a PCMCIA card. Incidently, the ease and relative low cost of wireless transmission is also what is currently fueling the drastic increase in home networking which allows computers in different rooms to not only share web access but also share files, printers, etc.

An Internet Service Provider (ISP)

If your school has full-time access through a network connection to the Internet, you have the shortest path of all. All you need to do is sit down at a terminal or workstation, log on, and get going. Most Internet connections have been made just like that — as connections between two networks, rather than between two computers. For example, a school's local-area network (LAN) might get access to the Internet by making a connection through a leased phone line to a regional network. Once that connection is made, in most cases, every computer on the local-area network has "full-time" access — meaning, the Internet is available all the time, day and night. Virtually all schools and libraries are connected, and most universities provide access throughout their campus and residence halls this way. Moreover, some schools allow their employees to log on to their system from home or other remote locations (LaQuey, 1994; NCES, 2002).

If your school does not have access or if you want access at home, you will need an Internet Service Provider (ISP). ISP's equip you with a gateway to the Internet by giving you the access, software you need to connect, technical help, and sometimes the hardware such as a cable modem). Most ISPs also include at least one e-mail account, website hosting services, and additional services such as e-commerce with companies and organizations that conduct business on the Internet. You may choose from local or national ISPs. To identify ISPs and online service providers in your area, look under "Internet products and services" or a similar topic in your local yellow pages, or search for them online through The List (http://thelist.internet.com/). Then call their customer service number and interview the representative about various aspects of their service. In addition, instead of relying on published statistics, advertised claims, or the testimony of a customer service representative for this information, you might also want to take advantage of a 30 day free trial. If the ISP does not offer a free trial period, it wouldn't hurt to ask for one. During your trial, pay attention to the nature of your service, especially connection speeds at different times of the day before making your decision. Be aware, however, that some ISP's will have you provide your credit card number before issuing your free trial and automatically begin to charge your account after the 30 days expire unless you take it upon yourself to cancel your subscription in writing. Smart ISP consumers pay special attention to features such as:

1. **Dialing in.** Does the ISP or online service provider offer service through a telephone number in your area? Does it offer a local telephone number or toll-free number in areas in which you expect to travel?

2. **Access.** How often will you actually get through, rather than get a busy signal, when you dial in? Note that dialing in and gaining access are not issues with cable modem access since the connection, like your television, is "always on".

3. **Transmission rates.** To appropriately transfer information and files over the Net, the transmission rate with which you connect must match the rate of the ISP. Therefore, even if you have a top-of-the-line 56K modem, if your ISP's fastest connection is 28.8K, your connection will typically drop down to 28.8K. It is important, then, to make certain that the ISP you choose offers a connection rate that can accommodate the fastest possible connection for which your computer is capable.

4. **Technical support and customer service.** Are there knowledgeable, friendly technical support and customer service people available whenever you need them? Is the telephone call toll-free? How long will you have to wait on hold? Can you get technical support and customer service online? Is technical support included in the package or is it extra? If technical support is extra, what is the fee schedule for using the service?

5. **E-mail.** How many e-mail accounts does the ISP provide, and can you access your account through another ISP if you're outside a local ISP's area? Is their server POP3 compatible which allows for collecting your mail through various clients such as Eudora, Outlook, Pegasus, Lotus, and Netscape. Does the ISP provide you access to your e-mail over the web?

6. **Web pages.** Can you post a Web site on the ISP's server? How much space can you get for your page and at what cost? Will you be charged based on the amount of traffic your page gets? Will the server support special functions of your page such as CGI scripting (necessary if your page includes a form or is password protected) or Microsoft Frontpage extensions? Will the ISP provide web authoring services and/or support and is this included in the monthly charges? Will the ISP help you establish your domain name? Do they provide backup services in the event that their system crashes or will backing up your web site be your responsibility?

7. **Training.** An ISP can not only connect you to the Internet, but might also provide online technical support. For example, an ISP might maintain a web site that offers special features and content such as Internet handbooks, manuals, useful links, and tips for enjoyable surfing.

8. **Confidentiality.** Does the ISP keep your personal profile information private or will it sell your information to interested companies? Will the company fulfill requests to identify you to others?

9. **Safety.** Does the ISP provide controls for accessing adult materials over the Net (in case you share your account with others, especially students)?

10. **Price.** Many services offer different monthly subscriptions, including unlimited access for a flat monthly fee and limited hours for a flat monthly fee with additional hours, as needed, for an extra charge. When you compare prices, consider the factors above as well as the special features and content that the online service providers offer. Thanks to

---

some hefty ISP competition, you can now purchase unlimited access to the Net for no more than $15 per month and sometimes for as much as $8. Some companies with which you already conduct business such as telephone and newspaper may have penetrated the ISP market and will offer substantial discounts to their customers. Some ISPs also charge a set-up fee of $20-$30 dollars which should also be considered when deciding on which company that you will contract. Like anything else, this might be negotiable.

No-cost ISP

Providing Internet Service to consumers has become relatively inexpensive, especially as compared to the cost of collecting marketing and demographic data. As a result, some companies now offer free Internet access at no cost in exchange for completing a survey about yourself and your interests. The other reason for providing free access is that it generates much greater traffic to the company's website which means that the company can then make a bigger profits from advertisement. When you dial in to a free ISP you will immediately notice an unremovable menu bar at the top of your computer which points you to the provider's advertiser sites. So what seems to be free access is really paid access except that other companies foot the bill instead of you. The advantage of signing up for free Internet service obviously includes the lack of cost although can also include extra flexibility or freedom. For instance, for travelers, your no-cost ISP may include local dial in numbers in the areas in which you most journey so that you may access the web and e-mail from outside your locale. Even for those that already have free Internet access as a benefit of employment, you may want to consider signing up for a no-cost ISP to do non-work related Internet activities. Four well known sites which offer free Internet access (for about 10 hours per month, then it costs) include www.netzero.com, www.myfreei.com, www.juno.com, and www.internet4free.net. To select the ISP best for you, pay attention to the features mentioned above for fee based ISP's.

Freenets

A freenet is a network of computers with Internet access which is created for the purpose of allowing Net access to a certain community. This is made possible by the creation of a not-for-profit organization that receives funding, mostly through corporate and institutional donations, for hardware and software. For instance, the Alachua Freenet (AFN) is a community supported and sponsored system in Gainesville, FL which gives access to the Internet and community resources to over 10,000 people. Alachua Freenet accounts are free for those living within the boundaries of the state of Florida in the USA. Those living outside of Florida are required to pay a $20 per year access fee to use an AFN account. The organization does not provide any local dial-up access for people outside of the Gainesville, FL calling area. If you live outside of that calling area and dial-up the Alachua Freenet computer system, your phone company will charge you accordingly. A listing of international free and community networks is available at http://www.lights.com/freenet/.

The Software

The first piece of software that you need to access the net is one that establishes the connection with your ISP. Such software is usually a part of your operating system and only needs to be initially configured with appropriate information such as phone numbers, your modem type, and the kind of account you have (e.g., PPP, TCP/IP, Network). Most ISPs will include tailored software when you subscribe which is already configured and may only require minimal customization. Schools and businesses usually connect their computers to the Internet using an Ethernet connection which is always "on." Ethernet connections are hardline connections, similar to your cable television connection, and only require that you launch your browser for instant Net access (similar to simply turning on your television to begin viewing the provided channels).

Once your connection is established, you will require a second piece of software to appropriately view the material you access from the Net called a browser. A browser interprets the rich content which you download, usually written in a code called hypertext markup language (HTML), and translates it into what you see on the screen. Moreover, a browser contains the basic software you need to download files, complete and transmit forms, view streaming audio and video, access bulletin boards, and send/receive messages across the Net.

Currently, the four most popular browsers, all free to anyone that will have them, include Microsoft's Internet Explorer (IE), Netscape's Navigator (Netscape), Mozilla, and Opera. All new computers will usually come with one or the other, usually already installed on the hard drive. Following are the download sites for each:

Browser	Download Site
Microsoft™ Internet Explorer	www.microsoft.com – click on downloads and then Internet Explorer
Netscape™ Navigator	www.netscape.com – click on Browser Central under Tools and then on Netscape Navigator.
Mozilla	www.mozilla.org/
Opera	www.opera.com/ download/

More About Browsers

Early in the development of web browsing, users could choose from various browsers including Cello, Mosaic, Navigator and several others. Today, however, IE and Netscape are the two browsers that dominate almost the entire market. The battle between the two is fervent, reminiscent of the battle between VHS and Beta video formats. The browser, or company that is, that endures will set the standards for how users browse the web, how developers will create content for it, and which programming languages will be used to build Internet applications. One benefit of the browser wars is that consumers are witnessing phenomenal advancements in both programs to make browsing a more heightened and productive endeavor.

So, which browser is better? Which browser should I use? Well, the answer to the first question is that neither browser has proven itself more useful or outperforms the other. Right now, the choice is a matter of preference, style, and industrial loyalty. Both browsers do the job, and do the job well. Choosing one over the other may be analogous to choosing a car in the same class, perhaps a Sedan, with a console that looks and feels different to the touch. Also, like some who buy only certain brands of automobile, some users whom have had good experi-

---

ences with one or the other may desire to re-main loyal to the company's product.

You can't go wrong with either Internet Explorer or Navigator (or Mozilla or Opera). Not too long ago, websites had a message planted somewhere that informed users which browser a user should be using to best view the site. That was true a couple of years ago, but not today. Both browsers are capable of displaying all the standard HTML tags and will display a site's information on your screen regardless of which browser you are using. At worst, you will notice some minor nuances between the two because each browser formats the information slightly differently. When it comes to some of the fancier sites that show off the latest technology using HTML extensions developed by one company, but not supported by the other's browser, the HTML tags will be ignored. The text will still be displayed, but it will not be formatted as origi-nally intended. For instance, when Navigator encounters one Microsoft extension called a marquee (fancy text that scrolls across the screen), it displays it as centered text, whereas IE users view it in all its glory.

With today's humongous hard drives, it may be typical for a user to have both IE and Netscape on their computers. You might down-load both IE (www.microsoft.com) and Naviga-tor (www.netscape.com) and take each browser for a test drive. Call up your favorite site and view it with one browser. Then view the same site with the other browser. Was the data dis-played differently? How do you like the toolbar? What options do you get when you right click the mouse? Can you customize the interface? Some people care a lot about these features. Others couldn't care less. It's up to you to decide which browser is right for you. You may take some comfort in knowing that, unlike purchas-ing a car, "trading in" one browser for the other costs nothing. And, because both browsers operate essentially the same, you can easily switch without having to overcome any learning curve. The examples in this text will rely heavily on IE although are easily applied to Netscape. Only the location of some buttons and some of their names change. For a few procedures that

are conducted significantly differently, I provide examples using each browser.

Plugins

Plugins are pieces of software that adds a specific feature or service to a larger system such as a browser. They are designed to extend the functionality of the browser and thus further the usefulness of using the Net. Most plugins work equally well with any of the more popular browsers. Following is a list of several highly useful and free plugins, a brief description, and, if necessary, the website URL for downloading (also see an online directory of browser plugins at http://dir.yahoo.com/ Computers_and_Internet/software/internet/ world_wide_web/browsers/plug_ins/):

Acrobat Reader. With free Acrobat Reader® software, you can view and print Adobe PDF files. http://www.adobe.com/products/acrobat/ readstep.html

Alexa. Alexa updates with site-specific informa-tion as you surf. This plugin will help you navi-gate the Web with related links for each page and make informed decisions about the value of each site you visit with site statistics, reviews, contact information, related news, and more. http://download.alexa.com/.

Ask Jeeves Toolbar is free to download and appears every time you open a new Internet Explorer window. http://sp.ask.com/docs/ toolbar/

Google Toolbar. The Google Toolbar increases your ability to find information from anywhere on the web and takes only seconds to install. http://toolbar.google.com/

iPIX Immersive Plug-in. The iPIX Immersive Plug-In enables your browser to display iPIX 360-degree images. The plug-in is supported by both Internet Explorer and Netscape on both Win-dows based PCs and Macintosh operating systems. http://www.ipix.com/support/ download.shtml

Macromedia Flash and Shockwave Player. With these players, you can enjoy multimedia games, learning applications, and product demonstrations on the Web, using exciting new 3D technology. http://sdc.shockwave.com/downloads/

Merriam-Webster Toolbar becomes a part of your Internet Explorer browser toolbar so you can instantly look up words in the Merriam-Webster Dictionary or Thesaurus no matter where you are on the Web. http://www.m-w.com/tools/toolbar/.

NY Times. Stay current throughout the day with The New York Times Explorer Bar. You can enjoy the day's top stories, breaking news updates every ten minutes, market information and access to stock quotes. http://www.nytimes.com/partners/ie50/ie5.html.

QuickTime Player. This plugin allows you to view QuickTime videos. http://www.apple.com/quicktime/download/

RealOne Player. RealOne Player allows you to tune into Internet radio stations, listen to music, watch video, and more live and on demand in real time (they start playing right away rather than making you wait until the entire file downloads). Visit www.real.com and look for the FREE RealOne download icon.

spIE (pronounced "spy") integrates with Internet Explorer to provide additional security and logging features to help prevent net abuse. These features can be useful for monitoring your children's web usage, or your employees web habits. You can also closely control which web pages are accessible from your computer. http://www.satacoy.com/spie/main.htm

Teoma Search Bar. Similar to AskJeeves and Google, this is a search engine toolbar. http://sp.ask.com/docs/teoma/toolbar/.

Windows Media player. This plugin allows you to view videos in Windows Media format. Visit www.microsoft.com and click on downloads.

Word 97/2000 Viewer. This plugin allows you to view Microsoft Word documents on the web, right in your browser. http://office.microsoft.com/downloads/2000/wd97vwr32.aspx

Yahoo! Companion is a free, personalizable toolbar that allows you to:

- Customize your toolbar with buttons for your favorite Yahoo! services.

- Save your favorite bookmarks online and access them from any computer.

- Get alerts when you have new Yahoo! Mail. http://companion.yahoo.com/

A Basic Overview of Internet Explorer

As of the first edition, this browser has made some significant improvements which makes using it even more rewarding than before. For instance, Internet Explorer (now version 6) offers a more stable and error-free browsing experience than before. New fault collection services help identify potential problems that need to be fixed in future updates to Windows Internet technologies. More functions are included, all with easy access at your fingertips, such as the Media Bar, Image toolbar, and Auto Image Resizing. When you point to pictures on your Web pages, the Image toolbar appears, giving you instant access to buttons which allow you to save, print, e-mail, or download the graphic. If pictures are too large to display in your browser window, automatic resizing makes them fit. You no longer need to scroll horizontally or vertically to view large pictures. In addition, if you navigate to pictures that fit within the browser window and then change the window dimensions, Internet Explorer automatically adjusts the pictures to fit the new window size. To prevent image distortion, Internet Explorer also adjusts both the picture height and width (even if only a single dimension needs adjusting). The Media Bar offers a seamless Web media experience. It provides a simple user interface for locating and playing media within the browser window. The Media Bar has simple controls that enable you to play music, video, or mixed-media files without opening a separate window. The Media Bar also lets you control the audio volume and choose which media files or tracks to play. It allows you to play Windows Media files, or listen to Internet radio stations, all on your computer or on the WindowsMedia.com Web site. You can also search for additional media on the Internet. For example, you can locate audio files on popular music storage Web sites. The remainder of this chapter focuses on the basics skills for setting up and using Internet Explorer.

Customizing Your Experience

After downloading IE from Microsoft (www.microsoft.com), the first thing you will want to do is customize how the browser looks and operates to meet your preferences and needs. There is probably not enough room on your monitor to see all available buttons or features and so you will need to choose the ones that you believe you will use the most in your work. Customizing is easy and so you can always change and re-change settings later. What are the buttons and toolbars that you will use most? Click on the [View] button on the Menu bar (usually located at the very top), then [Toolbars], and see a list of toolbars available. You can check or uncheck as many as you like to either view or hide them.

Here is a brief overview of selected options you most likely will use:

→ **Standard Buttons**: These are buttons across the top which help you to navigate the web and go to various parts of the browser. When it comes to your Standard Buttons, you can even pick and choose *which* buttons are shown; whether you want them to show up as text, icon, or both; appear as small or big icons; and in which order they appear. This is achieved by clicking on View, then Toolbars, and then Customize and then making your choices. If you are like me and you like to keep your hands on the keyboard when at all possible, you may not even need the Standard

Buttons shown because you might use the keyboard shortcut for each of the buttons. For example, instead of clicking the Back button, you can press ALT- Left Arrow. To go to your home page, press ALT - Home, etc.

→ **Address Bar**: It is a good idea to keep the address bar up so that you can quickly and easily enter website addresses. Without the address bar available, you would have to click on File and then Open (or press CTRL-O) and then enter a web address.

→ **Links**: The Links bar is very useful for storing your top 10 or so favorite and most used websites. Too add a button on the Links Bar, go to the website you want to add, drag the icon next to the address in the Address Bar (usually the blue letter "e") over to the Links Bar on the end or in between existing buttons. Now whenever you press one of those buttons, you are immediately taken to the associated websites. You can change (e.g., delete or rename) the buttons simply by

right-clicking over them and choosing the appropriate menu item.

→ **Other**: the remainder of available toolbars are those that you have installed (see previous Plugins section).

→ **Explorer Bar**: Further below on the View Menu is the Explorer Bar options. Here, you can choose what will appear in a framed window to the left of your website viewing area. To remove the Explorer Bar, click on the "X" to the top right.

→ **Text Size**: This allows you to make larger or smaller the size of text on the website that you are viewing. This may not work on some sites because the web author has used what is called fixed fonts although this is much more the exception than the rule. Incidently, you can also do this by holding the CTRL key down on your keyboard and using the mouse wheel (up for larger and down for smaller). Resizing the font size can help you see better and can also help you save paper when printing longer documents.

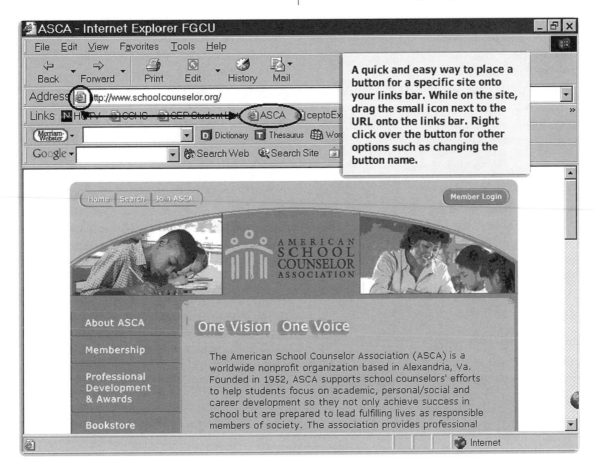

➔ **Full Screen**: Choosing this option will hide the toolbars shown on top of the browser and give you much more screen area to view the actual website. Pressing the F11 key is quicker and has the same effect. Once you settle on a website, you might do this to more easily study or use it.

The Standard Buttons Toolbar

The Internet Explorer Standard Buttons toolbar consists of buttons that are shortcuts for menu commands. They make browsing faster and easier. Here's a brief description of what each of these buttons do:

Back. Lets you return to pages you've viewed, beginning with the most recent. By clicking on the down arrow next to this  button, you may return to any one of the last 10 or so sites you've visited. (Keyboard shortcut is Backspace or ALT - Left Arrow).

Forward. Lets you move forward through pages you've viewed after using the Back button. Similar to the Back button, by clicking on the down arrow next to this button, you may return to any one of the last 10 or so sites you've visited after using the Back button. (Keyboard shortcut is ALT - Right Arrow).

Stop. Halts the process of downloading a Web page. Click this if you want to stop downloading a page for any reason such as if you're having trouble download- ing a site, for example. Or, if the site is taking unusually long to download and you don't want to wait, you may want to press Stop and try again later. (Keyboard shortcut is Esc key).

Refresh. Remember that when you access a site, you are actually requesting to download the information to your computer. When you return to that site, your browser, depending on how it is set up, will first check to see whether the site content resides on your computer. If it does, you will view the content on your computer which may happen to be outdated, even in a matter of days or minutes. The advantage of this set-up is that it is much quicker to access content from your computer than from a remote Internet site. The disadvantage of course is that you do not have any up-to-the-minute updates or changes to the site. To be certain that you are viewing the latest, click on [Refresh] which will update any Web page stored on your computer with the latest content. You can configure your browser to update or [Refresh] every time you visit a site even if you accessed it seconds ago. Most sites are not updated that quickly unless you are requesting stock market data. Therefore, it is probably best to only [Refresh] manually when needed. (Keyboard shortcut is F5). To check your set up, go to [Tools], [Internet Options], [General Tab], Temporary Internet Files [Settings], and then your preference (I recommend Automatic).

Home. Your homepage is the page you will view when initially launching your browser or can simply be a blank page. You will probably want to set up your home page as one that you most frequently visit such as a search engine or your school's website. No matter where you are on the Net, you can quickly return to your homepage by pressing this button (If you can't see the [Home] button, click the [View] menu, point to [Toolbar], and then click [Standard] buttons). To set up your home page, go to the page you want to appear when you first start Internet Explorer. On the [View] menu, click [Internet Options] and then click the [General] tab. In the [Home page] area, click [Use Current]. To restore your original home page, click [Use Default]. The quick way to set your new homepage is to drag the icon (remember that little "e" immediately to the left of the website address in the Address bar) over to the Home button on the Standards Button Bar, then choose Yes. (Keyboard shortcut is Alt-Home).

Search. This button displays a choice of popular Internet search engines in the left pane. Your search results appear in the left pane, too. When you click a link, the page appears in the right pane, so you don't lose sight of your search results. (Keyboard shortcut is Ctrl-E).

Favorites. This button displays a list of the sites (and the folders, files, and servers) that you've saved as Favorites. Click on any item in the list to jump to it. You can add to your list of favorite sites by clicking on this button and then choosing [Add to Favorites]. The advantage of including a site in your Favorites list is that you will thereafter never have to remember the site's address, only choose the site's title from your list of favorites. This is similar to the speed dial feature on your telephone. Once you enter Aunt Cathy's long phone number in once and name the button that dials the number, future calls to her only requires the press of a button. You can also organize your favorites under different folders. Before adding a favorite, choose [Create in >>] from the menu and click on the folder where the site should be stored. If there isn't an appropriate folder available, you can first create one by choosing [New Folder]. (Keyboard shortcut is Ctrl-I).

Print. Prints the page you're viewing which also includes page numbers and the site's address. IE will also give you the option to print at the end of the document

a table summary of all the links included on the page. And, you can even fully print all the documents that are linked to the original document (although be careful with this feature unless you plan to plant several trees in your spare time). (Keyboard shortcut is Ctrl-P).

Font. This button lets you display text in a larger or smaller font. This feature, I find, comes in handy when a website's content doesn't quite fit on the screen. I can reduce the font size a bit to contain the entire width of the page and save time by not having to scroll back and forth. Also, I might reduce the font to save paper before printing a web site. (Keyboard shortcut is Ctrl-mouse wheel).

Mail. Connects you to your default e-mail client such as Microsoft Outlook so you can read or send your e-mail which can include the link to the web site you are viewing. Or, you can choose to send a copy of the entire web page via e-mail.

Edit. Opens a web page in your default web page editor such as Microsoft Word, FrontPage, or Macromedia Dreamweaver.

History. By pressing this button, you can view the URLs for the sites you have previously visited. The number of sites logged into your History folder is determined

by the number of days you indicate to include in your historical record of sites traveled. To specify how many pages are saved in the History list, click on [View] in the browser, click [Internet Options], click the [General] tab. Then in the [History] area, change the number of days that Internet Explorer keeps track of your pages. To empty the History folder, click [Clear History]. This will free up disk space on your computer and prevent others from knowing where you have been. (Keyboard shortcut is Ctrl-H).

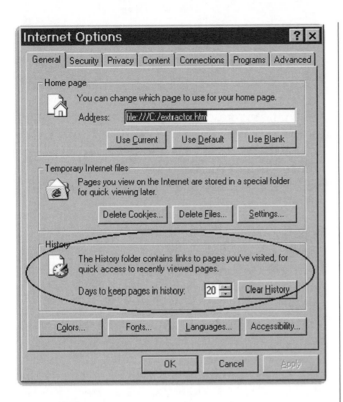

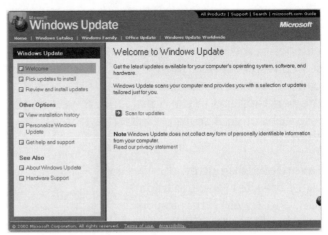

Full Screen. Toggles between displaying your web page on a full screen with a limited view of buttons or a more limited view of the web site with a larger display of buttons. (Keyboard shortcut is F11).

Address Bar. This is the white area that displays the current URL or web address. To change the address and go to another page, click inside the [Address] bar until the currently displayed address is highlighted. Then, start typing the address of your desired site. If you've visited the Web site before, the AutoComplete feature suggests a match as you type. The suggested match is highlighted in the [Address] bar. After you finish typing the Web address, or when AutoComplete finds a match, press [ENTER] on your keyboard. To view other matches, press the [DOWN ARROW] key.

Keeping IE Up to Date

With any software, it is important to periodically look for and install patches. A patch is a temporary fix to a program bug or glitch that will eventually be more permanently fixed in future versions of the software. Patches are commonly used for increasing the compatibility of software with various kinds of computers and peripherals; for resolving conflicts with hardware or other software; to add a feature to an existing program after a high volume of feedback; and especially important for web browsers — to literally patch up security holes in the software to ward off potential hackers. Microsoft Corporation has made it relatively simple to keep all of their products up to date. Simply visit http://v4.windowsupdate.microsoft.com/en/default.asp (or click on the [Tools] menu in Internet Explorer and choose [Windows Update]). Then click on Scan for Updates. Without collecting any form of personally identifiable information from your computer, the site will first scan your computer for Microsoft products, determine what patches are available and have not yet been installed for your software, and then allow you to pick and choose which to install. One of the choices is actually a piece of software that automatically checks for updates on a periodic basis called *Critical Update Notification*. It is an application for Windows 2000 and Windows 98 that notifies you when a new critical update is available from Windows Update. This is intended to proactively notify you when an important system patch is available for you to download and install. Critical Update Notification automatically runs daily as a scheduled job, and checks if you are connected to the Internet at that time. If so, it then checks if any critical patches apply to your computer. Note that some updates may require that you restart your computer. Save your work and close any open programs before beginning the installation process.

Other Internet Explorer Tricks

In case you were wondering ...

→ **Browsing your Computer**: In addition to the Web, Internet Explorer can be used to also browse the contents of your computer. In the address bar, type in c: and then press enter. You should see the contents of your hard drive. If you know the name of a folder (e.g. My Documents), you can actually type that into the address bar and go straight to that folder.

→ **Use a Blank Home Page**: Every time you launch IE, the browser takes you straight to whatever home page you set. This page may take some time to load — time you might not want to waste. So, eliminate a home page altogether and start up on a blank page. Do this by choosing the [Tools] menu and then [Internet Options], then click the [General] tab. In the Home Page area, click the Use Blank button. Or, you may type about:blank in the address bar and then drag the URL icon over to the Home button as previously described.

→ **Sharing Your Favorites**: To share your favorites with someone else, pull down the [File] menu and choose Import and Export which will launch the Export Wizard. Then choose Export Favorites, choose a location to save the file, and send this file to the other person. The other person should follow the same procedure except, instead of choosing Export Favorites, he or she will choose Import Favorites.

→ **Navigate With Just One Word**: Instead of typing in the entire website address, just type in the site's name (usually the middle part) and then press Ctrl-Enter to automatically add http://www and .com on each side of the word. For instance, to go to my website, type in schoolcounselor and press CTRL-Enter and you're there. Of course, this trick only works with websites ending in dot com.

→ **Hanging Websites:** If you're waiting for a page to load and it's taking too long, push the Stop button. Then click on Refresh to start over. Sometimes the path that the page takes to get to your computer contains what I call Internet hiccups that slow it down, and refreshing will send it back to you via a new, clearer route.

→ **Create Shortcut**: To place an icon on your Desktop that points to the web site, right click on any empty space on the website and choose Create Shortcut.

CHAPTER THREE

Go! ...
Seeking (and Finding) Web Nuggets

There is a wide range of estimates concerning the current size of the Web including the number of people online, the number of domains, and the number of web pages. Since the first edition of this book, the web has been estimated to grow from about 320 million pages to now over 4 billion! And by all accounts, the rate of growth continues to be exponential. So, how then, might school counselors find sites which are relevant and useful for a specific topic in a reasonable amount of time? There are typically three ways to find useful information on the Web, each having advantages and disadvantages. Counselors can (a) know the address for a Web page location, (b) navigate the Web using related hypertext links, or (c) conduct a more systematic electronic search using search engines.

Know the Web Location

Each site on the Web has it's own unique, case sensitive, electronic address called a universal resource locator (URL) that points a computer to the Web page's location. Users who discover a useful site might communicate to others, probably via electronic mail, the page's URL. A URL, usually consists of three parts: protocol, server (or domain), and file name. Sometimes, however, there's no path or file name. Here's an example of the anatomy of the "About" section of the SchoolCounselor.com website: http://www.schoolcounselor.com/about.htm

http:// is the protocol.

schoolcounselor.com is the server or domain.

about.htm is the file name

Domains divide World Wide Web sites into categories based on the nature of their owner, and they form part of a site's address, or uniform resource locator (URL). Many two, three, and four letter top-level domains abound and continue to be proposed (see http://www.norid.no/domenenavnbaser/domreg.html) . Common top-level domains that you are likely to see include:

.com	commercial enterprises.
.org	nonprofit organizations.
.net	networks.
.edu	educational institutions.
.gov	government organizations.
.mil	military services.
.int	organizations established by international treaty.

Once a URL is known, a user can simply type it into his or her Web browser and go directly to the intended site. For Netscape users, enter it directly into the [Location] or [Go] box located just under the toolbar. Sometimes, you don't even need to enter the full URL to go to a site. For example, the full URL for the Barnes and Noble online bookstore is http://www.barnesandnoble.com. However, you can also get there simply by typing barnesandnoble using Netscape Navigator which assumes the http://www. prefix and the .com suffix. This procedure is different for IE. Enter the full URL into the [Address] box to jump directly to that site. IE assumes just the http:// part of the URL, so to go to the Barnes and Noble site, you could enter just www.barnesandnoble.com. If you want to type in just barnesandnoble, you need to hold the CTRL key down before pressing ENTER key on your keyboard. Once at the site, a counselor can then place an electronic "bookmark" or Favorite that will allow him or her to point and click on the site's title without ever again having to recall the URL. This form of finding information on the Web is quickest and most desirable.

Bookmarking in Netscape

When you are at a site you would like to bookmark, go to the [Bookmarks] menu and select the [Add Bookmark] option. Click on the [Bookmarks] menu again, and you will notice the title of the current page has been added to the bottom of the menu. When you are at another site and want to jump back to the bookmarked page, simply select it from the [Bookmarks] menu. If you spend much time browsing the Web, you will quickly accumulate a long list of bookmarks. You will probably want to organize them in some manner to make returning to those sites easier. From the [Bookmarks] menu, select the [Go to Bookmarks] menu. All your bookmarks will be displayed. One method of organization is to group sites by topic, such as Counseling Departments, Grants, Fun Stuff, or Career Development. Click on the top item in the list (it will say something like Jane Counselor's Bookmarks), then, from the [Item] menu, select [Insert Folder]. In the [Name] box, enter a topic name for this new folder. Then click and drag your bookmarks into this folder. Repeat for all topics and bookmarks. If the names for your bookmarks aren't very clear, you can easily change them. Select a bookmark, then choose [Properties] from the [Item] menu. Here you can enter a new name for the bookmark. When you are finished organizing, close this window to return to your browser, and select the [Bookmarks] menu again. You should see the topic names with arrows next to them. Hold the cursor over one topic, and a pop-up list will appear showing all the bookmarks you have assigned to that topic.

Add a Favorite in Internet Explorer

Favorites can be added in one of two ways: by right clicking anywhere on the site (except a link) and selecting [Add to Favorites] or by selecting [Add to Favorites] from the [Favorites] menu. By default, the name assigned to the favorite is the title of the Web page, but you can change it to something more easily remembered. The "favorite" will automatically be added to the [Favorites] menu, or you can place it in a specific folder. To select a folder, click the [Create In] button and select one of the available folders, or to create a new folder, by clicking [New Folder]. To return to a favorite, simply open the Favorites menu and select it.

Some organizations have dedicated time and work towards compiling short descriptions of Web pages, with accompanying URLs, for a specific topic. Users can send an electronic message to the organization or visit their website requesting to receive these compilations (this is known as subscribing to a listserv). For instance:

→ **Blue Web'n** (http://www.kn.pacbell.com/wired/bluewebn/) is an online library of 1700+ outstanding Internet sites categorized by subject, grade level, and format (lessons, activities, projects, resources, references, & tools). You can search by grade level (Refined Search), broad subject area (Content Areas), or specific sub-categories (Subject Area). Each week 5 new sites are added. You can get a list and description of these additions sent to you by signing up on their web page for free weekly updates!

→ **EduHound** (http://www.eduhound.com), a division of T.H.E. Journal, is a highly specialized educational directory with built-in resource links offered free to educators, students and parents. EduHound.com seeks to harness the vast information resources of the Web, while enabling educators to use the Internet as a classroom tool. Since its launch in January 2000, the site boasts thousands of visitors per week and an ever-growing list of subscribers to their weekly newsletter, EduHound Weekly.

→ **Lockergnome**: (http://www.lockergnome.com). A variety of different and free newsletters that point to websites of interest related to technology solutions.

→ **ResearchBuzz**: (http://www.researchbuzz.com) This newsletter is designed to cover the world of Internet research. To that end this site provides almost daily updates on search engines, new data managing software, browser technology, large compendiums of information, Web directories, and more.

→ **SchoolCounselor.com Newsletter**: (http://schoolcounselor.com/newsletter) this newsletter is a FREE publication for the purpose of advancing technology literacy and application among school counselors.

→ **Scout Report** (http://scout.cs.wisc.edu/scout/report/) is a weekly publication of the InterNIC Net Scout project at the University of Wisconsin-Madison. It is provided as a fast, convenient way to stay informed about valuable resources on the Internet. Its purpose is to combine in one place new and newly discovered Internet resources and network tools, especially those of interest to researchers and educators.

→ **TOURBUS** (http://www.tourbus.com/) is a free e-mail newsletter published twice a week, and read by about 100,000 people in 130 countries around the globe. Your tour guides Bob Rankin and Patrick Crispen (also known as the "Click and Clack" of the online world) explain Internet technology in plain English, with a dash of humor. Since 1995, Tourbus riders have been getting the scoop on Search Engines, Spam, Viruses, Cookies, Urban Legends, and other topics. They also give you in-depth reviews of the most useful, fun and interesting sites on the Net.

Hundreds, or perhaps thousands of such lists exist on the Internet about a sundry of topics. To learn about such specialized lists, counselors can conduct an electronic search of available lists at http://www.liszt.com. Although this method for learning about available information does not require much time or work, it is sometimes not very practical. Waiting for others to present URLs forces one to wait until those are available which may not be very timely. Also, this method leaves to others' judgement the value and usefulness of the information. Counselors need to supplement this information with more immediate and personalized Web sources.

Navigate the Web

A second method for finding information is to rely on the hypertext feature of the Web and "jump" from one page to another using related links. This is affectionately known as "surfing the Web." You can tell whether an item on a page is a link by moving the mouse pointer over the item. If the pointer changes to a hand, the item is a link. A link can be a picture, a three-dimensional image, or colored text (usually blue and underlined). Click any link on a Web page to go to another page within that site or another site. As you surf the Web, you might bookmark and essentially create your own compilation of valuable Web sites. The advantage of surfing the Web is that it gives the user more control over what sites are deemed valuable. The disadvantage is that such a search is less than systematic and can be very time consuming and sometimes costly in the form of on-line charges.

At this point you might ask, "What would be a good starting point for my web travels?" An increasing number of universities, libraries, companies, organizations, and even volunteers are creating directories to catalog portions of the Internet. These directories are organized by subject and consist of links to Internet resources relating to these subjects. The major subject directories available on the Web tend to have overlapping but different databases. Most directories provide a search capability that allows you to query the database on your topic of interest. Subject directories differ significantly in selectivity. For example, the famous Yahoo! (www.yahoo.com) site's Directory is organized by subject. Sites are placed in categories by Yahoo! editors, who visit your web site, evaluate your suggestion, and decide where to place your site. This ensures that the directory is organized in the best possible way, so that it is easy to use, helpful, and fair to everyone. Similarly, each site in the About.com network is run by a professional Guide who is carefully screened and trained by the company. Guides build a comprehensive environment around each of their specific topics, including the best new content, relevant links, How-To's, Forums, and answers to just about any question. Google (www.google.com) uses a combination of people and machines. They start with a collection of websites selected by Open Directory volunteer editors. Then, Google applies its PageRank technology to rank the sites based on their importance.

Some directories have evolved into what is now known as web portals. A web portal is a site or service that offers a broad array of resources and services, such as e-mail, forums, search engines, and on-line shopping malls. The first Web portals were online services, such as America Online, that provided access to the Web, but by now most of the traditional search engines have transformed themselves into Web portals to attract and keep a larger audience. The four leading portals (in alphabetical order) are America Online (www.aol.com), Infoseek (http://infoseek.go.com/), Microsoft Network (www.msn.com), and Yahoo! (www.yahoo.com).

Use a Search Engine

One tool that has evolved for conducting research over the Web is the search engine. Most search engines have three parts: the spider, the index, and the actual search engine. First is the spider, also called the crawler. The spider visits a web page, reads it, and then follows links to other pages within the site. This is what it means when someone refers to a site being "spidered" or "crawled." The spider returns to the site on a regular basis, such as every month or two, to look for changes. Everything the spider finds goes into the second part of the search engine, the index. The index, sometimes called the catalog, is like a giant book containing a copy of every web page that the spider finds. If a web page changes, then this book is updated with new information. Sometimes it can take a while for new pages or changes that the spider finds to be added to the index. Thus, a web page may have been "spidered" but not yet "indexed." Until it is indexed it is not available to those searching with the search engine. Search engine software is the third part of a search engine. This is the program that sifts through the millions of

pages recorded in the index to find matches to a search and rank them in order of what it believes is most relevant (Sullivan, 2002).

No one search engine can index every web page available. So, if a specific site is not included in the results of a search, it does not necessarily mean that the page does not exist—only that the search engine has not included it in its index. Also, just because a site is indexed, does not necessarily mean that the site is still active. The Web is quite a dynamic place with sites being introduced and deleted all the time. It is wise, then, that serious web researchers conduct searches with more than one search engine. Better yet, you might conduct a metasearch with an appropriate search engine (e.g., http://www.dogpile.com or http://www.metacrawler.com), one that enters your search terms in more than one engine and presents the results from each of the various engines it queries. Copernic Agent Basic is a popular (and free; www.copernic.com) software program that aids in conducting metasearches by automatically checking up to 90 different search engines for your term and collating the results into one window. Which of the many search engines really matter? Sullivan (1998) writes, "...it's the search engines that are well-known and well-used. This is true whether you are a webmaster or a researcher. A well-known, commercially-backed search engine generally means more dependable results. These search engines are more likely to be well-maintained and upgraded when necessary, to keep pace with the growing web." Check out the search engine section of the Chapter 7 for a list of notable search engines to use.

Conducting Searches

I consider conducting effective searches similar to playing golf: mostly skill and some luck. The integrity of your results will depend in part on the search engine you use and mostly on the skill with which you perform your search. The Internet is a vast computer database. As such, its contents must be searched according to the rules of computer database searching. Much database searching is based on the principles of Boolean logic. Boolean logic refers to the logical relationship among search terms, and is named for the British mathematician George Boole (Cohen, 1998).

In general, the key Boolean operators are AND, NOT, OR and NEAR although can vary slightly depending on which search engine one uses. For instance, a search for school counseling jobs which excludes sites about financial counseling might look like this:

"school counseling" NEAR jobs NOT "financial counselor"

The keyword NEAR instructs the search engine to return sites where the word "jobs" is found within ten words or so of counseling. The use of quotations tells the computer to search for and return results with the phrase or term "school counseling" instead of pages with either word. In this case, the operator NOT excludes sites with the phrase "financial counselor." Another example which illustrates the importance of using quotation marks would be a search about peer pressure which should be entered as "peer pressure" so that you do not retrieve every indexed page with either the word peer or pressure (likely a more expansive set of results). Although not an operator, you can sometimes use the asterisk (*) as a wildcard to take the place of one or more characters so that a search for couns* should return sites on both counseling and counselor. Notice that Boolean operators must be in all caps and they must be separated on either side by a space. Also notice that the operator AND was not used in the example. This is because virtually all search engines assume this operator when encountering a space between words or phrases. Also, know that the operators I describe here are somewhat standard although may vary slightly. So, you should always consult the search engine site's section on advanced searching.

Using Boolean operators can often be the quickest way to enter and find what you are looking for. However, for counselors whom are more inclined, you would be interested in knowing that most search engines of today now allow such conditional searches by simply completing a form. Typically, the search form which allows you to pick and choose conditions for your search is located under a link called [Advanced Search]. Following are common choices you will have for both restricting and expanding your search:

→ search term(s);

→ specific languages (e.g., you may want to include sites only in English);

→ pages containing or not containing any words or phrases specified;

→ pages published within a specified period of time;

→ results which include only specified file types such as graphics, sound, films, PDF files, and more;

→ the number of results to be displayed and the length of each description;

→ block (i.e., prevent pages containing offensive content from being returned);

→ domain (i.e., your results should only come from a specific website or kind of website such as educational sites ending in .edu); and

→ similar pages (e.g., by entering a website address, search engines will now locate similar pages).

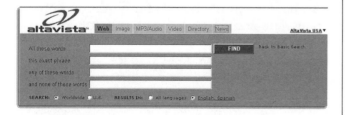

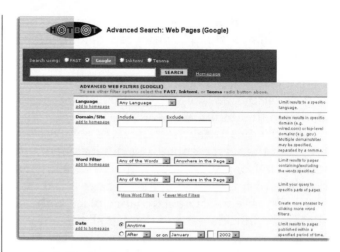

Before conducting any serious web searches, you might want to consider the following tips:

1. Pick one acclaimed search engine and read the directions provided for you at the site. Become expert for using the site by studying how the search engine works and practicing with small variations of a search term.

2. Supplement your search by using other search engines. No search engine indexes all web sites and web pages. So if your primary search doesn't produce the results you wanted, try searching with at least one other search engine. As mentioned before, you may want to try your hand at conducting metasearches.

3. If you have a multi-term search, be sure to determine which type of Boolean logic or Advanced Search conditions you should use.

4. Make certain that your spelling is correct because errors of one letter, space, or wrong punctuation mark may not be forgiven by a search engine. Some search engines do check for spelling and will suggest alternatives if needed.

5. Realize that some search engines are case sensitive.

6. If you have too many results, or results that are not relevant: Increase the number of key words and/or phrases (remember, phrases are words in quotes) that are specific to your topic. If available, you can conduct a search within a given set of results.

7. If you have too few results: reduce the number of keywords you used to broaden your subject. Add alternate terms or spellings for individual concepts and connect with the Boolean operator OR.

8. If you are having problems connecting to a site with a long URL, try deleting the information after the main part of the address or the site's home page. From there you can navigate the site via its on-page links.

Search engines continue to evolve and will surely change how we seek and find appropriate websites in the future. One area of progress is how search engines use natural language to help provide relevant results. Natural language is synonymous with human language which means that instead of using Boolean or other cryptic operators, we can simply ask the computer a question similar to how we would ask another human being. According to the Research Buzz (www.researchbuzz.com/articles/natlang.html), natural language searching is great for asking general questions or getting general information. But if you're trying to get really specific information, such as a source for a quote or specific song lyrics, regular Boolean expressions might get your answer faster. Natural language searching is a good choice when searching for the same information using Boolean expressions leads you to landslides of information. One of the first engines to boast natural language searches is Ask Jeeves (www.ask.com) although others are notable contenders such as AltaVista (www.av.com), InfoSeek (www.infoseek.com), and Lycos (www.lycos.com). My experience tells me that all the major search engines will receive a natural language questions and make adequate or good sense of it to formulate relevant results. For further reading about conducting effective searches, you may want to visit the Search Engine Watch website at http://www.searchenginewatch.com. For a user-friendly tutorial, visit the University of South Carolina Beaufort Library Search Engine Tutorial at http://www.sc.edu/beaufort/library/bones.html or Dr. Steven Hale's guide located at http://www.dc.peachnet.edu/~shale/humanities/composition/writers_tools/tips.html.

Search Engine Results

If you were to receive a list of results including 200 websites or more, how would you know the best way to attack it? What about results which include 400,000 websites which may be likely to happen? Fortunately, search engines usually report search results as ranked or arranged according to specific criteria. My experience is that the first 50-80 sites listed in a set of search results are applicable and useful. After that, the results seem to be repetitive or irrelevant. Following are the criteria that are typically used to rank and arrange search results:

1. **Location**. Word matches found in certain key document fields of a webpage (e.g., <title>, <header>, and <meta> tags for descriptions and keywords; headings tags;) and matches found on words located early on in the document.

2. **Frequency**. In general, the more frequently a search term is found in a web document, the higher its relevancy ranking. The practice of "spamming" or gratuitously duplicating certain keywords in web documents is sometimes used by web authors to try to manipulate this criterion. Some search engines have started applying a "spam penalty" — which decreases a document's ranking — to web documents that use this tactic.

3. **Proximity**. In general, the closer together your search terms are in a web document, the higher the relevancy ranking.

4. **Link frequency**. Some search engines add up the number of links that have been made to a particular web page and use that as a measure of its "popularity". The more links to a web document made by other web pages, the higher the relevancy ranking for that web document.

Becoming a Googler

Note: Parts of this section are reprinted from Google.com by permission.

One search engine that deserves special attention these days is Google (www.google.com) because of the way it has distinguished itself from the crowd. Google is a privately held company focused on search services. Named for the mathematical term "googol", Google operates a web site at www.google.com that is widely recognized as a search engine that is quite fast, accurate and easy to use. Google's uncanny ability to find exactly what you are looking for comes from its advanced search methods which include PageRank™, a breakthrough technology that evaluates the Web's link structure to determine most relevant results for user queries. Google has indexed more than four billion pages, arguably the largest index on the web, and updates their index on a regular basis to ensure fresh content.

Why Become a Googler?

Google is currently the most widely used search engine for many reasons, including power, ease, and speed. For instance, Google.com:

➔ conducts more than 150 million searches per day over more than 2 billion web pages.

➔ conducts very deep searches into more than just websites, but other files such as:

❏ Adobe Portable Document Format (pdf)

❏ Adobe PostScript (ps)

❏ Lotus 1-2-3 (wk1, wk2, wk3, wk4, wk5, wki, wks, wku)

❏ Lotus WordPro (lwp)

❏ MacWrite (mw)

❏ Microsoft Excel (xls)

❏ Microsoft PowerPoint (ppt)

❏ Microsoft Word (doc)

❏ Microsoft Works (wks, wps, wdb)

❏ Microsoft Write (wri)

❏ Rich Text Format (rtf)

❏ Text (ans, txt)

❏ Images: more than 390 million

❏ Usenet messages: Google has fully integrated the past 20 years of Usenet archives into Google Groups, which now offers access to more than 700 million messages dating back to 1981. This is by far the most complete collection of Usenet articles ever assembled and a fascinating first-hand historical account.

➔ has 82 different language interfaces (including Pig Latin;

➔ provides results in over 35 languages;

➔ examines more than 2 billion web pages to find the most relevant pages for any query and typically returns those results in less than half a second.

➔ can search for images, messages on electronic bulletin boards (usenet groups), and even many online shopping catalogs;

➔ checks the spelling of your search and suggests replacements;

➔ offers tools for translating web pages from one language to another;

➔ can conduct backward link searches. That is, Google.com can help you learn about other sites which are linked to a target site;

➔ can search the entire web or conduct a search of keywords restricted by a single site.

Going "Under the Hood"

Learning the details about how to use Google.com is important and can be achieved by studying the user-friendly Google.com Help Central page (http://www.google.com/help/index.html). My attempt in this book is to provide you with a convenient overview of using Google.com with some extra added tips and tricks I've learned along the way.

Conducting a Basic Search

To submit a query to Google, just type in a few descriptive words and hit the 'enter' key (or click on the Google Search button) for a list of relevant web pages. Since Google only returns web pages that contain all the words in your query, refining or narrowing your search is as simple as adding more words to the search terms you have already entered. Your new query will return a smaller subset of the pages Google found for your original "too-broad" query.

Choosing Keywords. For best results, it's important to choose your keywords wisely. Keep these tips in mind:

→ Try the obvious first. If you're looking for information on school counseling, use the phrase "school counseling" (including the quotes) rather than the simple word "counseling".

→ Use words likely to appear on a site with the information you want. "Lesson on career choices" gets better results than "teaching kids about their future careers".

→ Make keywords as specific as possible. "Learning more about your career interests" gets more relevant results than "career development".

Conducting an Advanced Search

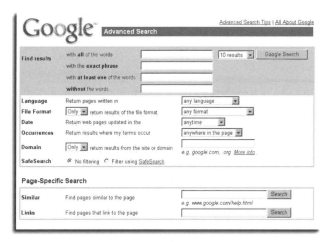

By going directly to http://www.google.com/advanced_search or clicking on [Advanced Search] on the Google.com homepage, you can restrict your search results to certain criteria including:

→ using keywords

→ using phrases (words found only together)

→ date of last update

→ words found on certain places of the page (e.g. title, body, in the site address, and more).

→ words found on a specific website

→ words found in the news

Also, Google.com also allows you to find results for specialized topic-specific searches. For example, if you wanted to do a search concerning a Microsoft® product, you would conduct your search at http://www.google.com/microsoft.html. Similarly, the following table provides addresses for other specific searches:

If you want to search pages related to:	Go to ...
Apple Macintosh	http:// www.google.com/ mac.html
Mail Order Catalogs	http:// catalogs.google.com/
Shopping	http:// froogle.google.com/
Images	http:// images.google.com/
News	http://news.google.com/
U.S. Government	http:// www.google.com/ unclesam
Universities	http:// www.google.com/ options/universities.html

Interpreting Your Results

Search results from Google.com should be reviewed carefully as a great deal of information and options are provided in a small amount of space. The following diagram (reproduced by permission) provides an overview of what is offered:

A. Advanced Search
Links to a page that enables you to restrict your search if necessary.

B. Preferences
Links to a page that enables you to set search preferences, including the default number of results per page, the interface language, and whether to screen results using our SafeSearch filter.

C. Language Tools
Tools for setting language preferences for pages to be searched, interface language and translation of results.

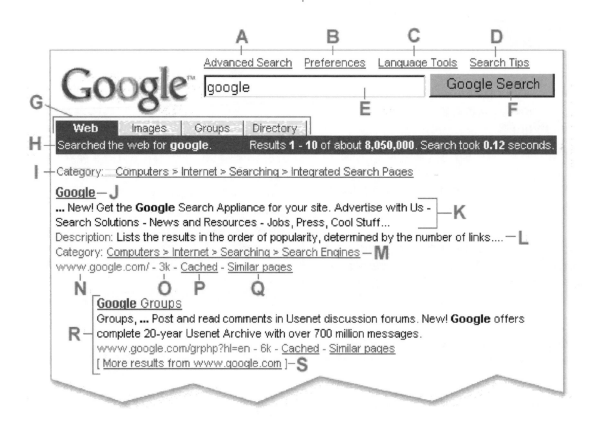

D. Search Tips

Links to information that will help you search more effectively. Tells you how Google differs from other search engines—from the way they handle basic queries to the special features that set us apart.

E. Search Field

To enter a query into Google, just type in a few descriptive keywords. Hit enter or click on the Google Search button for your list of relevant results.

F. Google Search Button

Click on this button to submit another search query. You can also submit a query by hitting the 'enter' key.

G. Tabs

Click the tab for the kind of search you want to conduct. Choose from a full web search, images only, Google Groups (Usenet discussion archive) or the Google Directory (the web organized into browsable categories).

H. Statistics Bar

This line describes your search and indicates the number of results returned as well as the amount of time it took to complete your search.

I. Category

If your search terms also appear in the web directory, these suggested categories may help you find more information related to your query. Click on them to browse for other links.

J. Page Title

The first line of the result is the title of the web page found. Sometimes, instead of a title there will be a URL, meaning that either the page has no title, or Google has not indexed the full content of that page. They still know it's a good match because of other web pages — which they have indexed — that have links to this returned page. If the text associated with these links matches your query, they may return the page as a result even though its full text has not been indexed.

K. Text Below the Title

This text is an excerpt from the returned result page with your query terms bolded. These excerpts let you see the context in which your search terms appear on the page, before you click on the result.

L. Description

If your search query is listed in the web directory, the description filed by the open directory author is displayed.

M. Category

If a site found by your search query is listed in the web directory, the category in which it appears is displayed below its description.

N. URL of Result

This is the web address of the returned result.

O. Size

This number is the size of the text portion of the found web page. It is omitted for sites they have not yet indexed.

P. Cached

Clicking the cached link will enable you to see the contents of the web page as of the time Google indexed it. If for some reason the site link does not connect you to the current page, you can still retrieve the cached version and may find the information you need there. Your search terms are highlighted on the cached version.

Q. Similar Pages

When you select the Similar Pages link for a particular result, Google automatically scouts the web for pages that are related to this result.

R. Indented Result

When Google finds multiple results from the same web site, the most relevant result is listed first with the other relevant pages from that same site indented below it.

S. More Results

If there are more than two results from the same site, the remaining results can be accessed by clicking on "More results from..." link.

Safe Search Filtering

Many Googlers prefer not to have adult sites included in their search results, especially if the terms they are using increase the likelihood of this happening (e.g., terms with the word sexual in them such as sexual harassment). Google's SafeSearch screens for sites that contain pornography and explicit sexual content and eliminates them from search results. While no filter is 100% accurate, Google's filter uses advanced proprietary technology that checks keywords and phrases, URLs and Open Directory categories.

By default, **moderate** filtering is set to exclude most explicit images from Google Image Search results. To apply Google's SafeSearch filtering to both web search and image search results, select the strict filtering option on the web search preferences page (http://www.google.com/preferences) and save your preferences. This will activate stricter filtering of images, as well as filtering of adult content in regular Google search results. To turn off filtering completely, select the "do not filter..." option. The filtering option you select on the Preferences page will remain on until you change and resave your preferences. You can also adjust your SafeSearch settings on the Advanced Search (http://www.google.com/advanced_search) or the Advanced Image Search pages (http://www.google.com/advanced_image_search) on a per search basis.

Google strives to keep the filtering information as current and comprehensive as possible through continual crawling of the Web and by incorporating updates from user suggestions. If you find sites that contain offensive content in your results, even with SafeSearch activated, you can send an e-mail with the site's URL to safesearch@google.com and they will investigate it.

The Free Google Toolbar

Another reason that Google.com is a popular search engine is because the company provides a powerful browser toolbar. The toolbar increases your ability to find information from any website you happen to be on and takes only seconds to install and configure. When the Google Toolbar is installed, it automatically appears along with the Internet Explorer (version 5.0 and higher) toolbar (it is not currently available for other browsers). This means you can quickly and easily use Google to search from any website location, without returning to the Google home page to begin another search.

To install the toolbar, go to http://toolbar.google.com/ and follow the directions. Once installed, you can customize which buttons/features you want to readily show across the toolbar by clicking on the first button which shows the colorful Google logo (this is the Google Menu button) and clicking on [Toolbar Options]. Following are among the choices:

Google Menu: Clicking on the "Google" logo on the Google Toolbar brings up a menu of handy items, including toolbar options, help, and feedback links.

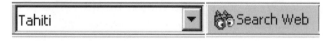

Search Box: Allows you to do a Google search from your browser toolbar. Enter your search terms in the text box, and then hit Enter or click "Search" to do a Google search on those terms. Recent searches can be accessed in the drop-down menu below the search box. You can press

Alt-G to move the keyboard focus to the Search Box (i.e., place your cursor in the Google search bar without taking your hands off the keyboard).

Quick Tip: Hold the Shift key before pressing Enter to display the results of your search in a new window.

Search Site: Allows you to search the website you are looking at for pages contain-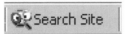
ing your query terms. Enter your search terms in the text box, and then click "Search Site" to do a search of those terms on the current website. So, for instance, if you were visiting a page any-where on the ASCA website and wanted to quickly find the ethical standards, you can type in the word ethics and click on this button to find that page.

I'm Feeling Lucky™: Automatically takes you to the first web page Google returned for your query. You will not see the search results page at all. An 'I'm Feeling Lucky' search means less time searching for Web pages and more time looking at them. This button is absent in the Toolbar's default setting. You can turn any search into an 'I'm Feeling Lucky' search by holding down the Alt key when you click on the search button.

Search Images: Gives you access to Google's Image Search. Just enter a query in the Toolbar Search Box and hit the Search Images button. This button is absent in the Toolbar's default setting.

Search Groups: Allows you to easily search within Google Groups, Google's Usenet archive. Google Groups contains the entire archive of Usenet discussion groups dating back to 1981. These discussions cover the full range of human discourse and provide a fascinating look at evolving viewpoints, debate and advice on every subject from politics to technology (and including school counseling). Google's search feature enables users to access this wealth of information with the speed and efficiency of a Google web search, providing relevant results from a database containing more than 700 million posts. To use this function, just

enter your search text into the Toolbar Search Box and click the Search Groups button. To learn more, visit http://groups.google.com/googlegroups/help.html. Note: This button is also absent in the Toolbar's default setting.

Search Directory: Allows you to search the Google Web Directory without leaving the current web page you're viewing. To learn more about the Directory, visit http://www.google.com/dirhelp.html. This button is absent in the Toolbar's default setting.

News: Allows you to navigate to the Google News site. Google News presents information culled from thousands of news sources worldwide and automatically arranged to present the most relevant news first. Topics are updated continu-ously throughout the day, so you will see new stories each time you check the page. To use this function, just click on the News button or select Google News from the toolbar menu. To learn more, visit http://news.google.com/help/about_news_search.html.

Voting buttons: If you especially like or dislike a page, you can vote for or against the page by using these but-tons. Just click the happy or unhappy faces to tell Google that you like or dislike a page as you surf. These buttons can also be used to report espe-cially good or bad results after searching on Google. Indicate satisfaction or dissatisfaction with your results by clicking the appropriate button after performing a Google search. This feature is in testing; for now, you will not see any immediate effects by voting for or against a page.

PageRank™ : Displays the PageRank of the page currently in your browser. In order to automati-cally update this display for each page you visit, the Toolbar sends information about the page you are viewing to the Google servers. Although Google, Inc. does not collect information that directly identifies you (e.g., your name, e-mail address) and will not sell or provide personally identifiable information to any third parties, you may wish to read their privacy policy and/or disable this sending of information. PageRank relies on the uniquely democratic nature of the web by using its vast link structure as an indicator of an individual page's value. In essence, Google interprets a link from page A to page B as a vote, by page A, for page B. But, Google looks at more than the sheer volume of votes, or links a page receives; it also analyzes the page that casts the vote. Votes cast by pages that are themselves "important" weigh more heavily and help to make other pages "important." Important, high-quality sites receive a higher PageRank, which Google remembers each time it conducts a search. Of course, important pages mean nothing to you if they don't match your query. So, Google combines PageRank with sophisticated text-matching techniques to find pages that are both important and relevant to your search. Google goes far beyond the number of times a term appears on a page and examines all aspects of the page's content (and the content of the pages linking to it) to determine if it's a good match for your query.

Category: Allows you to access related page information in the Google Web Directory. If the web page you are viewing has a related category in the Google Web Directory, clicking this button takes you to that category page in the Google Web Directory.

Page Info Menu: Gives you access to more information about the page that you are viewing. From this menu, you can also choose the following options:

→ Cached Version of Page: Allows you to see a snapshot of the current page as it looked when Google crawled it.

→ Similar Pages: Finds web pages similar to the current page.

→ Backward Links: Enables you to see which pages link to the current page.

→ Translate into English: Translates search results into your default interface language.

Up: Allows you to navigate up one directory in the current URL. For example, if you are currently viewing http://www.schoolcounselor.com/newsletter/november2002.htm, clicking UP will take you to http://www.schoolcounselor.com/newsletter/. Clicking UP again will take you to http://www.schoolcounselor.com/. You can use the drop down list to navigate directly to the top level. Click the drop down list and select the URL you want to see.

Highlight: Allows you to highlight terms on the current page. Click the highlight button to toggle highlighting on and off. Each search term found on the current page will be highlighted in a different background color. Note that you do not have to run a search on the terms to have them highlighted. Simply enter terms in the search box (do not hit the Enter key) and click the "Highlight" button.

Word Find: Allows you to find words on the page and navigate to them. When you enter your search terms in the search box, extra buttons containing these terms will appear on the right end of the Toolbar. Click on these buttons to jump to the next occurrence of that word on the page. Hold the Shift key while clicking a Word Find button to move backwards and find previous occurrences of the word. Each word has its own button. If you want to search for a phrase, put it in quotes (for example, "cat food"). If you want to search only for exact matches of a word, hold the Ctrl key while clicking a Word Find button. As with the highlight button, you do not have to run a search on the terms to use the word find buttons. Simply enter the terms in the text box (do not hit the Enter key) and click one of the word find buttons. Click on the button again to jump to the next occurrence of that term on the page.

Other Google Tips

If you see a set of double arrows (called chevrons) appear on your Toolbar (or any toolbar for that matter), click on them to view the rest of your Toolbar buttons. Some of your Toolbar buttons are folded under the arrows when your browser window or your monitor's viewing area is not large enough to display all of your selected Toolbar buttons.

Drag and Drop Functionality: You can drag any text or URL, from the current page you are viewing, onto the Google Toolbar in order to run a search. Simply highlight the desired text and drag it to the toolbar. The Google Toolbar will then run a search on those terms or that URL.

Right-Click Functionality: Another way to search the Internet for text on the current page you're viewing is to highlight that text, right-click your mouse and select "Google Search" from the pop-up menu.

Frequently Asked Questions and Answers about Google

Q: **Does it matter if I use capital or small letters?**

A: No. Google searches are NOT case sensitive. All letters, regardless of how you type them, will be understood as lower case. For example, searches for "school counseling", "School Counseling", and "ScHoOl CoUnSeLiNg" will all return the same results.

Q: **Does Google.com support wild cards (a symbol, usually an asterisk, which holds the place of using any letters).**

A: No. To provide the most accurate results, Google does not use "stemming" or support "wildcard" searches. In other words, Google searches for exactly the words that you enter in the search box. Searching for "googl" or "googl*" will not yield "googler" or "googlin". If in doubt, try both forms: "school counselor" and "school counseling," for instance.

Q: **Why isn't my web site in the index?**

A: Google.com adds new sites to their index each time they "crawl (update their index)," and may have missed your site for one of many reasons. You can submit your page to be considered by visiting their "Add URL" page (http://www.google.com/addurl.html). Only the top-level domain is necessary; you do not need to submit each individual page. Their crawler, Googlebot, will be able to find the rest. You should also know that Google finds most of its pages when their robots crawl the web and jump from page to page via hyperlinks. The best way to ensure a high listing on Google is for your page to be linked from lots of other pages.

Q: **How can I keep up to date with new developments at Google.com?**

A: You can subscribe to the Google-Friends mailing list by going to http://www.google.com/contact/newsletter.html. Messages include updates on Google search features, business partnerships, and products in development.

Q: **How can I find out when a new version of the Google Toolbar is available?**

A: The Google Toolbar automatically updates itself when a new version is available. The toolbar may not update itself immediately, but it will sooner or later; if you learn that there's a new version and you're really eager for it, you can reinstall the Toolbar. (You may need to uninstall first, though this shouldn't normally be necessary.)

Navigational Errors

Now and then, you will unsuccessfully try to access a site and receive an error message. This happens most often due to human error, especially incorrectly typing in a URL. The Net can be quite unforgiving when it comes to mistyped URL's and will issue you an error message even when you are off by a punctuation mark, character, and very often — a space. The following is a list of the more common error messages you might come across and suggestions for pursuing should help:

400—Bad Request

This error message indicates that the server cannot identify the URL or address you are requesting. The error is often the result of incorrect URL syntax. Check for incorrect spelling, punctuation, and the presence of spaces. Try retyping the URL while experimenting with different likely variations.

401—Unauthorized

As you may have guessed, this error occurs when the site you requested to access is protected and the server did not receive the correct password or other identification necessary for access. Retype your user identification and/or password making sure that it is correct in spelling and syntax, especially since some servers are sensitive to case sensitive passwords. Also know that you may receive this error from servers that deny access from certain domain types. For example, some universities pay for and allow access to special databases for conducting research among students and faculty. Access to such databases are granted only from connections from the university's computers or server domain. If you believe you should have access to the site, try sending an e-mail to whomever maintains the Web site. His or her e-mail address is often on the main page of the Web site, or you can try sending e-mail to the "Webmaster" of the site. If the Web address looks like http://www.xyz.com/, then the Webmaster's address will probably be "webmaster@xyz.com."

403—Forbidden or Connection Refused by Host

Quite similar to the 401 error, the 403 error message usually occurs when a server denies access because of your domain, some sort of security restrictions, or because you must first register for the site. Sometimes, this error message is generated by Web servers when you try to access a file that has not been correctly configured by whomever maintains it. (The file needs to be set with "read permissions" for all users.) In other words, you can't view the page because whomever maintains the site set it up incorrectly. The latter occurrence is most often the cause when you have had consistent access which is suddenly refused. In all likelihood, the webauthor updated the site and mistakenly configured the access settings.

404—Not Found or File Not Found

By far the most popular, a 404 error means that there was no web page with the name you specified for the web site. This could happen for a variety of reasons. Make certain that the web address (URL) you entered exactly matches the address you intended to use. Check that the capitalization is the same, that all words are correctly spelled, and that all punctuation are correctly placed (especially using the forward slash "/" and not the backward slash "\"). Remember that there are no spaces allowed in web addresses. This error may also be the result of a renamed, moved, or deleted web. Or, you may not be logged on so make sure that you are properly connected to the Internet. The good news about a 404 error is that it is telling you that there exists a Web site at the address, just not the particular page you were looking for. You might try backtracking by deleting the portion of the URL that follows the last slash.

500—Server Error

Web pages are stored on servers, machines that contain files and allow other servers (computers) to download files from them. If the server has been incorrectly set up or is experiencing mechanical problems, it will return this error. If you entered the URL manually, make sure it matches the URL exactly. Spelling, punctuation, and capitalization errors can prevent you from seeing the page you re seeking. If you continually receive this error message, you should wait and try again later until the problem has been resolved by the server's administrators.

Service Unavailable

There are a variety of possibilities for reasons this error avails: your access provider's server may be down, your school's gateway (the connection between the LAN and the Internet) may be broken, or your own system isn't working. You might try to wait a minute or two and try again. If the error persists, identify the culprit (access provider, gateway, or your system) by process of elimination.

Bad File Request

This error indicates a problem with HTML coding at the site. Your browser supports forms complete with data-entry fields and drop-down lists, but not the form you're trying to access. Perhaps there's an error or unsupported feature in the form. In this case, you might send an e-mail to the webmaster and try the form again some other day.

Connection Refused by Host

Quite similar to 403—Forbidden, this code indicates that you may not be allowed to access this page, probably because it's either blocked to your domain or it's password-protected. If you know the password, carefully try again. If you don't know the password but think you're eligible for one, contact the site's Webmaster and ask for it.

Failed DNS Lookup

The domain name system or DNS (the conventions for naming hosts and the way the names are handled across the Internet) can't translate the URL to a valid Internet address. This is either a harmless anomaly or the result of a mistyped URL (specifically the host name). Anomalies in DNS lookup are common, and often you can rectify this by clicking the Reload button. If that doesn't work, check your typing of the URL carefully. If the problem persists, try again after an hour or so. If you are connected via a modem and you continue to get this error for every page you try to access, chances are good that there is a problem with your connection. Try to reconnect and re-launch your browser.

File Contains No Data

This error intimates that the site you have accessed is correct although there are no web page documents on it. You may have stumbled upon this site just as updated versions are being uploaded. Try the URL again, carefully. If that doesn't help, try again later.

Host Unavailable or Host Unknown

Encountering this error usually means that the machine that hosts this site is probably down for maintenance. Wait a while and then try to reload.

Network Connection Was Refused by the Server or

Too Many Connections—Try Again Later

This error means that the server is probably too busy to handle one more user, but it's not configured to generate its own message, so this generic message shows up instead. As always, keep trying by reloading or refreshing the document.

Permission Denied

Several reasons for this error occurring are plausible: you are trying to upload a file to an FTP (File Transfer Protocol) site against the wishes of the site's administrator. Alternatively, you're using the wrong syntax when trying to get a file. Or, maybe the site is currently too busy to handle your upload. First check that you used the correct syntax. Then try again later. If the problem persists, send e-mail to the web-master and ask how you can upload a file to that site.

Unable to Locate the Server

You have either mistyped the URL, or the server doesn't exist (you may have outdated information). Check with your source to verify that the URL is correct. Or, you may have to conduct a relevant Internet search using one of the search engines.

You Can't Log on as an Anonymous User

Some FTP sites allow people who are not members and some do not. Others may allow nonmembers, but limit the number of visitors. Another possibility is that your browser doesn't support anonymous FTP access. The way most browsers handle this is to submit "anonymous" as the user ID and your e-mail address as the password. To correct for this error, either try again later during a less busy time or enter your user ID and password manually by using FTP software (e.g., WS-FTP).

CHAPTER FOUR

What To Do When You Get There

Once you locate what you are looking for, you must decide how to handle it. The following chapter describes various ways of dealing with websites which should further help you with effectively and efficiently using the web. If you are certain that the website is exactly the one that you are looking for and it is of high quality (e.g., the website of a well known and reputable professional organization), then it's time to move ahead. If however, you land on an unfamiliar website, you ought to review it first to determine whether the information is valid and reliable by using the criteria for evaluating websites presented next. Remember, anyone can put almost anything up on a website and purport to be an authoritative source. Just as any professional, you need to be especially careful of becoming a smart consumer of literature as it exists on the web.

Evaluating Website Information

One website hoax that still haunts me is the following: Radio, print, and television media all over the world reported on July 14, 1998 that two 18-year-olds would lose their virginity on the Internet, in the full glare of the public. The couple would have their first sexual encounter while a camera would broadcast the event over the Internet for all the world to see. The Internet's alleged first-sex event was supposedly inspired by the girl's beliefs in freedom of speech and by seeing a birth on-line (which actually happened when, only a month before, a 40-year-old Florida woman gave birth to a baby boy in the first-ever live on-line birth before an estimated audience of two million people). One justification as noted by the teenagers on their website was that they "wanted to show that the act of making love, which is the first step that brought that live birth about, is just as beautiful—and nothing to be ashamed about." Further, the event's sponsors billed the purpose of the episode to change repressive sexual attitudes among some people and to make a statement about safe sex and freedom of choice. Only a week later, after much discussion over the Internet and around the workplace was the story discovered as a publicity stunt for a new pornography site. Even more spectacular than the actual hoax was that many millions of people (including me) immediately believed and responded to it. Even today, I continue to be surprised and disappointed that I fell for this hoax when I should have known better. Interestingly though, it serves as a stark reminder of the need to critically evaluate web content. Hundreds of other Internet hoaxes and urban legends also exist such as those documented at http://www.urbanlegends.com.

Being able to quickly and critically evaluate a long list of links or titles is a very useful skill. According to Schrock (1998), knowing what type of information is appropriate for particular purposes, knowing how to find such information easily, and evaluating information, is called information literacy, digital literacy, media literacy, or technoliteracy. Gilster (1997) defined the concept in his book, Digital Literacy: "Digital literacy is the ability to understand and use information in multiple formats from a wide range of sources when it is presented via computers... (Not) only must you acquire the skill of finding things, you must also acquire the ability to use those things in your life. Acquiring digital literacy for Internet use involves mastering a set of core competencies. The most essential of these is the ability to make informed judgments about what you find on-line."

One of the best ways counselors can practice critical evaluation of Internet sources is by conducting searches on topics with which they are familiar. Using an evaluation checklist such as the one provided below, counselors should be able to evaluate sites critically, examine the technical aspects of the site, the authority of the writer, and the validity of the writer's content. At the end of the evaluation, when the entire process is completed, counselors should ask themselves whether the site provides the information they need to solve their information problem. If it did not, they should ask themselves how the process could be varied to obtain the needed results. Self-assessment at the end of the information seeking process is a higher-order thinking skill that information consumers should understand and apply. Critical evaluation of information can be applied to all information sources including World Wide Web sites (Grassian, 1998; Schrock, 1998).

Criteria for Evaluating Website Information

The following is a checklist of questions to ask yourself for effectively evaluating website content and format (also see http://info.lib.uh.edu/pr/v8/n3/smit8n3.html):

❏ **Accessibility, Availability**. How accessible is the information? How easy is it to find and use? How much time does it take to access the resource? How stable is the information resource or its provider? Will it be available again if you need it at a later date? Be aware that some Internet information can be very transitory or short lived. Also, does the site allow for reasonable download time? If a site is rated by you as excellent in all other aspects, it would remain an unusable site if it required an unreasonable wait time just to see it. Consistently slow access to a site may be due to a high volume of traffic to the site. In this case, it would be an option for the site server to "beef up" on their hardware to allow for more connections or for you to view the site offline. Access to the site may also be slowed by too many graphics. Webauthors should limit the number of graphics to those that are necessary for the content. Additionally, graphics might be compressed or saved in the format which allows for desirable viewing with minimum file size. Finally, is the site accessible to those with disabilities (e.g., large print and graphics options; audio; alternative text for graphics)?

❏ **Are facts documented?** Does the information contained in the site confirm information from other sources? Are the other sources clearly cited and/or linked?

❏ **Authoritativeness, Scholarship**. Who wrote, created or published the information? How easy is it to clearly identify the authority of the authors? Is the author's perspective culturally diverse, or narrowly focused? How well has the author documented the sources of the information presented? Does the site provide contact information for the author, especially a link to his/her e-mail?

❏ **Balance, Objectivity, Bias, Accuracy**. What is the intended purpose of the information? Why is the information being presented, or made available? What is the perspective of the publication(s)? Is the information presented accurately and objectively? How can you tell? What clues are present to help you judge?

Russell A. Sabella, Ph.D.

❑ **Cost**. Is the information free, or is there a fee required for access? Is the cost worth having the information and time saved? Also remember, information isn't free if it takes too much of your time to find, print, read or manage. With so much Internet information available, it is easy to suffer from information anxiety. Before clicking on a link, decide whether further investigation of the site satisfies your research needs or simply your curiosity? When in doubt, you might download the information or bookmark the site for later perusal instead of immediately studying it.

❑ **Ease of navigation**. Does a site leave you buried deep somewhere without any hope of getting back to another of its pages? A site should be easy to explore and review. Navigation that changes to reflect your current location (by dimming out the navigation button for your present location, using a different color for the current link, or providing a clear header that tells where you are) helps people to orient themselves. This sort of feedback may be simple, but it's also a valuable tool for users. It's important that people know where they are, where they can go, and how they will get back to where they started (Websitejournal, 1998). Also, is the site laid out clearly and logically with well organized subsections? Does the site include an index which includes all available information in an outline form? If the site is especially large, does it include a search engine which can point to keywords directly within the site?

❑ **Format**. Can you clearly identify what type of information it is? Is it a Web Home page? Is it a newsgroup posting? Is it a file or downloadable software? Is it a government report? Is it an advertisement? Is the information in an appropriate or useful format for your needs? Does it have the features you need? How complete is the information?

❑ **Links**. Are links relevant and appropriate? Be sure to investigate additional sites on the topic before assuming that the linked sites are the best available. Also, are links up to date or do they point to sites which no longer exist or have moved (i.e., broken links)?

❑ **Originality**. Is it primary information or secondary information? Is the originality of the information important for your research?

❑ **Pervasiveness**. Is this a site that others have found helpful and useful? Has the site been awarded recognition by reputable organizations as evidenced by an award icon? Does a search of the site's URL produce many different results which indicate that other sites reference the site in question?

❑ **Quality**. What kind of information is it? Is it facts or opinions? Is there any documentation? Are any major findings presented? How does the information compare to other related sources? Most important, is the text well written?

❑ **Search Engine Rank**. Put some keywords relevant to the website into a search engine and see where the particular site ranks. Of course, higher ranks probably indicate a more popular website which may underscore other evidence that already supports it. Relatedly, you can see how many other websites are linked to the site in question by using the Backwards Links feature of most popular search engines. For instance in Google, put the website address in the search field and then click on [Find web pages that link to ...].

❑ **Security**. If you need to transmit confidential or otherwise sensitive information, does the site incorporate encryption over a secure server?

❑ **Timeliness**. When was the information produced? Is the information too old, or too new for the needs of your research?

❑ **Usefulness**. How useful is the information for your particular need? If you can't identify it's usefulness immediately, it should be considered a low priority to save, print or read online.

After you have determined that the site you found is relevant, useful, and adequately meets the above criteria for quality sites, then you may begin using the site with the remainder of this chapter as a guide.

Searching Within a *Site*

You may be certain that the information or link you are seeking is located somewhere on a particular website. If the site is designed well, you should be able to find it quite easily and quickly. Sometimes however, especially among the larger sites, you may need to conduct a quick search within the site. There are two ways to do this. First, the actual site may have a search feature which allows you to find keywords and/or phrases within the site. Second, you can use a commercial search engine typically used to search the entire World Wide Web to conduct a search only on a particular site. Restricting a search to a particular site is usually available after clicking on Advanced Search in all of the popular search engines.

Searching Within a *Page*

Once you have located the site and the particular page that contains the information you need, you may find that the page is very long. Instead of reading a long document, you may want to conduct a page search using certain keywords. Before I tell you how to do that, let's review lest you might be getting confused at this point. There are three levels of searching: the entire web, only a particular website, and only a particular page within a website. To search a page in Internet Explorer, click on [Edit] and then [Find (on this page)] or press CTRL-F on the keyboard as a shortcut. Then simply put in your keywords and press Enter or [Find Next]. Notice that you can check or uncheck certain options such as to search up the page or down the page. You can also restrict your search to whole words only and find an exact match which takes into consideration capitalization.

Note: Some people begin getting confused at this point about where to type in their search terms. Remember to enter keywords only in a search engine bar and not the address or URL bar.

Russell A. Sabella, Ph.D.

Saving to Disk

When you see text or graphics on a Web page that you like or want to refer to later, you can save them on your computer's hard disk. Later, you can open the saved file and review and use it offline. To save a text or source file:

1. On the toolbar, click [File,] and then click [Save As].

2. Choose the default file name or retype one that better suits you.

3. Choose the location for where you want the file to reside on your hard drive.

4. Select the format, text or HTML, for the file. Saving in text format will strip away most HTML coding and leave you with simple text. HTML format will retain all coding which can be a plus if you want to get an inside look at how web pages do what they do (and if you want to retain the active links). Notice that you can also save the entire website on your computer by picking [Web page complete] as the format choice. This will download a near exact copy, graphics and all, on your computer which you can then navigate using a browser similar to looking at it on the web. The advantages of "off line" browsing is that it loads faster and you don't need an Internet connection.

5. Finally, click [Save] to save the file.

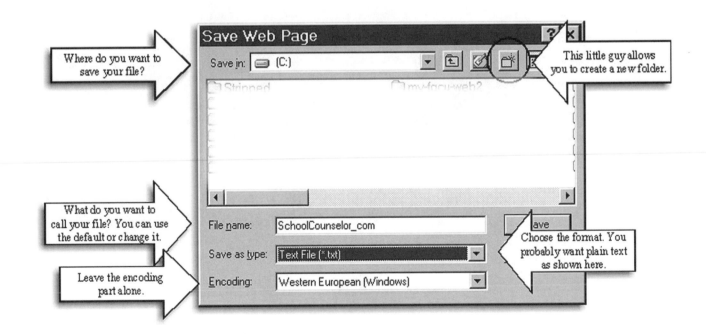

Saving Graphics and Text

To save an inline graphic (a graphic presented to you on a webpage) using Internet Explorer (or, almost identically in Netscape Navigator):

1. Place your mouse arrow over the graphic you want to save and **Right**-click on it. On the shortcut menu that appears, click [Save Picture As]. Notice too that you can choose [Copy] which saves the graphic in memory and then allows you to Paste it into another application such as a word processor or multimedia presentation program. To save text from a web page into memory, block or highlight the text you want to save, Right-click over it, then choose [Copy].

2. [Browse] to the folder where you would like to save the file.

3. Click [Save] to save the file.

If you have installed the latest update to Internet Explorer, you will also notice that when you hover over a graphic using your mouse, a menu pops up which allows you to save, print, or e-mail the graphic too. In addition, if the graphic is larger than is actually viewed, you can click on an expander button to enlarge it to its normal size.

To open a saved file in HTML, double-click it from the folder where you've saved it and you browser should start automatically and your saved file will appear in the browser window. Files saved as text can be opened by any basic word processing program and are easily read by both Windows and MacIntosh compatible computers. You can open graphics with any program that can handle the graphic's format, typically GIF or JPEG, such as the latest word processors or graphic suite programs.

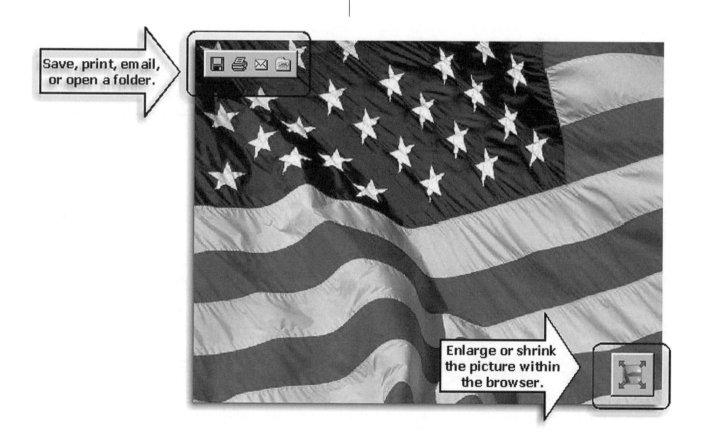

Save, print, email, or open a folder.

Enlarge or shrink the picture within the browser.

Russell A. Sabella, Ph.D.

Saving Data Files

For the purposes of this chapter, data files include everything except web or HTML pages such as spreadsheets, movies, sound, multimedia, etc. There are two methods by which you can download a data file from the Internet: via your web browser or via an FTP (File Transfer Protocol) program. Generally speaking, using your Web browser is by far the easiest and most popular. I highly recommend that you read the section in this book about safety and security before you start downloading so that you reduce the risk of infecting your computer (and the computers of others) with a nasty virus.

So, to download a file from the web using your browser:

1. If available, click on the [Download] link or button on the webpage next to the target file and your browser will automatically ask you what you want to do with the file: open it from the current location or save it to disk. Tell your browser to save the file to disk by selecting the appropriate option. You'll then be asked where to save your file. I have created a directory on my hard drive called c:\downloads where I store all my downloaded software. If you don't have such a folder you can create one.

   OR,

2. Sometimes, if a link points directly to a file such as a word processed document or spreadsheet, and you have installed a viewer as a browser plugin for such a file, you can click on it and view it right inside your browser.

   OR,

3. If a link points directly to a file, you can Right-click over it and choose [Save Target As]. Then, follow the directions as mentioned before for saving graphics to your computer. One way that you can tell that a link is pointing to a certain file is to hover over it with your mouse and look on the bottom left corner of your browser. Notice the last three letters of the file which indicates the type of file it is (e.g., doc is usually a Microsoft Word document, ppt is a Microsoft PowerPoint presentation, and xls is a Microsoft Excel spreadsheet file). Visit http://members.aol.com/donnaskani/filetypes.html for an excellent page entitled Common File Formats and How to Open Them.

Once downloading is complete, determine what kind of file it is and use the appropriate software, if needed, to deal with it as described below.

Executables (e.g., exe, bat, vb, com)

This type of file, most commonly ending in exe is in one in which the computer can directly execute or run (i.e., to perform an action). You need to be especially cautious with this type of file that what you download is free of viruses or other malicious code. Sometimes, an executable file is actually a set of compressed files which make up a software program. In this case by clicking on the exe file, you actually have it first uncompress the files and then begin an installation process.

Shareware

On the Internet you will find literally hundreds of thousands of great programs, utilities, games, screen savers, etc. that you can download for free (freeware). In the case of shareware, however, you are allowed to try out the software for some period of time (typically 30 days). If you find the shareware useful, the author expects you to send in a registration fee, usually between $5 and $50, with some fancier programs costing up to $99. In return, you receive something more, like a password that unlocks additional program functionality, or a printed manual. If you realize that the software isn't right for you, just uninstall or delete it from your hard drive and consider it a free test drive.

Shareware was a concept born out of the need for software programmers and small companies to more effectively compete with conglomerates. A software author can distribute his or her programs essentially for free by uploading them to online services, Bulletin Board Services (BBS), and the Web. This effectively eliminates the need to go through traditional distribution procedures. Users in turn get to download the software for free and try it out before making a decision to purchase. Several of my favorite shareware sites include www.shareware.com, www.hotfiles.com, www.jumbo.com, and www.pccomputing.com. Once you have found the shareware you want, it's time to download it as described in the section on saving files to disk. It may take a while depending on the size of the file and your connection speed. Very often, a shareware program is compressed into a "zip" file which is described next.

Compressed Files (.zip)

What if you had a set of 1^ or even 100 or 1000 files you want to share with others. It would be very difficult to send them all because of the sheer number and also because of the size. One solution is to send only one compressed file with all the files inside. Compressed files save time and space, and make downloading software and transferring e-mail attachments faster. You need special software to both compress and uncompress files. One of the most pervasive is called WinZip for the Windows operating system, itself a shareware program, is available at www.winzip.com. Virtually all shareware available on the web is in the form of a "zip" file. For the Macintosh, you might want to try ZipIt (http://www.maczipit.com) or Stuffit (http://www.stuffit.com). Once you have used a program such as WinZip and extracted the compressed files, look for the appropriate installation files (usually setup.exe or install.exe) and install the program. Sometimes, the WinZip will offer this as an option right inside the program. Check out http://autumnweb.com/Roxys/2Tutorials/4WinzipTutorial.html for a good tutorial about winzip.

Portable Document Files

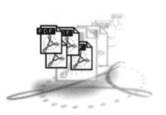

PDF files, short for Portable Document Format, is a file format developed by Adobe Systems which captures formatting information from a variety of desktop publishing applications. This software makes it possible to send formatted documents and have them appear on the recipient's monitor or printer as they were intended. In other words, people viewing a PDF file (or document) with the free reader (download the Adobe Acrobat Reader from www.adobe.com) see the document with the exact layout intended by the author. This is its main advantage over other electronic formats such as HTML, where the layout can vary depending on the software being used to view it. If your document contains particularities such as graphics, columns, tables, charts, and multiple colors, the PDF format is highly desirable. If so intended, PDF files can also contain hyperlinks which take you to specific locations on the web or another place in the document. Advanced forms of PDF files may also contain forms which allow readers to enter customized information which is then integrated into a printable document. For example, I might send to you an award or certificate template with fancy graphics and text in PDF format. Once you receive the file, you can then enter an awardees name which is automatically formatted for type size and color and then prepared for printing. The best example I know (and most unpleasant) comes from the myriad of fill-in forms from the Internal Revenue Service (www.irs.gov).

There are two ways to view a PDF file that is located online: either download and view directly from your computer or view it directly within your browser. I prefer to download the PDF file directly to my computer and then open it right from there. The reason for this is that viewing and/or printing is faster and I can more easily take advantage of the reader's many capabilities. Also, I can then much more easily share the file with others with whom I work or around the world by sending it via e-mail. Once you locate a PDF file online, you simply need to download it to your computer as previously described. Once on your computer, locate the PDF file and click twice on it to open it in the reader. From here you may search for text within the document, insert bookmarks or print it in part or in whole. You can also copy text to paste into other applications. What you may not do is edit the document. Sometimes you may want to choose the second option and view the PDF file from directly online, especially if it is a small document that you will use only once. To do this, you must make certain that your browser is updated with the Adobe Acrobat reader plug-in from www.adobe.com. To see if your browser is capable of viewing PDF documents online, simply locate a PDF document and attempt to view it. If your browser is not capable, you will get a pop-up window which will ask you what program you want to use to view the PDF file. Close this and go to www.adobe.com to download the free viewer. Then, try again.

Macromedia Shockwave (.swf)

Shockwaves are highly extensible multimedia content files which include advanced 3D games and learning applications deployable across multiple media, especially the web. The files are created using a piece of software called Macromedia Director. The lighter version of Shockwave is called Macromedia Flash which includes more simple designs, animations, and user interfaces. To appropriately view a Shockwave and Flash file, you need to have installed each of the free respective Macromedia players located at http://www.macromedia.com/downloads. Also, you must have a later version of the browser you use such as Microsoft Internet Explorer 4.0 or later, Netscape 4.0 or later, or AOL 4.0 or later. As an example of the power and potential of these types of files, try these games, animations, and tools on for size which I found by using Google.com and entering filetype:swf after my search term (separated by a space):

❏ http://www.people.fas.harvard.edu/~pyang/flash/miniputt.swf

❏ http://www.seussville.com/seussville/grinch/coloring.swf

❏ http://www.mcps.k12.md.us/schools/takomaparkms/academics/cs/flashprojects/tictactoe/tic-tac-toe.swf

❏ http://www.practialdesigns.com/flash/calculator.swf

❏ http://pieria.forthnet.gr/~aiginio/cuckoo-clock.swf

❏ http://clte.asu.edu/active/StopWatch.swf

Video or Movie Files
(e.g., avi, asf, mov, ra, qu, and mpeg)

Movie files come in many different types because they are manufactured by different companies. Many movie players can play more than one format, however, such as Windows Media Player (www.microsoft.com), RealOne Player (www.real.com), and QuickTime (www.apple.com/quicktime). Similar to PDF files, you can usually download and view a movie or view it directly online. Be forewarned, however, that these files can grow quite large and can take some time to download over a dial-up connection. Some are so large that they would literally require an overnight download. Also, most readily available movies (also known as clips or briefs) are not currently counseling oriented. Worse, there is a great deal of pornography briefs available on the web as well as other gruesome footage. Today's digital video cameras and high speed connections make it quite easy and fast to put these on the web and make them available to the world. At your own volition and risk, you can view for yourself what I'm talking about by going to one of these websites: www.steakandcheese.com or www.consumptionjunction.com, only two of many.

One special type of video is streaming video. As contrasted with other video files which must be completely downloaded before they begin playing, streaming video buffers a few seconds of video and begins playing while it continues downloading. The result is that you can watch huge video files without speedy connections. If you think you might be interested in streaming video from a website, know that it costs quite a bit of money because it requires a special server and software. However, companies can do this for you for about $15 per hour that the video is streamed from the site which can add up quickly over many users. A good example of streaming video is ifilm (www.ifilm.com) which streams short films, movie clips, and more. One of my favorite things to do is find short and funny clips that I can use in my Microsoft PowerPoint presentations to add an effect or underscore a message (e.g., http://users.ev1.net/~medosier/Vidclips.htm).

Sound Files
(e.g., wav, mp3, aiff, mp4, au)

Sound files are used on the web quite similar to video clips – they can be downloaded, heard online, or streamed. And, of course, sounds can be incorporated into many other applications such as documents, multimedia presentations, and websites. The most pervasive sound file today is probably MP3 (currently evolving into mp4) because they are highly compressed (small) and of high quality. Because MP3 files are small, they can easily be transferred across the Internet. Also, very small appliances or gadgets have evolved which can hold and play many hours of these file types which also makes them attractive. Problems currently exists when copyrighted songs are sold and distributed illegally off of Web sites. On the other hand, musicians and others may be able to use this technology to distribute their own songs from their own Web sites to their listeners, thus eliminating the need for record companies. Counselors could, for instance, easily share with supervisors counseling sessions in this format or other sound files which may be used in their work such as in classroom guidance.

Streaming sound is used a great deal for listening to live and archived radio broadcasts. One website, Radio-Locator (http://www.radio-locator.com/), has a comprehensive radio station search engine on the Internet with links to over 10,000 radio station web pages and over 2500 audio streams from radio stations in the U.S. and around the world. Or you can search for radio stations right within some media players such as the RealOne player previously mentioned. If you are looking for short sound bytes, you should try http://www.findsounds.com.

Other Files

The following list includes other common files that you may find on the web and includes the file extension (the few letters at the end of the file) and the application with which they are associated. Check out the Computer User High Tech Dictionary at http://www.computeruser.com/resources/dictionary/filetypes.html for a more inclusive list.

File Description	Extension
ASCII text file. Common text format opened by any word processor.	ASC or TXT
AVI movie format.	AVI
Bitmap. Common graphic file.	BMP
Claris Works file.	CWK
Common Gateway Interface. A file that makes it possible for HTTP servers to interface with computer programs to provide interactive functions like fill-out forms.	CGI
Document File usually associated with Corel WordPerfect.	WPD
Document File usually associated with Microsoft Word.	DOC
MPEG Layer III compressed audio. This file can be played with QuickTime Player, Real Player, and some other sound players.	MP3
Microsoft Access Database file.	MDB
Microsoft Excel Spreadsheet	XLS
Portable Network Graphics bitmap (type of graphic format)	PNG
PowerPoint SlideShow.	PPS
PowerPoint presentation.	PPT
TIFF graphics file	TIF
True Type Font	TTF
Windows icon graphic	ICO
Windows screen saver.	SCR

If you happen not to have an appropriate application for opening or otherwise viewing a file, there are several things you can do:

1. Send it to a friend via e-mail who can print it out or resave it into a format you can read. For instance, if you use Microsoft Word and you want to view a Corel WordPerfect file, a friend who owns the latter can open the document and resave it in a different, more common format such as Rich Text File (RTF). Understand, however, that the document may lose some of its features. Ideally, your friend can convert the document to PDF to maintain its integrity.

2. Check online for a free viewer that you can download and install. Many companies offer free viewers as a way to increase the popularity of their proprietary formats, thus increasing sales.

3. Download a trial version of the application for free. Of course when the trial is up, you will have to either purchase or uninstall it from your computer.

4. Locate and download a conversion filter for an application that you do have. For instance, sometimes students send me documents in Microsoft Works which I could not open. I did install a converter for the application that I do have, Microsoft Word, so that I can now seamlessly open Works files into Word (by the way, the filter is located at http://office.microsoft.com/downloads/2002/wp6rtf.aspx).

Printing Web Pages

The most straight-forward way to print a webpage is to click on the Print icon on the toolbar or press CRTL-P. Following, however, are a few tips or tricks to print exactly how and what you want:

1. **Multiple Pages On One Sheet**. To save paper, you may want to print two regular pages onto one 8 ¹/₂ x 11 inch sheet (or legal size for that matter) in the landscape orientation (i.e., on its side). This can be done inside the printing menu for most printers of today. For example, for me, I press CTRL-P, then Properties, then Features, then Multiple Pages per Sheets. It may be slightly different for you. This feature may not be available for older printers. Incidently, some software programs (e.g., http://www.fineprint.com) allow you to print actual booklets from your websites.

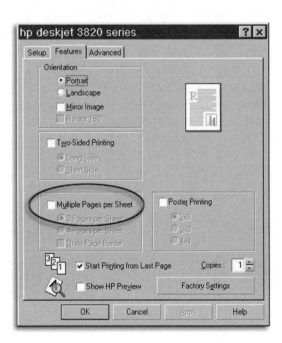

2. **Draft Mode.** To save expensive ink, you may also want to go to the print menu and choose draft mode, especially if what you are printing is not being presented to others.

3. **Remove Background.** You can also save ink by not printing out a website's background color and images. To do this, click on [Tools], [Internet Options], [Advanced], and then uncheck [Print background color and images].

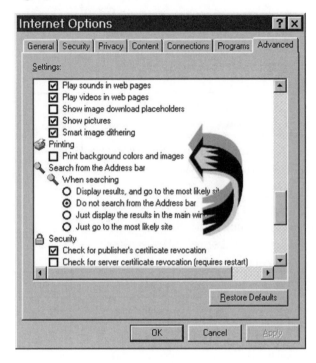

4. **Changing the Header and/or Footer.** When you print a web page, you should have a header across the top that, by default, includes the name of the website and the page numbers. On the bottom or footer, you should see the web site address and the date it was printed. What if you wanted to edit or add to these? For example, if you print on a networked printer, you may want instead to put "Printed for: Your Name" across the top or bottom? To do this, click on [File], [Page Setup], and change Headers or Footers. Also on this menu, you may also choose the margins and paper orientation.

5. **Print a Table of Links.** After clicking on the Print icon or pressing CTRL-P, check the box toward the bottom and enable Print Table of Links. At the end of your printout, you'll get a table of all links and their respective URLs on that page.

6. **Print All Linked Documents.** If you want to do the opposite of saving ink and paper, check off this option after selecting Print. This will print the entire pages to which the current page links.

E-mailing Web Pages

Sometimes you may want to e-mail only a site's URL to someone which is easily accomplished by copying the address, switching over to your e-mail client, and pasting it in (or clicking on the Mail icon in the tools bar and selecting Send a Link). However, perhaps you may want to send a copy of the actual web page entirely with graphics, links, etc. To do this, click on the [Mail] icon and then click on [Send Page]. If the recipient's e-mail software is set up to automatically view HTML files, he or she should see it right inside their e-mail. Or else, they will see it as an attachment icon which will open the web page from their computer. Another way to do this is to copy the entire contents of a web page into memory by clicking on [Edit] and then [Select All] or CTRL-A, then [Edit, Copy] or CTRL-C, and then pasting it into an e-mail message (Edit, Paste or CTRL-V). The e-mail message must be in HTML format however or else this will not work. E-mailing messages in the same format as the web (HTML) is one reason why we can use fancy stationary in the first place when sending out e-mails.

A Note About Copyright

Although much of this chapter discusses ways to download graphics, text, software, and other content, it is not always appropriate to use the content you access. When downloading and using anything on the web (or other media for  that matter), it is legally and ethically responsible to follow appropriate copyright and fair use laws. Because it is so very simple to access, duplicate, and share digital information, this has been a very difficult and often controversial topic around intellectual property discussion circles. The outcome of conversations which focus on the limitations and extent to which people own and share intellectual property has major implications for a range of endeavors from education to business. So much so, that the Digital Millennium Copyright Act (DMCA) was signed into law by President Clinton on October 28, 1998 as an update to U.S. copyright law for the digital age (see http://www.loc.gov/copyright/legislation/dmca.pdf for an introduction and overview and http://www.educause.edu/issues/dmca.html for links to related and helpful documents). This legislation represents the most comprehensive reform of United States copyright law in a generation.

The concept of *Fair Use* is relevant and important to school counselors and other educators (e.g., see http://fairuse.stanford.edu) because of how we rely on resources to teach and facilitate change. The "fair use" exemption to copyright law was created to allow things such as commentary, parody, news reporting, research and education about copyrighted works without the permission of the author. Intent, and damage to the commercial value of the work are important considerations. Are you reproducing an article from the New York Times because you need it in order to criticize the quality of the New York Times, or because you couldn't find time to write your own story, or didn't want

your readers to have to pay to log onto the online services with the story or buy a copy of the paper? The former is probably fair use, the latter probably aren't (Templeton, 2003). The same principle translates to graphics and other files. My nonlegal guideline and standard recommendation to fair use is: "When in doubt either contact the author for permission or don't do it."

The web has come a long way since its humble beginnings in providing counselors with valuable information and resources. It continues to become faster, more organized, and highly interactive. New and more functional methods for locating and using information are witnessing steady progress. Also developing are methods for delivering guidance and counseling services to students and others over this medium. How exactly will this ensue is truly an exciting mystery. One thing is certain though, the future of the Web is happening every day.

CHAPTER FIVE

Counselor as Content Provider

Great websites, like great pieces of literature, are easy to follow and enjoyable to partake. Both present ideas and stories that seem simple yet stimulate our resourcefulness and imagination. For school counselors, a website can eloquently tell a story which informs and engages our many audiences. Today's websites are also online tools and systems which can help us to collaborate, communicate, analyze data, and even deliver interventions. A website can help you to reach farther in less time by bringing your clients and their care givers to you. The technical side of a site has all but become a non-issue due to the powerful and user-friendly software now available to webauthors. Indeed, the hard part is getting the ideas right — making sure that the words and pictures on your Website represent the best of what your counseling program offers. In addition to providing information, creating a counseling website may also help you to provide students and others with important tools. For instance, one online GPA Calculator provided by the University of Maryland (http://www.sis.umd.edu/gpacalc/java.html) allows a student to calculate a list of possibilities for reaching their desired GPA given their current GPA and number of credits. Another site (http://cyberguidance.net) allows secondary students to request a copy of various scholarships by completing an online form. This same site which was created by Mr. Bob Turba, counselor at Stanton College Preparatory School located in Duval County, Jacksonville, Florida, has many other tools and ideas for infusing technology into your school counseling program. I consider it a model site for all school counselors.

This chapter provides some suggestions for building your website and how to get people to use it. Before constructing your website, you should definitely spend some time planning. Ask yourself the following questions:

1. **What is your school's acceptable use policy?** Your site must follow the guidelines set forth by your district. An acceptable use policy (AUP) governs the responsibilities of the school administration, students, teachers and parents regarding software, the use of the Internet and adherence to copyright laws. If your district does not have an acceptable use policy, you might review such documents provided online by other schools to help you create one (see Willard, 1996). Most Acceptable Use Policies include the following components (Virginia Department of Education, 2003):

   a. a description of the instructional philosophies and strategies to be supported by Internet access in schools;

   b. a statement on the educational uses and advantages of the Internet in your school or division;

   c. a list of the responsibilities of educators, parents, and students for using the Internet;

   d. a code of conduct governing behavior on the Internet;

   e. a description of the consequences of violating the AUP;

   f. a description of what constitutes acceptable and unacceptable use of the Internet;

   g. a disclaimer absolving the school division, under specific circumstances, from responsibility;

h. a statement reminding users that Internet access and the use of computer networks is a privilege;

i. a statement that the AUP is in compliance with state and national telecommunication rules and regulations; and

j. a signature form for teachers, parents, and students indicating their intent to abide by the AUP.

2. **Who will help create the site?** Even the best of webmasters have an advisory group to assist in making important decisions concerning their site. For those whom are just getting started, it is highly advisable to delegate webauthoring responsibilities among an established team or committee. Members of your web development team can write content and assemble photos for the various sections of the site. Luckily, many schools have computer courses and labs where, as part of their assignment, students can help design various parts of your site. You might also include talented parents and nearby college students who would like to provide a community service. In this instance, you might take the role of editor: the person who guides others into developing appropriate and fitting material, makes any needed changes, and integrates the material with the total body of information in a way that is logical and easy to follow.

3. **How much time will I need to effectively maintain my site?** Develop a schedule for site updates. Perhaps twice per month, you might allow yourself a couple of hours to make pertinent changes. To the contrary, you can spend too much time by making minor changes more frequently. Keep a file of any edits that need to be made (by you, or hopefully, others), and then make them all at once during your scheduled time.

4. **What will the site's directory structure look like?** Outline the various sections of your website and what would most appropriately be placed within those sections (i.e., content, writing style, length, etc.). Many people find it most efficient to develop this scheme in the form of a flowchart. Even if you have little or no content for a section (e.g., News and Events), it will be easier to proceed and create the section if you anticipate future content. Remember that all of the content for your site will not necessarily have to be created. You will find that current school documents and photos already include much of what you will need for your website and, with some editing, may be quite useful. For instance, a list of student homework resources, event calendar, or contact information may already exist. Also, you might create links to other important information that already exists on the Web. One suggestion for this part of the process is to consult other similar sites for ideas.

5. **What tools do I have available for maintaining my site?** To make life easy for you in your webauthoring endeavor, you will need tools to automate otherwise difficult tasks such as editing, scanning photos, uploading to a server, creating forms, and creating images. Survey your school and district for available resources such as computer software, hardware, and consultants. Determine if the available resources will be sufficient. If not, what will you require and what will be the cost? How can you acquire any missing resources through purchases or donations? At the minimum, you will need a computer, webauthoring software such as Microsoft FrontPage or Adobe Dreamweaver, a scanner, a camera (hopefully digital), and photo editing software.

Your Personal Webspace

Before you can publish a website, you need a unique address for the site. This address is your *domain name*. Domain names are user friendly words that are actually associated with a *domain number*. So, instead of having to remember and type in a number such as http://216.58.174.218/, you can type in www.schoolcounselor.com which is my domain name associated with my domain number, similar to a speed dial on a telephone. Some Internet Service Providers set aside portions of their hard-disk space for subscribers' web pages that require no domain registration. In all likelihood, you will be using your school district's web server which means you probably already have a domain name. When you use your school's server to put your website on, they become your webhost. Most school counseling websites are located directly beneath (i.e., as a subfolder) their school's website. In this case, your site is typically called a subweb. For example, the Pottsville School District web page is located at http://apache.afsc.k12.ar.us/. The counselor at Pottsville High School, created a subweb at http://apache.afsc.k12.ar.us/highschool/counselor, a couple of directories directly under the district's website.

Sometimes, you may want to use a webhost other than your school such as a private webhosting company. Often, you can take care of securing webhost services and register a domain name all in one place because most webhosting companies offer domain name registration services as well (and provide an e-mail system to boot; e.g., www.webstrikesolutions.com). Some companies will actually provide educators with free webhosting services and also make it easy to publish content. For instance, check out School-Notes (www.schoolnotes.com), HighWired.org (www.highwired.com/), and GeoCities (http://geocities.yahoo.com/). On the other hand, if you want to only register a domain name without having it point to a web server, you will need to use a domain registration service such as Network Solutions (www.networksolutions.com), Register.com, (www.register.com), or dotster (http://web.dotster.com) to name but only a few. When visiting the registration site, you will first have to query a database (the whois database) to see if the name you want is available. If it is, you can then purchase it for about $15-$35 per year.

Webauthoring Tools

I began webauthoring in 1995 by studying the source code of sites that I respected and by reading about HTML. Then, by using my word processor, I was off and running conducting the tedious task of writing, editing, and frequently rewriting all the HTML "tags" to properly show some basic text with a few graphics and a table. The procedure alone made me wonder why anyone would ever want to do such a thing. I'm extremely pleased to report that such programming efforts are largely foregone and have been replaced with sophisticated software that makes creating "eye-popping" web pages a snap — without any knowledge of HTML coding.

Most popular webauthoring products come with site creation and management tools that allow you to create frames, draw tables, add rich graphics, and include support for an interactive database. Additionally, leading webauthoring programs allow you to view your site's navigational structure, directories of information, hyperlinks, hyperlink status, or all of your files at once. Some also include automatic hyperlink maintenance which allows you the freedom to make changes without worrying about broken links. With most programs, too, you can start your page from scratch or begin with one or

more of many professionally designed, customizable templates (e.g., see http://www.steves-templates.com or http://www.freelayouts.com). Others templates are reasonably priced, about $5-$25 dollars such as those found at OutFront (www.outfront.net). As if it couldn't get easier, virtually all webauthoring packages also include thousands of high-quality clip-art images, photographs, web-art graphics, fonts, animated GIF files, color schemes, and many other design elements to create publications that reflect your individual needs and personality.

Something else you should know before you go out to your nearest software store and spend between $50 and $1000 on webauthoring software: Today's leading word processing programs, especially Microsoft's Word and Corel's WordPerfect, will "mark up" or convert a document into HTML for uploading to your site's server. Different word processors make this happen somewhat differently, but basically, you either click on a menu item that says "send to HTML" or manually save your document in HTML format by finding this option on the [Save] menu. One word of caution however: make sure that you make a backup copy of your document in case you find that your word processor writes over your original file and vanishes it forever. One way around this is to make certain to rename the file too. My experience is that this kind of conversion is not perfect and still has a way to go. That is, the way my document is layed out as a document does not exactly look the same when converted to HTML for the web. "Cleaning up" the document while viewing it in HTML, though, is still easier than having to entirely recreate it.

What Should Reside on My Site?

The first and most important task is to consider your website audience. Who will be accessing it? What will they be looking for? What kind of specific format might appeal to them? Many different people will access your site for many different reasons. You might want to create a general introduction, description about you and your program, and different links for parents, community members, students, faculty and people from other schools that will lead them to information of special interest to them. For instance, consider the following lists of web content for each:

General Info

1. Most people know the school as a building and a place they walk into each day. There are many ways to represent the school building, and especially your office, on your Website: with a photograph; with a diagram or map; with a drawing by a student or with a written description of the architecture. On the site, show your office up-close-and-personal by using a photo and include students (with permission) in the picture so the school appears as a live space.

2. A profile of you and your background.

3. Executive summary of the School Counseling National Standards as defined by the American School Counselor Association.

4. Special features of your counseling program (e.g., photos and descriptions of peer helper projects). Use photos and frequently-updated stories to let people know what students are accomplishing and performing outside of the academic program.

5. Introduction to the members of your school counseling program committee.

6. This year's guidance and counseling goals and objectives.

7. Accountability data that allows others to recognize the kinds of tasks and activities that you are involved.

8. According to the American School Directory (www.asd.com) you might publish a "wish list." Do you need magazines for an upcoming small group counseling unit that calls for a collage? Could you use more computers? Are you in need of new books for your own professional development? These are just a few of the hundreds of items that might be posted on your Counselor Wish List. If you ask for a few things of reasonable value you are likely to be successful in receiving donations. Don't forget to let people know how to respond to you, update your list frequently, and include a list of thank-you's as well.

9. You might also choose to include a text based, or if you want to get fancy, a streaming video message from your principal or superintendent that supports your work and program.

10. One of the things that motivates others to return to your site is new and updated information, even in the form of a new inspirational quote of the day (or week).

11. Clear contact information that makes it simple for others, especially parents, to communicate with you and other counselors.

12. Any honors or awards that you or your program have received (don't forget to include any photos).

13. A list of important dates and events and how to prepare for them.

14. A way to collect data either by creating surveys yourself or using a free or almost free company (e.g., http://free-online-surveys.co.uk/).

Parents

1. Tips for parent involvement in your school which might include a list of projects and "how to help."

2. Various educational "brochures" about parenting topics.

3. Upcoming parent opportunities for training and development, perhaps sponsored with the PTA.

4. School and district resources for parents and respective contact numbers.

5. Pertinent aspects of your schedule such as times for parent conferences.

Community Members

1. Tips for community involvement in your school which might include a list of projects and "how to help."

2. Profiles of community members whom have participated in special guidance and counseling projects (e.g., tutoring, mentoring, or activity sponsorship).

3. How your work serves the interests of the community (e.g., school-to-work or career development activities).

4. Information about adult education services.

Students

1. Various educational "brochures" about student success topics such as homework help, time management, conflict resolution, and school adjustment to name a very few.

2. Information relevant to school success ranging from studying, making friends, choosing a college or career, to calculating your GPA.

3. Information for alumni to stay in contact.

4. Interactive guidance units.

Faculty

1. Curriculum for use within a teacher-as-advisor program.

2. Various educational "brochures" about teaching topics such as classroom management, discipline options, working effectively with ADHD children, and team building to name a few.

3. Opportunities for teacher consultation which includes the nature of school consultation and its effects. For instance, you might describe the opportunity of having you consult with a teacher for approximately four meetings to discuss ways to enhance student growth and development known to support academic achievement.

Elements of a Website

What are the essential traits of great websites? After you visit a site and find yourself staying awhile, what makes you stay? A sense of humor helps. Flashy graphics are nice. But the fundamental traits that make a site work are more elusive. Original content is the most important trait of a great website. Sites that provide only links to other sites are essentially meta-lists, while sites that have some information that's useful to the user stand out and will be revisited. Additionally, sites which are well organized, customized for specific audiences, and somewhat interactive, are considered highly desirable (WebReference, 1998).

After deciding what type of information and level of interactivity your website will offer, it is time to consider how exactly this will be layed out. The next level in planning is to decide how best to present your website with one or more of various elements. The following are elements which are most pervasive, although certainly not exhaustive, of all the possibilities you might include to build your counseling site:

Animated GIFs (Graphic Interchange Format). Animated GIFS are called so because they are actually a very special kind of graphic file. They are actually a series of single graphic files compressed into one file. When displayed by the web browser, each individual GIF is displayed in sequence to create the intended motion much like a very short film. Many of the more popular web authoring programs contain GIF animators so that you may create your own. However, just like everything else, there are available thousands of free animated GIFS throughout the Net (e.g., see http://www.animfactory.com and http://www.gifs.net/animate/giflist.htm). Animated images are popular on the web because they can be very creative and fun to watch. They do, however, contribute to a greater overall file size of the site which can significantly increase download time. You should also be aware that some viewers find animations distracting or annoying at best. The size, purpose, and importance of an animated GIF should be considered in your decision to include them.

Background. Page backgrounds can be plain white, colored, textured or comprise a graphical image or photo. If you want your background to be a simple color, just change it from a menu of background colors offered to you by your webauthoring software. Image backgrounds are customized by creating a computer graphic using a graphics editing program or they may be one of thousands available for free throughout the Net (conduct a search with the key terms "free web graphics" or begin at http://www.mediabuilder.com) or included in webauthoring software . Sometimes, backgrounds appear as texture such as wood, cloth, or marble which is digitally created or sometimes scanned and altered. Background images are usually created as tiles or borders. Tiles use a small square of image that is repeated or tiled as a background. Border backgrounds are usually long skinny strips with a color or image along one side or the top, and another image or color for the body. These are also repeated to create the background. Using the method of repeating the image allows for the use of an image without increasing the file size of the page appreciably. The main advantage of this method is that it is conducive to efficient downloading.

Backgrounds provide individuality, and creativity to a site. However, care should be given that the background not become so complex it confuses the purpose of the page. Also, attention to print color in relation to background color, positioning of images, etc. is important to keeping the site easily readable to visitors.

CGI Scripts. Common Gateway Interface (CGI) scripts are mini computer programs written in any programming language (e.g., C, Perl, Java, or Visual Basic) and run via a web browser. CGI programs are the most common way for web servers to interact dynamically with users. The more popular CGI programs allow web authors, for example, to maintain a guest book, count the number of times a page is viewed, insert the current date, secure a part of the website for specific users with appropriate passwords (e.g., organization members), or automatically forward a user to a new page. Other scripts can help you create highly useful interactive menu/button systems, scrollers, and eye catching effects. Although using CGI scripts are not necessary, they may also automate more complex tasks such as collecting or sending data. Scripts, too, are pervasive on the web for free such as at www.dynamicdrive.com, www.cgi-resources.com, and http://www.scriptarchive.com.

Formatted Text. Text, like any other good document, should be easy to read and make sense. Similar to word processing, you may format webpage text in various sizes, shapes, or fonts. The main thing to remember is to make your site look uniform and simple. Also, you should know that the fonts you use on a website will be viewed correctly only if the receiver has the same font on his or her computer. If not, the computer will determine the next best font which means that the site may not be viewed the same as how you view it. Several fonts have been designated as website safe fonts because they are easy to read on a computer monitor or television and because they are pervasive. Such fonts include Arial, Comic Sans, Courier, Georgia, Impact, Times New Roman, Tahoma, Trebuchet, and Verdana.

Forms. Web forms are formatted documents containing blank fields that users can fill in with data. With paper forms, it is usually necessary for someone to transfer the data from the paper to a computer database, where the results can then be analyzed. Some OCR (optical character recognition) systems can do this automatically, but they're generally limited to forms containing just check boxes. They can't handle handwritten text. Electronic forms solve this problem by entirely skipping the paper stage. Instead, the form appears on the user's display screen and the user fills it in by selecting options with a pointing device or typing in text from the computer keyboard. The data is then sent directly to a forms processing application, which enters the information into a database. Electronic forms are especially common on the World Wide Web because the HTML language has built-in codes for displaying form elements such as text fields and check boxes. Typically, the data entered into a Web-based form is processed by a CGI program (Webopedia, 2003). Once entered, data

can then be e-mailed to others, analyzed, or displayed in a report. Reports that are generated from a website always contain the most recent data. For instance, I conduct a yearly survey among school counselors to determine the kinds of software they use and for what purpose (see http://www.schoolcounselor.com/software-survey.asp). Counselors who visit the site complete a form. As soon as they click on [Submit], the information they entered is instantaneously included in a report of software titles and descriptions.

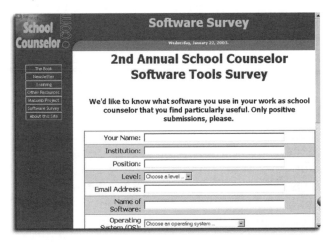

Frames. Many sites are now organized with the use of frames which is essentially the presentation of two or more webpages at the same time. One frame may be used on the left side of a page to continually present a table of contents. Sometimes, authors will include a "header" frame which, as you might guess, is a frame across the top of a site which constantly shows a type of letterhead. Always included is the main frame which presents the primary web page. Although using frames tends to make navigating somewhat easier, there are serious problems with using them. Considering the following issues with frames may motivate you to abstain from using them:

➔ some older versions of browsers do not support the use of frames and, when encountering a page with frames, runs into trouble. Specifically, a browser that does not support frames will simply skip over these instructions and display nothing in its place.

➜ there is no mechanism to keep track of where a user is, so the "current location" cannot be expressed using a URL.

➜ printing a page with frames can sometimes result in mistargeted print jobs. That is, you may end up printing the wrong frame or each frame as a separate print job.

Graphics. Including images are a way to present information more visually palatable. The two most popular image formats for the Web are GIF (Graphics Interchange Format) and JPEG (Joint Photographic Experts Group). It's not a hard-and-fast rule, but JPEG is usually a better format for photographs, while GIF is better for small line drawings, transparencies, and animations.

The use of images will necessarily slow down the loading of a page to some extent. So, they should have a valid purpose and be kept as small in file size as possible. This can be done through a number of techniques. One is to keep images physically small. Another is to "optimize" the images using graphic manipulation software, a process that reduces file size by eliminating redundant pixels and limiting the number of colors. All web images should be optimized as much as possible without losing essential quality. This improves website load time and preserves bandwidth on the Net. If larger images are important to a site, as in showing individual who won a contest, an option is to offer thumbnail images or text which link to larger images. This technique allows the main page to load more quickly and offers your visitors the option of waiting while a larger image loads. Check out http://www.webreference.com/dev/gifanim/ for detailed information about the efficient use of graphics, especially GIFs.

Image Map. An image map is a single graphic image containing more than one "hot spot" which can be used as a navigation tool in addition to hyperlinked buttons and text. The most lucid example is an image of the United States which takes a user to state specific information when he or she clicks on a specific state. Image maps are created by delineating a space or shape within an image and "mapping" it to a hypertext link. A counselor might have a picture of a filing cabinet with each drawer labeled for different areas of his/her website and mapped to specific sites.

Critics would tell us to avoid putting image maps on your pages unless you have a really good reason for using them. Fancy image maps can be far more confusing than a well-formatted text list or a simple set of buttons. In many cases, they say, it is difficult to tell just where to click. This is especially true if the map contains both images and words. Unlike regular text links which change color after being clicked on, image maps give no clue about what's been seen and what hasn't. This makes it more difficult for the user to navigate your site. However, used sparingly, image maps can help you to keep your site organized and they also look pretty cool.

Links. Your web page should be highly connected to the rest of the school and district. So, include links on all your pages, whenever possible, that point visitors to other valuable resources. Lists of links should be short, well organized, and truly resourceful. After reviewing the list of websites in this book, you might highlight several that are especially pertinent to you and include them as links on your website.

Marquee. On web pages, this is a scrolling area of text. Starting with Version 2, Microsoft Internet Explorer supports a special tag for creating these areas. Netscape Navigator, however, does not support this tag. You can also create marquees with Java applets and Dynamic HTML which are compatible with both browsers.

Multimedia Presentations. Programs such as Microsoft PowerPoint© and Corel Presentations© allow users to create attention grabbing slides which contain sounds, graphics, animated objects, animated texts, and other elements. These programs also allow you to convert your multimedia slide shows to HTML and upload them to your site. The result is a series of highly stylized images for slide shows and reports. Multimedia slide shows can include various types of charts, graphs and text in a variety of fonts. Most systems enable you to import data from a spreadsheet application to create the charts and graphs. The conversion accuracy from multimedia to HTML varies with each version of the program although continues to get better.

According to Sabella and Booker (in review), the importance of placing your multimedia presentation (MMP) on the World Wide Web lies in making your message easily accessible to both a regional and global audience. Community members, business, industry, parents, and others outside of the school environment can more conveniently and readily learn about your guidance and counseling program. A presentation that is easily accessed and which contains rich, meaningful, and useful information can positively contribute to the profession's credibility while lending support to it's members. Similarly, counselors may elect to use the power of this technology for providing consultation to other stake holders in the form of online training and development. Counselors who make available to parents and others MMPs about best practices in areas such as communication, studying, career development, or other academic, personal, and social endeavors stand to provide timely and much needed assistance while also promoting their own program.

PowerPoint makes it relatively easy to save one's presentation to the World Wide Web. The program first requires that you save the document as an HTML (hypertext markup language) document by clicking on [File] and then [Save as a web page]. The resulting menu allows the counselor to choose (a) the destination folder for the files generated by the program; (b) the title of the presentation which will later become the

title of the web page; and (c) the name of the file which becomes the name of the file that users will point to in their web browsers. The next step is to click on the [Publish] button which presents a final menu that allows the counselor to customize the look and format of the web page. Customizing includes options for colors, whether the presentation will be animated on the web or not, and whether the presentation will include speaker notes, among others. If your computer is directly connected to your webhost, then you can simply publish to the host. Immediately after it is published, it will be accessible over the web. Otherwise, you will have to use your webauthoring software to copy the folder with your new PowerPoint files and ultimately publish them up to your webhost.

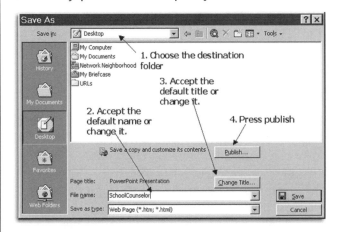

You can also check out www.msofficemag.net/features/2001/08/vba200108pr_f/vba200108pr_f.asp for a tutorial about publishing your PowerPoint to the web.

Search Engine. The leading website authoring software allows you to include on your website a search tool which users can use to locate information across your site. Also, you may want to include a search bar from one of the major search engines which will allow users to search the entire web from your website (e.g., www.google.com/services/free.html). To do this, visit the search engine and look for a link such as "Put this search bar on your site." Once you sign up, you will receive a snippet of HTML code to include on your site, and whalla!

Server Side Includes (SSI). When shopping around for a webhost, make sure that they include support for SSIs. These are a type of HTML comment that directs the Web server to dynamically generate data for the Web page whenever it is requested (Webopedia, 2003). SSIs are activated every time someone visits the page in which they reside and so they are constantly updated which means that you can have dynamic content which is continually refreshing. So, for instance, you can go to www.weather.com and grab the SSI code that, when inserted into your webpage, will generate a weather map for your area. One online bookstore, Amazon.com, provides SSI's which allow other websites to automatically have a selection of books or other resources available for any given topic. The Life Mentoring website (www.lifementoring.com/wm.html) allows you to put daily motivational quotes on your site while Vibrant Media (www.vibrantmedia.com) provides daily news feeds for various business topics.

Short Films (AVI and MPEG). AVI stands for Audio Video Interleave and is the most common format for audio/video data on the PC. Inserting an AVI file is very similar to inserting a link. Once the short film is inserted, a user simply needs to click on the link which will cause the AVI file to be downloaded or viewed from the server. The browser recognizes that the AVI file is not a typical document. Then, the browser invokes a helper application that can play the AVI file, such as Windows Media Player, and the movie will appear in a separate window. Sometimes, the browser may have a plug-in that provides support for AVI, in which case the video window will appear embedded in the HTML page. In both Internet Explorer and Netscape, the user can configure the browser to use helper applications or plug-ins as desired.

The procedure is the same for MPEG and other similar movie formats. Pronounced m-peg, this type of movie refers to the family of digital video compression standards and file formats developed by the Moving Picture Experts Group. MPEG generally produces better-quality video than competing formats because it plays at a high compression rate by storing only the changes from one frame to another, instead of each entire frame.

There are plenty of free, fun, and informative movie files floating around the Net. These can be downloaded and inserted into your web page. To create your own movie clip, you must either use a digital video recorder or convert more traditional tape formats to digital. According to Sabella and Booker (in review), one way to make the transfer is to connect your computer to a computer projector that has the appropriate inputs (from the VCR) and outputs (to the computer). In this case, the computer projector is the converter and also the monitor. However, counselors may want to consider purchasing and installing a piece of computer hardware such as a PC Video card (installed on the inside of the computer) or a Video Bus (an external device connected outside of the computer. For example, see www.ati.com, www.cdw.com, or www.belkin.com/videobus2), which easily allows for this kind of transfer. At one time, such hardware were cost prohibitive although many are now under $100. Typically included with the device is video editing software for adding text and special transition effects to your resulting video. The limited bandwidth of the Internet is the bane of effective use of video on a Web page. So, video clips on a web page need to be small. Even then, downloading a video clip can take several minutes or hours over a dial-up connection. The longer the wait, the better the video should be.

Russell A. Sabella, Ph.D.

Site Index. Leading web authoring software can help you to easily generate an outline or table of contents of your website pages. This is an easy way for visitors to locate exactly what they want.

Sound. Having sound on a site can help you keep your visitors' attention and facilitate communication and interactivity. For instance, you might record your own voice and present a welcome message. You may personally narrate an event or program. Many sites contain sound effects which bring other graphics or events alive. There are several popular sound file formats which include:

→ RealAudio (RA), from Progressive Networks, is a tool to stream audio-content in realtime over the Internet. You can start listening right from the moment you start downloading. This is the main difference to sound-files in conventional sound-formats, which you must download completely before playing. A RealAudio connection is interactive: you can start, stop and pause the playback, as well as adjust the volume — much as you would operate a local tape recorder. To listen to a RA file, you must download and install a free player from www.realaudio.com.

→ WAV is the format for storing sound in files developed jointly by Microsoft and IBM. Support for WAV files was built into Windows 95 making it the de facto standard for sound on PCs. WAV sound files end with a .wav extension and can be played by nearly all Windows applications that support sound. WAV files can be recorded with software which comes with Microsoft Windows (sound recorder) or downloaded from the Net (e.g., check out http://www.dailywav.com/)

→ Musical Instrument Digital Interface (MIDI): Pronounced middy, this format is the standard adopted by the electronic music industry for controlling devices, such as synthesizers and sound cards, that emit music. At minimum, a MIDI representation of a sound includes values for the note's pitch, length, and volume. It can also include additional characteristics, such as attack and delay time. The MIDI standard is supported by most synthesizers, so sounds created on one synthesizer can be played and manipulated on another synthesizer. Computers that have a MIDI interface can record sounds created by a synthesizer and then manipulate the data to produce new sounds. For example, you can change the key of a composition with a single keystroke. A number of software programs are available for composing and editing music that conforms to the MIDI standard. They offer a variety of functions: for instance, when you play a tune on a keyboard connected to a computer, a music program can translate what you play into a written score (Webopedia, 2003).

Tables. Similar to tables in word processors, website content can be displayed in various cells within rows and columns. Tables allows for exact placement of content such as with a newsletter or table of data.

Text Art. Text art is simply text with some very fancy changes such as representing a word or phrase in three dimensions. Ultimately, it is saved into a graphic  file of any format. Text art is usually created with desktop publishing, word processing, or multimedia software. Once saved, the file is then inserted into the web page.

How Do I Get My Site Noticed?

Once your site is up, running, and presentable, you will want to make your hard work pay off. There are several things you can do to publicize your new webpage and its offerings:

→ Submit your website information to several popular search engines.

→ Announce your new website to listservs which comprise members who should find your site of particular interest. Realize though that many listservs do not allow you to post messages unless you are a member of the group. Therefore, you will either have to temporarily subscribe or have the message forwarded by a member of the group that you know. Be aware that if your description sounds as if you are selling a product, this is considered to be "spam" and is virtually always considered inappropriate. Some users who receive spam get angry and sometimes will try to punish you by filling up your e-mail box with tons of unflattering messages and files. Some users will log official complaints with your ISP (or school) which can result in you losing your account. So, be certain to emphasize that your site provides free and relevant information.

→ Post your site information on relevant news groups. You can identify relevant news groups by conducting a keyword search of news groups using Google (http://groups.google.com/). Then, follow the instructions for posting information to the group. Again, be careful not to accidentally spam your audience.

→ You can market your website by using flyers, cards, buttons, etc. at various functions such as conferences, meetings, and in newsletters.

→ Create a brochure about your site which can be handed to parents and others at the reception area.

→ Include information about your site in your schools handbook and any other pertinent sources of communication.

How Do I Get My Site Used?

Although creating a website can be fun and intrinsically rewarding, most webauthors would like to know that their sites are useful to others in some way. School counselors would probably like to know that their website assists them in reaching their guidance and counseling goals and advancing the program mission. So how can counselors help others to make use of their site? Several tips follow:

→ **Make your site valuable**. If the information is useful and valuable, people will stream to your site to get it. If it is information they need and want, and if it is not available elsewhere, you can be assured that your intended audience will be connecting regularly. On the other hand, if there is nothing on the site that is not already published somewhere else, or if the information is old, or if it is information that no one really needs, then you cannot expect to see many visitors.

→ **Make your site timely**. One reason to use the Internet rather than the printed handbook is the ability to reflect last-minute changes. For most schools, daily or weekly updates of information will allow the website to provide things that are available nowhere else. Regular changes will keep people coming back. Reasonably frequent updates make a site much more useful to its audience.

→ **Make your site user-friendly**. If the material on the site is easy to find and easy to read, it will be used more. A clear writing style allows people to read quickly and to find the ideas they need. Accurate labels and titles and subheadings also make it easier for the user to find content for which he or she is looking. Do not be afraid to divide an article into short sections with subheadings.

→ **Help teachers to be involved**. If teachers have been involved from the beginning in the planning and development of the site, then you are on the right track. Teachers are key to utilization of the school's Website. Teachers will provide new material to keep the site updated; teachers will tell their students to connect to the site, and these students will tell their parents. The more you can involve teachers in the authoring of the various sections of the Website, the more likely you are to find your site well used. If your teachers are not familiar with the World Wide Web, then provide a short in-service training program. You can also arrange a training program of your own, perhaps calling on the school librarian or technology coordinator, who are often well-versed in using the Internet.

→ **Help students to be involved**. Many schools find that students are the chief users of the school Website. Students have a big stake in their school. They are familiar with the new technologies, and they love to see their own works published on the Web. The more you call on students to develop and update different parts of your site, the more they will encourage use of the Website among their friends. You may find, as many schools have, that students are quite willing and prepared to locate and type the daily and weekly updates of information that are essential to a well-used site. Also, to get students using the site early on, consider a contest of some sort. Provide clues on your site that change each day; students who collect all the clues might win a school sweatshirt or other valuable prize. You might also conduct training sessions in the computer lab or library, to show students how to connect to the school Website, and how to find the information that is valuable for them.

→ **Help parents and the community to be involved**. Use every means possible to let the parents and community know your site is up and ready. Send notices home with students. Conduct a "School Counseling Web Night" at school, with hands-on introduction to the Internet for parents and community. Put a notice in the school newspaper and in the local paper. Recruit a parent volunteer to post a notice of the site in all the large workplaces in the community. Better yet, involve parents in authoring parts of your site, perhaps a parenting support section. You might also consider an informational evening for parents, in cooperation with local Internet Service Providers. Show people how easy it is to connect to the Internet from home, give them advice on getting connected, and answer their questions on what they would need at home to become part of the "information infrastructure."

→ **Help everyone remember your site**. Take every opportunity to let people know that you have a Website. Include your site's URL on your school stationery and on your business card. Include it in the school newspaper and at the bottom of all relevant announcements that go from school to home. Post it in the front hall, and on the sign in front of the school. Make a big banner of the URL, and hang it at basketball and football games. This will let everyone in the school community know that the school counselor is publishing on the Web.

A counseling website can assist you in interacting with your students and other stakeholders, post valuable and timely information, and increase your program's presence throughout the school and community. Web authoring software has made the task much easier and more fun. Like everything else, you will want to regulate your time, especially limiting yourself to those parts of web authoring which you believe truly augment your efficiency and effectiveness. The interactions with others, especially students, as part of your website development should also serve to build healthy and productive working relationships. Stay focused on your web authoring purpose and prepare to be excited by the possibilities.

Russell A. Sabella, Ph.D.

CHAPTER SIX

Speed Bumps, Traps, and Slippery Roads on the Information Superhighway

The Web's power as a medium for communication, collaboration, service deliver, electronic transfer, etc. lies in its ability to transcend limitations of space and time. Internet users enjoy the freedom of conducting all types of transactions, including counseling, over the Net. With this freedom, however, comes an important responsibility to use the Internet in a manner which is safe, secure, ethical, and contributes to the overall welfare of all involved. This chapter intends to help counselors become more aware of the dangers involved in traveling the information superhighway. With increased awareness, counselors can more effectively make decisions about their online behavior. Further, school counselors must familiarize themselves with the possible negative effects of accessing the web as technology related counseling/educational issues are continually surfacing. Modern school counselors need to understand such issues to effectively plan appropriate interventions for their clients and families as well as develop approaches to help prevent them from occurring.

CyberAddictions

"One more minute," a typical Internet user often says to a spouse or parent who yearns for their attention during a long on-line session. But before they know how or why it happened, that minute invariably turns into one or more hours — at the cost of the people and activities that more and more often are ignored (Caplan, 2002; Freeman-Longo, 2000; Hansen, 2002; Howard & Hall, 2000; Tsai, & Sunny, 2001; Young, 1998). Various types of cyberaddictions now exist and may include one or more of the following:

1. Cybersexual Addiction: compulsive use of adult web sites for cybersex and cyberporn.

2. Cyber-relationship Addiction: over-involvement in online relationships.

3. Net Compulsions: obsessive online gambling, shopping, or online trading.

4. Information Overload: compulsive web surfing or database searches.

5. Computer Addiction: obsessive interaction with computer applications, especially game playing (e.g., Doom, Myst, or Solitaire).

These cyberaddictions are likely to occur in places where people can use computers and access the Internet in isolation or disguised as an appropriate behavior such as conducting research. High speed connections to the Internet, also known as broadband, is now readily available in K-12 and postsecondary institutions. Colleges and universities in particular are now likely to include broadband connections throughout their campus – in libraries, computer labs, and increasingly in every campus residence hall room. Some are suggesting that one reason for an increasing college drop-out rate is that some students frequently choose to be on the computer instead of attending class (Fox & Straw, 1998). Moreover, some estimate that these cyber addictions now account for between 5 and 10% of those in recovery programs. And, as the availability of broadband connections for residential neighborhoods continues to steadily grow, families will have to contend with technology that either help them to become stronger or perhaps weaker. Consider these Internet addiction briefs:

→ Counterculturalist Timothy Leary was one of the first to liken computers to LSD, noting the mind-expanding, mesmerizing and ritualistic similarities between the two.

→ One of many "Netaholic" websites offers this Serenity Prayer, "Almighty webmaster, grant me the serenity to know when to log off, the courage to know when to check e-mail, and the wisdom to stay away from chat rooms."

→ A 24-year-old Ohio University graduate student, started his "Webaholics" home page in 1994 after two of his classmates ended up dropping out of school because they spent all their time on the web. "It's all tongue-in-cheek," He said. "Obviously, alcoholics don't have AA meetings in bars. But some of the people who sign into the support group definitely have problems. I've talked to some of these people; they're really looking for help." One anonymous visitor wrote: "The web has practically ruined my life. I once actually used to be popular and good at sports. . . . (Now) I have no friends, a bad attitude, and my grades dropped big time. I also get eye strain from staring at the screen for such periods of time." (Grumman, 1996).

→ In April, 1998, police in a Milwaukee suburb reported one of the first known cases of an Internet-induced spat turning to physical violence. When a woman decided she'd had enough with her husband's obsession with the Internet (and with an Australian woman he met in a chat room), she took to the phone wires outside her house with a pair of scissors, according to local police. The incident escalated into a shoving and punching match, and the couple wound up in separate jail cells for the night on charges of battery and criminal damage to property (Grumman, 1996).

→ In another case, a Maryland woman destroyed her marriage and neglected her children because she was on-line as much as 21 hours a day. She wasn't taking (her children) to the doctor, they were running out of heating oil in the winter and not having enough food because she was spending all her time on the Net (Grumman, 1996).

→ Dr. Young's Center for On-line Addiction (http://netaddiction.com/) offers training for psychologists, educators and human resource managers on how to identify and deal with individuals who spend excessive amounts of time on the Internet. As part of a three year study that she conducted, results indicated that nearly 6% of 17,251 respondents met the criteria for compulsive Internet use and over 30% report using the Net to escape from negative feelings. The vast majority admitted to feelings of time distortion, accelerated intimacy, and feeling uninhibited when on-line (Young, 1998)

→ An 18-year old from Portland, Oregon signs onto the Internet every day and spends hours telling people he has never met about his life and his dreams. He tells them things he wouldn't dare tell his high school buddies. Eventually, his grades suffered; he doesn't visit his grandparents as often as he used to; and he starts feeling restless if he goes more than a day without connecting to the World Wide Web. In an interview, he stated, "I once went two days without being on-line. I didn't like it. I was bored. Talking to real people just wasn't as exciting." (Grumman, 1996).

→ After her husband died the day before Christmas in 1997, June L. found herself living alone in her apartment in northern New Jersey. Cruising the Internet one day, the senior citizen discovered Web sites where she could play casino games such as blackjack and poker right from her home. At first, she won some of the time. In fact, on four occasions she won $10,000, and it was indeed sent to her. But the winning didn't last. Soon she was maxing out her credit cards to pay for her losses. She ran through a $60,000 insurance settlement, then the rest of her savings. "I even spent the money for my burial," she says. "I cashed that in, too." Eventually she lost about $110,000 and went bankrupt. "My children wouldn't even talk with me anymore," she recalls. "They were disgusted with what I was doing. I just couldn't seem to stop myself." (Lamb, 2003).

→ In April 2002, a 17-year-old middle school student in Nanchang, the capital city of east China's Jiangxi Province died suddenly from over excitement when playing games in an Internet café (Guangzhou, 2002).

→ In 2001, Serena Williams, a famous tennis player, admitted to being treated for a compulsive online shopping habit. "Every day I was in my room and I was online," she said. "I wasn't able to stop and I bought, bought, bought. I was just out of control (Pacienza, 2002)."

→ Will Lee, a 15-year-old freshman at Chamberlain High School, chose a different approach in dealing with his mother's frustration about his pursuit of a very popular virtual reality online game. He ignored her, as his grades plummeted to straight D's in middle school. Lee calculated that the hours he spent playing one character equaled "three months and two weeks." One evening, "My mom got my cable cord ... she pulled it and ripped it out," says Lee, still a bit wide-eyed at the memory. Later, his mother knocked down a locked door. "I've learned not to mess with my mom," he says (Thompson, 2002).

→ The following is the first paragraph of a website (http://home.fuse.net/jsburns/main.html) which tells the story of one Internet addict: "If you're an Internet Addict, I don't need to tell you how I felt the first time I heard the modem on MY computer connecting. I was embarking on a new frontier. At that moment, I went through a whole range of emotions and was euphoric. In the early days I was content to do research, send and receive e-mail, play games

and download files. Had I not been so inquisitive, I may never have become as addicted as I became. It was a snowy Colorado day when I stumbled into a chat room. That day was the beginning of the end. Once I got my bearings and knew what I was doing, chat became my life."

→ What does it feel like to be addicted to the Internet? ABCNEWS.com readers who completed a comprehensive survey on Internet addiction answered that question, and the responses may shock you. One woman writes that she had to smash her fiancé's monitor with a wrench to get him off the Net. Another reader tells of staying up all night waiting to get on a bulletin board to chat. Visit (http://abcnews.go.com/sections/living/DailyNews/netaddictletters032699.html) to read more.

→ In an online Internet addiction website (complete with online support group; http://www.webaddiction.com/), one contributor described his wife's Internet addiction as follows: "My wife and I have been married twenty years. I thought I would bring us into the real world, so my kids can do homework, research, and use the computers as such. But my wife found out how to use chat rooms, at first we did them together, then before I knew it, they became her friends. It started out talking with other couples, then as the months went by it turned into all men she talks with now. She is or has been threatening to leave the kids and I, this has been on going. She started out just a little time on the computer to what now I consider an addiction. She is always talking of her friends, to our real friends, and they don't want to hear about it, she is losing her real friends, no one wants to be around her when we go to an event or to the local bar. She has told everyone that she is going to leave me, because her needs aren't being met at home. She spends hours on the computer."

John Suler, PhD, a professor of psychology at Rider University and a practicing clinical psychologist writes that, "With the explosion of excitement about the Internet, some people seem to be a bit too excited. Some people spend way too much time there." He asks, "Is this yet another type of addiction that has invaded the human psyche?" Addiction specialists are not even sure yet what to call this phenomenon. Some label it an "Internet Addiction Disorder." Some cyberspace addictions are game and competition oriented, some fulfill more social needs, some simply may be an extension of workaholicism. Nevertheless, some people are definitely hurting themselves by their addiction to computers and cyberspace. When people lose their jobs, or flunk out of school, or are divorced by their spouses because they cannot resist devoting all of their time to virtual lands, they are pathologically addicted. These extreme cases are clear cut. But as in all addictions, the problem is where to draw the line between "normal" enthusiasm and "abnormal" preoccupation. "Addictions" — defined very loosely — can be healthy, unhealthy, or a mixture of both. If you are fascinated by a hobby, feel devoted to it, would like to spend as much time as possible pursuing it — this could be an outlet for learning, creativity, and self-expression. Even in some unhealthy addictions you can find these positive features embedded within (and thus maintaining) the problem. But in truly pathological addictions, the scale has tipped. The bad outweighs the good, resulting in serious disturbances in one's ability to function in the "real" world (Suler, 1999).

Psychiatrist Nathan Shapira of the University of Cincinnati College of Medicine, conducted a study that provided evidence suggesting that people who seem addicted to the Internet often show a bumper crop of psychiatric disorders like manic-depression, and treating those other conditions might help them rein in their urge to be online. He and colleagues studied 14 people who spent so much time online that they were facing problems like broken relationships, job loss and dropping out of school. One 31-year-old man was online more than 100 hours a week, ignoring family and friends and stopping only to sleep. A 21-year-old man flunked out of college after he stopped going to class. When he disappeared for a week, campus police found him in the university computer lab, where he'd spent seven days straight online. The study participants, whose average age was 35, were interviewed for three to five hours with standard questions to look for psychiatric disorders. Being hooked on the Internet is not a recognized disorder. Shapira writes that it is unclear whether the Internet problem should be considered a disorder or just a symptom of something else, or whether certain disorders promote excessive online use (Associated Press, 1998).

What makes the Internet addictive? According to Young (1998), the Internet itself is a term which represents different types of functions that are accessible on-line. Generally speaking, Internet addicts tend to form an emotional attachment to the on-line friends and activities they create inside their computer screens. They enjoy those aspects of the Internet which allowed them to meet, socialize, and exchange ideas with new people through highly interactive Internet applications (such as chatting, playing on-line games, or being involved with several news groups).

These virtual communities create a vehicle to escape from reality and seek out a means to fulfill an unmet emotional and psychological need. On the Internet, you can conceal your real name, age, occupation, appearance, and your physical responses to anyone or anything you encounter on-line. Internet users, especially those who are lonely and insecure in real-life situations, take that freedom and quickly pour out their strongest feelings, darkest secrets, and deepest desires. This leads to the illusion of intimacy, but when reality underscores the severe limitations of relying on a faceless community for the love and caring that can only come from actual people, Internet addicts experience very real disappointment and pain. On-line personas may be created whereby they are able to alter their identities and pretend to be someone other then who they are in "real life." People who use such on-line personas help build their confidence, express repressed feelings, and cultivate a certain type of "fantasy world" inside their computer screens. Those with the highest risk for creating a secret on-line life are those who suffer from low self-esteem, feelings of inadequacy, and fear of disapproval from others. Such negative self-concepts lead to clinical problems of depression and anxiety, which also may be intertwined with excessive Net use and manipulated self-presentations.

A special type of Net addict is the user who hurts him/herself and others by engaging in cyberporn and/or cybersex, especially with children. The abundance and accessibility of such material makes it effortless to fall into compulsive patterns of use for sexual gratification or exploitation. This creates special problems for those who suffer from sexual addiction or deviance only to use the Internet as another vehicle to fulfill their needs. For others, cybersexual addiction is a unique problem in their lives. Sexual feelings are awakened through the anonymity of private chat rooms and other eager participants.

What are the warning signs for the development of Cybersexual Addiction? According to Young (1998), several include:

1. Methodically spending significant amounts of time in chat rooms and private messaging with the sole purpose of finding cybersex.

2. Feeling preoccupied with using the Internet to find on-line sexual partners.

3. Frequently using anonymous communication to engage in sexual fantasies not typically carried out in real-life.

4. Anticipating your next on-line session with the expectation that you will find sexual arousal or gratification.

5. Finding that you frequently move from cybersex to phone sex (or even real-life meetings).

6. Hiding your on-line interactions from your significant other.

7. Feeling guilt or shame from your on-line use.

8. Accidentally being aroused by cybersex at first, and then finding that you actively seek it out when you log on-line.

9. Masturbating while on-line and engaged in erotic chat.

10. Less investment with your real-life sexual partner only to prefer cybersex as a primary form of sexual gratification.

A Behavioral Perspective

Internet addiction may also be effectively explained by behavioral principles. Specifically, Net surfing is a behavior that may be highly sustained, both in frequency and duration, due to the chaotic nature of the Net. Finding special resources is sometimes easy and can be accomplished in very few attempts. At other times though, the process is difficult and requires extensive searches and sifting through many sites. The unpredictability of results may inadvertently reinforce users for staying online with a variable interval or variable ratio schedule of reinforcement. Similar to gambling, Net surfers may find themselves continually playing until they hit the "jackpot," in this case, that perfect site (better known as the web nugget). Of course, the nature of the jackpot varies among users and depends on what is considered reinforcing. A site may be highly rewarding because it translates into high levels of sexual gratification. Others may find gratifying experiences which include power ("I know something you don't know."), prestige ("Look at what I was able to find and you couldn't."), belongingness ("I share with you this unique information."), connection ("I found you!") popularity ("Ask Mary, she knows everything about the Web."), or attention ("I wonder who may have sent me an e-mail since I checked three minutes ago?"). Behaviorists would help us manage our on-line experience by rewarding behaviors which promote self-discipline and time management.

Tips for Preventing Net Addiction

The following are tips to consider, especially for those that believe they may be susceptible to an online addiction:

1. Allow yourself a set period of time, perhaps one hour, to stay online. If you need to, set a timer with an alarm (perhaps a computer program) that reminds you to log off. When you hear the alarm, remind yourself that there is always another site of interest that can be discovered later. Also, remind yourself that there exists no website or e-mail communication that will make or break your career or professional effectiveness if you were to disregard it.

2. Install software that keeps track of the time you spend online and report it to someone else who can help you monitor your online usage.

3. Let others surf the Internet for you to find web nuggets. That is, subscribe to one or more of the many available listservs that provide annotated descriptions of websites of particular interest. After you receive the posting, visit the sites of particular interest and create a bookmark for those sites so that you can visit them during your next scheduled surf session. For instance, when I'm developing a new classroom activity, I conduct a search of my computer's hard drive for files containing relevant terms. Included in the results are the websites which I have bookmarked which contain those terms. Then, I simply focus on those specific sites with a clear purpose in mind rather than spending much time researching and re-evaluating.

4. If appropriate, only maintain Internet access from your work rather than also obtaining access from your home. This will help to foster clear parameters for work, family, and leisure.

5. Use a debit card rather than a credit card when signing up with your Internet Service Provider so that you will not accrue any undue debt. With a debit card, if you do not have funds in your checking account to cover the expense, you will lose your Internet access.

6. When surfing for leisure, consider it an activity you might share with your significant other. This way, it will be more difficult for you to submit to adult web sites which can easily strain a relationship.

7. Prioritize your tasks. For example, if a task is pressing, postpone checking your e-mail until tomorrow.

Russell A. Sabella, Ph.D.

Equitable Access

Nations are leaders because of their invention and innovation with tools and processes. Whether the topic be counseling, agriculture, medicine, the economy, the military, or influence on the masses (mass media), the status of a nation in the world community continues to be determined by the ability to invent or acquire modern tools and to master innovative processes with these tools. The tools and processes of this generation relate to information technologies, and it is on the basis of capacity for information processing that national haves and have-nots are emerging (Thomas & Knezek, 1998). As modern technology threatens to take over many tasks performed by unskilled workers, there is a danger that displaced workers who have no technology skills will see their standard of living — indeed their very ability to earn a living — nose dive amid significant technology-based economic success by the nation. According to the U.S. Department of Labor's Occupational Outlook Handbook (see www.bls.gov/oco/ocos042.htm), systems analysts, computers scientists, and database administrators are expected to be the among the fastest growing occupations through 2010. Employment of these computer specialists is expected to increase *much faster* than the average for all occupations as organizations continue to adopt and integrate increasingly sophisticated technologies. Growth will be driven by very rapid growth in computer and data processing services, which is projected to be the fastest growing industry in the U.S. economy. In addition, many job openings will arise annually from the need to replace workers who move into managerial positions or other occupations or who leave the labor force. It is vital, therefore, that as the U.S. positions itself for continued world technology leadership that capacity be built among all its citizens for understanding, coping with and applying emerging technologies – beginning with our children.

Schools already show significant disparities in resources, even within the same district. Internet access, especially throughout a school and district, is still quite costly to initiate and especially maintain. Could it be that more affluent schools that provide the advantages of technologies such as Internet access perpetuate the privileges already afforded to their students? Could it be that poorer schools and districts that cannot yet afford the relative luxury of Internet access face yet another hurdle that keeps students further behind? Internet literacy is known to be a desirable and even critical competency that our future workforce may not be able to do without. So, the lack of Internet access may imply that students not only learn less effectively, but may be less equipped to meet the needs of their future workplace. Consider that the expansion in computer-related industries accounted for more than one-quarter of the U.S. economy's growth for the past five years, according to statistics by the Commerce Department as of April 1998. According to the department, the industry will need 1.3 million new workers in the next 10 years. In addition, the computer-illiterate will not be able to participate in many daily functions that the World Wide Web is taking over. For example, the Commerce Department notes that consumers bought $1 billion worth of travel bookings online. In the next three years, that number is expected to jump to $8 billion (Weinraub, 1998).

On the "front burner" of the equitable access issue is how incorporating Internet advantages in learning may be systematically leaving out ethnic minorities whom may disproportionately represent poorer schools. The inequity in Internet access at school may not be reconciled by other forms of access either such as having a computer at home. The current landscape of equitable access shows both good news and bad news.

The good news...

According to one governmental study entitled *Falling Through the Net: Toward Digital Inclusion* (U.S. Department of Commerce, 2000), the overall level of U.S. digital inclusion is rapidly increasing (also see National Telecommunications and Information Administration, 2002):

→ The share of households with Internet access soared by 58%, rising from 26.2% in December 1998 to 41.5% in August 2000.

→ More than half of all households (51.0%) have computers, up from 42.1% in December 1998.

→ There were 116.5 million Americans online at some location in August 2000, 31.9 million more than there were only 20 months earlier.

→ The share of individuals using the Internet rose by a third, from 32.7% in December 1998 to 44.4% in August 2000.

And, even better news:

The rapid uptake of new technologies is occurring among most groups of Americans, regardless of income, education, race or ethnicity, location, age, or gender, suggesting that digital inclusion is a realizable goal. Groups that have traditionally been digital "have nots" are now making dramatic gains:

→ The gap between households in rural areas and households nationwide that access the Internet has narrowed from 4.0 percentage points in 1998 to 2.6 percentage points in 2000. Rural households moved closer to the nationwide Internet penetration rate of 41.5%. In rural areas this year, 38.9% of the households had Internet access, a 75% increase from 22.2% in December 1998.

→ Americans at every income level are connecting at far higher rates from their homes, particularly at the middle income levels. Internet access among households earning $35,000 to $49,000 rose from 29.0% in December 1998 to 46.1% in August 2000. In 2001, more than two-thirds of all households earning more than $50,000 had Internet connections (60.9% for households earning $50,000 to $74,999 and 77.7% for households earning above $75,000).

→ Access to the Internet is also expanding across every education level, particularly for those with some high school or college education. Households headed by someone with "some college experience" showed the greatest expansion in Internet penetration of all education levels, rising from 30.2% in December 1998 to 49.0% in August 2000.

→ Blacks and Hispanics still lag behind other groups but have shown impressive gains in Internet access. Black households are now more than twice as likely to have home access than they were 20 months ago, rising from 11.2% to 23.5%. Hispanic households have also experienced a tremendous growth rate during this period, rising from 12.6% to 23.6%.

→ The disparity in Internet usage between men and women has largely disappeared. In December 1998, 34.2% of men and 31.4% of women were using the Internet. By August 2000, 44.6% of men and 44.2% of women were Internet users.

→ Individuals 50 years of age and older — while still less likely than younger Americans to use the Internet — experienced the highest rates of growth in Internet usage of all age groups: 53% from December 1998 to August 2000, compared to a 35% growth rate for individual Internet usage nationwide.

Although the bad news ..

Nonetheless, a digital divide remains or has expanded slightly in some cases, even while Internet access and computer ownership are rising rapidly for almost all groups. For example, most recent data show that divides still exist between those with different levels of income and education, different racial and ethnic groups, old and young, single and dual-parent families, and those with and without disabilities.

→ People with a disability are only half as likely to have access to the Internet as those without a disability: 21.6% compared to 42.1%. And while just under 25% of people without a disability have never used a personal computer, close to 60% of people with a disability fall into that category.

➔ Among people with a disability, those who have impaired vision and problems with manual dexterity have even lower rates of Internet access and are less likely to use a computer regularly than people with hearing difficulties. This difference holds in the aggregate, as well as across age groups.

➔ Large gaps also remain regarding Internet penetration rates among households of different races and ethnic origins. Asian Americans and Pacific Islanders have maintained the highest level of home Internet access at 56.8%. Blacks and Hispanics, at the other end of the spectrum, continue to experience the lowest household Internet penetration rates at 23.5% and 23.6%, respectively.

➔ Large gaps for Blacks and Hispanics remain when measured against the national average Internet penetration rate.

— The divide between Internet access rates for Black households and the national average rate was 18 percentage points in August 2000 (a 23.5% penetration rate for Black households, compared to 41.5% for households nationally). That gap is 3 percentage points wider than the 15 percentage point gap that existed in December 1998.

— The Internet divide between Hispanic households and the national average rate was 18 percentage points in August 2000 (a 23.6% penetration rate for Hispanic households, compared to 41.5% for households nationally). That gap is 4 percentage points wider than the 14 percentage point gap that existed in December 1998.

— With respect to individuals, while about a third of the U.S. population uses the Internet at home, only 16.1% of Hispanics and 18.9% of Blacks use the Internet at home.

— Differences in income and education do not fully account for this facet of the digital divide. Estimates of what Internet access rates for Black and Hispanic households would have been if they had incomes and education levels as high as the nation as a whole show that these two factors account for about one-half of the differences.

➔ With regard to computer ownership, the divide appears to have stabilized, although it remains large.

— The August 2000 divide between Black households and the national average rate with regard to computer ownership was 18 percentage points (a 32.6% penetration rate for Black households, compared to 51.0% for households nationally). That gap is statistically no different from the gap that existed in December 1998.

— Similarly, the 17 percentage point difference between the share of Hispanic households with a computer (33.7%) and the national average (51.%) did not register a statistically significant change from the December 1998 computer divide.

➔ Individuals 50 years of age and older are among the least likely to be Internet users. The Internet use rate for this group was only 29.6% in 2000. However, individuals in this age group were almost three times as likely to be Internet users if they were in the labor force than if they were not.

➔ Two-parent households are nearly twice as likely to have Internet access as single-parent households (60.6% for dual-parent, compared to 35.7% for male-headed households and 30.0% for female-headed households). In central cities, only 22.8% of female-headed households have Internet access.

➔ Even with broadband services, a relatively new technology used by only 10.7% of online households, there are disparities. Rural areas, for example, are now lagging behind central cities and urban areas in broadband penetration at 7.3%, compared to 12.2% and 11.8%, respectively.

The reports conclusion is that "Internet access is no longer a luxury item, but a resource used by many. Overall, the findings in this report show that there has been tremendous progress in just 20 months, but much work remains to be done. Computer ownership and Internet access rates are rapidly rising nationwide and for almost all groups. Nonetheless, there are still sectors of Americans that are not digitally connected."

The Federal government recognizes the importance of technologically literate Americans and has thus allocated a great deal of financial resources towards this endeavor. For instance, the Clinton Administration announced on September 22, 1998 that 20 school district partnerships in 17 states would be awarded grants totaling $30 million to help provide the additional support to meet the challenge of preparing new teachers, and supporting existing ones, to teach effectively using technology. The Technology Innovative Challenge Grant Program served as a catalyst for positive change for schools. It supports educators, industry partners, communities, parents, and others who are using new technologies to help bring high quality education to every classroom and neighborhood.

On Jan. 8, 2002, President Bush signed into law the *No Child Left Behind Act* of 2001 (NCLB; see http://www.nclb.gov). This new law represents his education reform plan and contains the most sweeping changes to the Elementary and Secondary Education Act (ESEA) since it was enacted in 1965. It changes the federal government's role in K-12 education by asking America's schools to describe their success in terms of what each student accomplishes. The act contains the President's four basic education reform principles: stronger accountability for results, increased flexibility and local control, expanded options for parents, and an emphasis on teaching methods that have been proven to work. The NCLB promises to further support and integrate the use of technology into teaching and learning. For instance, as part of the NCLB, U.S. Secretary of Education Rod Paige announced a new Enhancing Education Through Technology (ED Tech) initiative. The goals of Ed

Tech grants are to (www.nclb.gov/start/facts/21centtech.html):

→ Improve student academic achievement through the use of technology in elementary schools and secondary schools.

→ Assist students to become technologically literate by the time they finish the eighth grade.

→ Ensure that teachers are able to integrate technology into the curriculum to improve student achievement.

NetDay

NetDay began in 1995 as a grassroots volunteer effort by companies, educators, families, and communities to wire the nation's K-12 classrooms for Internet access. The organization, headquartered in Irvine, CA, was founded by John Gage from Sun Microsystems and Michael Kaufman from KQED. The first National Wiring Event was held on March 9, 1996 in California, where an estimated 50,000 volunteers wired 4,000 schools — approximately one-third of California's K-12 schools. In his weekly radio address to the country on April 19, 1996, President Clinton described NetDay and its benefits when he said:

NetDay is a great example of how America works best when we all work together. It's like an old-fashioned barn-raising, neighbor joins with neighbor to do something for the good of the entire community. Students, teachers, parents, community groups, government, business unions — all pulling together to pull cable, hook up our schools and put the future at the fingertips of all our young people. Once we reach our goal of linking our schools to the Internet, for the first time in history, children in the most isolated rural schools, the most comfortable suburbs, the poorest inner-city schools, all of them will have the same access to the same universe of knowledge. That means a boy in Lake Charles, Louisiana can visit a museum halfway around the world, a girl in

Juneau, Alaska can visit the Library of Congress on line. Since the first NetDay just over a year ago, nearly a quarter million volunteers have wired 50,000 classrooms around our country.

Today, NetDay activities are occurring in more than 40 states. .... Today I am directing every department and agency in our national government to develop educational Internet services targeted to our young people. With this action, we are one step closer to giving young people the tools they need to be the best they can be in the 21st century.

Since then, NetDay has expanded to 40 states and mobilized over 500,000 volunteers to wire more than 75,000 classrooms in states across the country (for more details, visit http://www.netday.org/). The mission of the organization has expanded to connect every child to a brighter future by helping educators meet educational goals through the effective use of technology.

Internet access and technology literacy are of consequential concern to counselors because they facilitate our mission to, in short, assist all students to become successful and responsible lifelong learners. We as counselors might help seize the opportunity to obtain federal funding, coordinate professional development, and work with others to ensure rightful access and competent use of modern-age tools. Counselors can help to develop community and business partnerships which provide both equipment, access, and training to all involved. Counselors may use their skills to negotiate collaborations with local organizations and especially university Colleges of Education.

E-Rate

On May 7, 1997, the Federal Communications Commission (FCC) adopted a Universal Service Order outlining a plan to guarantee that all eligible schools, libraries and rural health care providers have affordable connections to the Internet. By making $2.5 billion available annually, this program provides discounts (commonly known as the E-rate) to eligible organizations on certain telecommunications services. The plan also created a $400 million fund to lower the prices rural health care providers pay for telecommunications services. The following is a list of resources containing background information, instructions, application forms, help lines and other useful information related to the E-rate (Fulton, 1998).

1. **FCC Universal Service Home Page**. For the latest official government information, FCC orders are available electronically from the http://www.fcc.gov/ccb/universal_service/

2. **Services and Functionalities Eligible for Discounts**. http://www.fcc.gov/Bureaus/Common_Carrier/Public_Notices/1997/da971374.html#2

3. **FCC LearnNet**. The FCC's Informal Education Page dealing with FCC policy and education initiatives. Contains press releases, FCC Orders, recent E-rate public notices, and FAQ's. http://www.fcc.gov/learnnet/

4. **Universal Service Administrative Company**. Apply for an e-rate here! http://www.sl.universalservice.org/

5. **Nine Steps You Can Take Now to Prepare for the Schools and Libraries Universal Service Program**. http://www.ed.gov/Technology/ninestep.html

6. **Questions and Answers on Implementation of the Universal Service Program for Schools and Libraries**. http://www.ed.gov/Technology/qanda.html

7. **National Center for Education Statistics School (NCES) Codes**. The E-rate application forms require the district or school NCES (National Center for Educational Statistics) code. This site will help you find those codes. http://nces.ed.gov/ccd/schoolsearch/

8. **Consortium for School Networking**. CoSN, a non-profit organization, promotes the use of telecommunications in K-12 education to improve learning. This site contains recent SLC Fact Sheets, E-Rate forms, and links to state education departments. http://www.cosn.org/

9. **Kellogg Consulting, LLC** has been helping schools with the E-rate program since its inception in 1997. We are currently providing E-rate services for over 150 school districts. We can assist your school district in all aspects of the E-rate program from preparing your Technology Plan to filing for reimbursement. http://www.kelloggllc.com/erate.html

10. **U.S. Department of Education** Discounted Telecommunications Services for Schools and Libraries E-Rate Fact Sheet. http://www.ed.gov/Technology/comm-mit.html

Gender Equity

Throughout the last half of the 1990's, research confirmed what teachers were generally observing since they started using computers in the mathematics classroom. In general, girls just aren't as interested in technology as boys are. The American Association of American Women's (AAUW) 1998 study, *Gender Gaps: Where Schools Still Fail Our Children* (see http://www.aauw.org/2000/gg.html) documents a diminishing gender gap in achievement in mathematics and science, with one exception — technology. The study concluded, "While girls have narrowed the gender gaps in math and science, technology has become the new 'boys' club.'"

The AAUW study also concluded that:

❖ Girls are significantly more likely than boys to enroll in clerical and data-entry classes, the 1990s version of typing. Boys are more likely to enroll in advanced computer science and graphics courses.

❖ School software programs often reinforce gender bias and stereotypical gender roles.

❖ Girls consistently rate themselves significantly lower than boys on computer ability, and boys exhibit higher self-confidence and a more positive attitude about computers than do girls.

❖ Girls use computers less often outside of school. Boys enter the classroom with more prior experience with computers and other technology than girls.

Although there is available some research that shows the gender equity gap for math and science currently closing, current research in the area of technology is all but nonexistent. The following websites should prove valuable in learning and combating gender based inequities to technological careers.

❖ **Girls and Technology: Closing the Gender Gap (Merrow Report)**. You can listen to the program and/or download a transcript. http://www.pbs.org/merrow/tmr_radio/girltech/guests.html

❖ **Girl Tech**. According to the site, "The Internet is full of research about girls and their issues in education, sports, health and more. Unfortunately, when one does a search for "girls" on the Internet, one must sift through much pornography to get to quality information. We have made this information easier to find by creating a Girl Powered Search Engine. We also provide Girl Tech's research, information on girl development and direct links to many articles, essays, and areas on the Internet devoted to girls and women. We hope you find it helpful and useful." http://www.girltech.com/

❖ **GAP (Girls are Powerful)**. Online girls technology club. http://math.rice.edu/~lanius/club/

❖ **Voices of Girls in Science, Mathematics, and Technology**. http://www.ael.org/nsf/voices/index.htm

❖ **Girlstart** is a non-profit organization created to educate and empower girls in math, science, and technology. http://www.girlstart.org/

❖ **GirlsTech**. A website to help teachers, parents, librarians, and other youth leaders evaluate web sites, CD-ROMS, games, and other electronic information resources to judge their likely appeal to girls and young women and stimulate their interest in science and technology. http://girlstech.douglass.rutgers.edu/

Pornography on the Web

On September 2, 1998, an event made news headlines in every major newspaper in the world. About 100 people in 14 countries were arrested in what police said was the biggest ever worldwide swoop of alleged pedophiles using the Internet. Dozens of addresses were raided, including 32 in the United States alone. The raids were based on an investigation of a pedophilia ring known as the "Wonderland Club," which used sophisticated encryption codes originally developed by the KGB. And so it continues ...

The Internet, from the very beginning, has been a tool for distributing a wide variety of information across a large number of people, and until recently, has not been a place where particularly young children would frequent. With the introduction of user-friendly online systems and the World Wide Web, and the introduction of the Internet to the classroom, more and more children are taking advantage of the power of the Internet. Its potential for education, communication, and a sense of global community is practically limitless. However, the Internet remains largely an adult forum, and so it carries with it adult subjects. This raises the question: What happens when the adult themes and a child's naive explorations meet?

Amidst the material available on the Internet that is of enormous educational potential, there is also material that even the hardiest civil libertarian would probably agree is not appropriate for small children — for example, graphical depiction of child pornography, vicious racism from bigots of various stripes, and detailed instructions on how to build bombs from some highly destructive people are all there. In some cases this material can raise questions that go beyond those of appropriateness and taste: its distribution and ownership may also be illegal, particularly within certain jurisdictions. For example, possession of child pornography is illegal as well as reprehensible. In most cases, pornography is also readily available from non-Internet sources (your local Adult Bookstore, for example), but its availability on the Net is a particularly sensitive issue because it is harder to monitor the age of persons accessing material on the Net than to check the age of patrons at the adult bookstore. The analogy might be walking into a video store where the Disney movies are mixed in with the adult videos. Further, the titles may only differ in a few letters (e.g., www.whitehouse.com versus www.whitehouse.gov).

Sex and pornography occur in every part of the Internet. This includes the World Wide Web, Virtual Communities, online simulation games, chatrooms, and newsgroups. The presentation of sexually explicit materials differs from platform to platform, as does the degree of obscenity or indecency. While some are more visible than others, sexually explicit material can be easily found on all of them. The Web is the most visible aspect of the Internet, and the way that most people explore it. The nature of the Web itself — a multimedia carnival of pictures, movies, sounds, and colors — makes it much more popular with the general public than the other platforms. The multimedia aspect of the Web also makes it a place where all kinds of sexual material can be displayed, and many people have taken advantage of this whether for profit or for fun. One example of a type of pornography that is specific to the Web is live "video conferencing" in which the "caller" interacts with one or more individuals who perform sexual activities at the prompting of the user. These live shows vary from the tame to the lewd, and can include any number of users all typing or speaking commands simultaneously.

A simple search for any one of a number of sexually explicit words, especially slang terms for genitalia and/or sexual intercourse, on any search engine will yield a list of countless pornographic sites. Some of these are more of a soft-core nature, displaying "simple nudes" — Playboy and Penthouse are prime examples. These sites tend to make available material much like that displayed in their paper publications, which are indecent to be sure, but may not be obscene. On the opposite end of the spectrum, there are a great number of hard-core sites — far

more numerous than their softer cousins. These sites display blatant indecency such as penetration of the vaginal, anal, and oral orifices of men and women by penises, hands, and various devices. They show hetero- and homosexual intercourse, bestiality, bondage, and fetishes involving various forms of human excrement, to name but a few. Since all of these sites have a common goal — profit — they tend to have a built-in security device. Namely, they only display a sampling for free, and further access is limited to credit card holders who are willing to pay a fee. This certainly helps to keep younger children from having full access to such sites, but even without ever gaining full access to any service, the amount of pornographic pictures, movies, and sounds that someone can compile for free and without ever encountering any age verification roadblocks, is enough to fill a hard drive (ACCA, 1999).

One other type of page on which pornography can be found is a personal homepage. The number of personal homepages — pages maintained for individuals, by individuals, and for no profit, is tremendous, and the content of these pages are as varied as the people who maintain them. Any level of sexual material can be found on any person's individual/personal homepage, from soft-core to hard-core. While many sexual homepages follow the design of a shrine to a celebrity, others display their owners engaged in sexual activities, and yet others display movies, sounds, or pictures from their favorite X-Rated movies. Finally, although most Internet Service Providers do not allow pornographic advertising on space not designated to contain it, some individuals use their homepages to advertise and sell their own homemade sex tapes, or various sundries such as sex toys, or used undergarments. These personal pages present even a tougher challenge for regulation for a couple of reasons. First, unlike commercial sites, they are not as widely recognized. Second, there are no measures taken to regulate these pages and prevent minors from accessing them, not even semi-effective measures such as credit card authorization.

Legislation to Help Protect Children

The nature of Internet pornography and the sort of person who uses it has resulted in a war that is being waged on the Internet, in children's homes, and on Capitol Hill. The debate has raised not only questions of obscenity, harassment, free speech, and censorship, but also of government control over the Internet. Whatever legislation ends up being imposed in this arena, it will set a precedent for how the government deals with the exchange of information in the future. Is the Internet a free forum for discussion, or is it a broadcasting service, and therefore subject to the same restrictions as television, print, or radio? Are communications on the Internet covered by the right to privacy? And who is accountable for what happens on it?

Legislation continues to further the cause of protecting children online. Two in particular, the Communications Decency Act and the Children's Online Privacy Protection Act are of special interest:

→ In February, 1996, the Communications Decency Act (CDA; see http://www.fcc.gov/Speeches/Chong/separate_statements/cda.txt) was passed. Many people found the CDA unconstitutional, and its passing prompted an Internet-wide protest. Since then, the CDA has been challenged and overturned, and then taken to the Supreme court where it was soundly defeated on the basis of it being unconstitutional. Whether or not Internet-specific regulations exist or not, actions which are illegal in general are still illegal on the Internet. For example, child pornography in any form is illegal. Hence, no further laws involving Internet child pornography are needed. Interestingly, though it is clearly illegal, and although there are cut-and-dry laws involving child pornography, examples of it can still be found on the Internet. Posted as often as the child pornography itself are messages from others damning the posters to Hell and warning them of imminent arrest, but, in general, no actions seem to be taken in the real world to serve to dissuade the child pornography posters, as their material invariably appear a few days later with other similar posts.

→ On October 20, 1999, the Federal Trade Commission issued the final rule to implement the *Children's Online Privacy Protection Act of 1998* (COPPA). The main goal of the COPPA and the rule is to protect the privacy of children using the Internet. Publication of the rule means that, as of April 21, 2000, certain commercial Web sites must obtain parental consent before collecting, using, or disclosing personal information from children under 13. The COPPA Commission, a congressionally appointed panel, was mandated by the Child Online Protection Act, which was approved by Congress in October 1998. The primary purpose of the Commission is to "identify technological or other methods that will help reduce access by minors to material that is harmful to minors on the Internet."

Decreasing Student Risk

There exists no guarantee that young students will not somehow access inappropriate, illegal, or obscene material over the Net. However, there are methods which schools and parents can employ to significantly decrease the danger and risk to such access among our children. Realize however, that what one person may find offensive, another might find aesthetic. Some people have proposed "tagging" all items on the Internet with a rating similar to the American motion picture ratings. This scheme is not a workable one, since even well-intentioned content authors will have difficulty rating their material in a manner that agree with your values as a counselor, parent, or educator. So what can counselors and other caring adults do to help protect children from viewing potentially abusive material on the Net? Following are several suggestions which can be implemented in schools and sometimes at home.

Supervision. "Hold hands while crossing the street" is good advice in reality and makes perfect sense on the Internet too. Adult supervision is a method for shielding our children from adult material more effective than the most advanced technology yet developed for this purpose. There exists no substitute for sitting down with your students or children and exploring the World Wide Web together. This is true when surfing for leisure, doing homework, or conducting counseling related activities. Similar to watching television together, adults and children whom surf the Web together share an experience which can prove to be beneficial to the relationship. Further, the Web provides much opportunity for discussing scores of topics and issues favorable for learning. Besides, if a student or class in your custody accesses pornographic material on the Net because you were not appropriately supervising, you may place yourself and your school at legal risk and consequently endanger your career.

Realistically however, when a group of student simultaneously access the Web, controlling which sites they enter is very difficult at best if not humanly possible. Therefore, adequately protecting students from harmful material requires both human and technological assistance. Parents and community stakeholder can help supervise and even conduct lab exercises when using the Net. Additionally, schools can incorporate hardware and software solutions for filtering and blocking (discussed later) potentially obscene materials from entering the school's walls.

Acceptable Use Policies (AUP). With Internet access becoming increasingly common within our schools, it is apparent that a clear set of guidelines for the use of the resources that this access provides are needed for the guidance of the students, teachers, administrators, parents, and board members. Using the Internet such as with classroom guidance can be somewhat risky. It is advisable to obtain consent forms from all parents at the beginning of the school year emphasizing that, while all efforts will be directed toward seeing that children access appropriate material, common sense dictates that no monitoring system is foolproof, and in the final analysis students must also assume responsibility for accessing only appropriate material. An Acceptable Use Policy is a document which establishes parameters for those who use the Internet at school. The document addresses appropriate use of the school's system, the rights of all parties involved, protocols and procedures

for infractions, and liabilities such as in the case of loss or damage. For an AUP template, you may visit http://education.otago.ac.nz/NZLNet/safety/template.html. Also, check out HISD's Armadillo — The Texas Studies Gopher (http://chico.rice.edu/armadillo/Rice/Resources/acceptable.html) which began collecting AUP resources a number of years ago and should prove to be helpful as a starting place.

According to Willard (1996), some school districts have established a policy of having a "sponsoring teacher" sign a student's Internet use agreement affirming that they will supervise the student's use of the account. The practical reality is that the sponsoring teacher of a secondary school student will not be in always be in a position to monitor an individual student's activities, therefore it is unclear what why such a signature is required. Sponsoring teachers will be directly in the firing line if a parent is displeased with their child's actions on the Internet. All district personnel should have general supervisory responsibility when their students are using the Internet. Counselors might be well advised to follow Willard's (1996) advice to teachers:

> My advice to teachers is that they should not sign any agreement that places responsibility on them for supervising specific students in their use of the Internet. A signature indicating specific responsibility is an invitation to trouble, including the potential of being listed as a defendant in a law suit. While it is unlikely that a teacher would be held personally responsible, being a defendant in a law suit does not rank high on anyone's list of fun and games. p. 10

Provide Students with Tools. Self-defense is more than just common sense on the Internet. Of course, all the rules in the real world also hold true in cyberspace. That is, don't talk to strangers, don't give out your personal information, and watch where you're going. However, the Internet is pervaded by savvy and cunning users who can obtain information such as your system origin (e.g., visit http://www.anonymizer.com), use this to decipher your personal e-mail address, find your home address and instantly create a map to your house (e.g., see http://www.anywho.com). This information can be gathered infinitely more quickly than in real life. Thus, helping students stay on a safe and secure path of exploring the Internet by making them aware of potential hazards.

Although children should always be supervised when online, they should also follow some "rules of the road" which should lead to having a better time in cyberspace, stay safe, and keep you and their parents worrying less. The following is an example of a "contract" that your students should read, understand, and follow (Magid, 1996; available as printable bookmarks at http://www.franklin.k12.wi.us/Pages/Programs/Registration%20Forms/My%20Rules%20for%20Online%20Safety.pdf).

☞ I will not give out personal information such as my address, telephone number, parents' work address/telephone number, or the name and location of my school without my parents' permission.

☞ I will tell my parents right away if I come across any information that makes me feel uncomfortable.

☞ I will never agree to get together with someone I "meet" online without first checking with my parents. If my parents agree to the meeting, I will be sure that it is in a public place and bring my mother or father along.

☞ I will never send a person my picture or anything else without first checking with my parents.

☞ I will not respond to any messages that are mean or in any way make me feel uncomfortable. It is not my fault if I get a message like that. If I do I will tell my parents right away so that they can contact the service provider.

☞ I will talk with my parents so that we can set up rules for going online. We will decide upon the time of day that I can be online, the length of time I can be online, and appropriate areas for me to visit.

☞ I will not access other areas or break these rules without their permission.

Blocking and Filtering Software

Software solutions to preventing access to harmful material falls into two general classes. Solutions that (a) block net access to certain addresses deemed to contain objectionable material (i.e., blocking); and (b) block access based on the appearance of certain words or phrases in the data being downloaded (filtering).

Neither of these approaches is foolproof. One can never know all sites which might contain objectionable material, and monitoring based on the occurrence of certain words or phrases might easily screen out daily newspapers or even the Bible. For instance, typical sites mistakenly blocked by word filters may include chicken recipe sites, blocked for the word "breast," the White House Web site, blocked for the word "couple," and a county government site blocked for the phrase "Middlesex County." One the other hand, a word filter will frequently allow a picture from a pornographic site to appear in the browser before triggering a block. This is because many porn sites purposely represent all the "words" in the opening page in the form of graphics in order to defeat any word filter. And, of course, once a picture is on the computer screen it can be saved, printed, e-mailed, or posted just about anywhere else on the Net. Willard (1996) also points out that using screening software is expensive and might take resources that could better be used to provide training and support for teachers, counselors, students, and parents.

She also indicates that such software places a reliance on barriers, instead of a focus on assisting students to make appropriate choices guided by school rules and personal values.

Several blocking/filtering software resources include:

→ Since children of all ages use America On Line (AOL), the company has created features to help parents make sure their children have a fun and enriching experience online, while limiting access to some features of AOL and the Internet. These Parental Controls allow parents to designate different levels of access for each child. http://www.aol.com. Also, MSN has a fully featured parental control as well (www.msn.com).

→ Bess filtering software works with a wide variety of implementations to meet the needs of schools and libraries. Whichever device you prefer, every Bess product uses the categorized filtering database recognized as the most effective available. (http://www.n2h2.com/products/bess_home.php)

→ Cyber Patrol is used to manage Internet access, limit the total time spent online and restrict access to Internet sites that you deem inappropriate. http://www.cyberpatrol.com

→ Cyber Sentinel allows user to block inappropriate material (web pages, e-mail, pictures, and word processing documents) no matter what format it is in, or what it is. It also allows the owner to configure the program to run in stealth mode (so the end user doesn't know it is running). The owner can then run Cyber Sentinel later and see screen shots of when the user was viewing inappropriate material. http://www.securitysoft.com/

→ CyberSitter is an award winning filtering software which I use personally. http://www.cybersitter.com

→ Pearl Software, Inc. provides network-enabled Internet monitoring software to schools, colleges, universities and libraries. Their focus is to provide teachers, administrators and librarians with a realistic means to supervise and educate students in a dynamic world of interactive Internet communications. http://www.pearlsw.com/

→ FamilyConnect Blocks 15 different categories, including pornography, file sharing, chat and illegal activity (drugs, bombs, hacking, etc.). http://www.familyconnect.com

→ DiskTracy allows adults to monitor what children are doing on the Internet without filtering or restricting access. It finds and displays text and graphics files, hidden graphics and compressed files and a listing of all websites visited. http://www.disktracy.com/

→ Net Nanny allows you to monitor, screen and block access to anything residing on, or running in your PC, whether you are connected to the Internet or not, and in real time. http://www.netnanny.com

→ SafeSurf is an organization dedicated to making the Internet safe for your children without censorship. They are developing and are implementing an Internet Rating Standard that is bringing together parents, providers, publishers, developers, and all the resources available on the Internet to achieve this goal. It involves marking sites with the SafeSurf Wave. http://www.safesurf.com/

→ While no filtering program is 100 percent effective, SurfWatch claims to shield users from 90-95% percent of the explicit material on the Net. http://www.safesurf.com

Child/Family Friendly Internet Service Providers

Some Internet Service Providers (e.g., www.integrityonline.com and www.cleanweb.net) have automatic controls of content, both web and e-mail, before it is even allowed to enter your computer. Given hundreds or thousands of dial-up numbers, you can enjoy filtered web surfing and e-mail correspondence from throughout the country. When using a filtered ISP, you typically do not have to worry about keeping your filtering or blocking software updated because the filtering occurs at the ISP level, not at your computer.

Russell A. Sabella, Ph.D.

Online Sexual Harassment

When Sue first met Simon, she knew that maintaining a relationship with someone from a different country would be difficult. Later, however, she realized that ending the relationship would actually be the difficult part. Immediately upon terminating the relationship Sue began receiving e-mails, almost hourly, from Simon. She then started receiving e-mails from men she did not know, soliciting her for sex. Apparently, Simon posted her phone number on the Internet, inviting men to "call for a good time." Finally, Simon posted her address and encouraged local men to stop by and see Sue (Bevilacqua, 1997).

In another incident at a Midwest university, a student posted four graphically violent stories on the Internet using the name of a female student from his class. University officials removed the story from their server, but Internet users continued to post and re-post it. The student posted his fictionalized stories to the biggest pornography bulletin board on the Internet with approximately 270,000 users internationally. In his stories, the student posted the female's first, middle and last name, complete with the student's detailed physical description. Fortunately, the story was seen and reported to university officials by a University of Michigan alumnus in Moscow. Interestingly enough, the case went to court and was dismissed because the court claimed that the student's words were protected under the First Amendment. This ruling, without surprise, caused a wave of clamor across the country. The government appealed the dismissed 1995 case, but, in January 1997, the 6th U.S. District Court of Appeals in Cincinnati also dismissed charges against the student, claiming that no threat was intended to the female student (Arnold, 1998).

Both men and women who use the Web, other online services, or even internal networks report receiving invitations and messages of a sexually explicit nature in real-time "chats" or via e-mail. These messages are variously analogous to obscene phone calls or "cat calls" in the street depending on their tone. However, they take on an added annoyance factor for those who are paying to utilize the resources of the online environment. Additionally, these messages may be experienced repeatedly by women, perhaps because of similar reasons that it happens to more females offline. Women looking for information online are often surprised to see that a female first name can bring a distracting and ultimately expensive volume of unsolicited contact. The problem is pervasive and annoying enough that many women choose to switch to non-gender-specific login names, for example, or to post to women-only conferences or mailing lists.

The official website of one organization dedicated to confronting online harassment, Women Halting On-line Abuse (W.H.O.A.; www.haltabuse.org), endeavors to educate the Internet community about online harassment, empower victims of harassment, and formulate voluntary policies that systems can adopt in order to create harassment-free environments. W.H.O.A. fully supports the right to free speech both online and off, but asserts that free speech is not protected when it involves threats to the emotional or physical safety of anyone. Another organization, the CyberAngels (http://www.cyberangels.org), seeks to prevent online harassment and various other online crimes through education, legislation, and other efforts. In the corporate world, employers increasingly are using e-mail surveillance software to guard against sexual harassment lawsuits and the loss of trade secrets. Evidence of the trend remains largely anecdotal, according to e-mail administrators and industry experts. However, many believe that content-filtering of workplace e-mail will become commonplace with the maturation of server-based applications.

According to Barton (http://www.wizard.net/~barton/harassment/harass4.html), you might take the following steps if you experience online harassment:

1. **Archive Every Piece of Mail Relating to the Situation.** Save every piece of communication you get from this person. Send copies of each harassing communication to your postmaster and the harasser's. Don't forget to save communications to postmasters, system administrators, police, supervisors at work, and security specialists.

2. **Start a Log.** In addition to your archive of communications, start a log that explains the situation in more detail. Document how the harassment is affecting your life, and document what steps you're taking to stop it.

3. **Tell the Harasser To Cease and Desist.** It's important that you contact your harasser directly telling him or her in simple, strong, and formal terms to stop contacting you. You must state that the communications are unwanted and inappropriate and that you will take further action if it does not stop. Don't worry about whether your letter sounds too harsh – make sure it's professional and to the point. Copy (CC:) your postmaster and your harasser's. Archive the mail you've saved, and note that you sent it in your log. After you send this mail, your communication to this person must stop. Any further communication can feed the situation. The harasser's behavior will be rewarded by your attention, so it will continue. Also, if the case goes to court, your harasser can report that the communication was going both ways, and it could damage your case. It's best to keep quiet no matter how tempted you are to defend yourself. It's important that you tell your friends not to communicate with the harasser in your defense for the same reasons.

4. **Tell the Right People.** Report the situation to your system administrator(s), your friends, family, and coworkers. Tell your supervisor and work security personnel. Tell your apartment building's security people. Report the situation to your local police. The FBI will also take down a complaint, and they'll follow up on it if they have the manpower.

5. **Take Police Action.** Many states have modified their stalking laws to include electronic communications. Many states will let you file for a restraining order in cases like this, and the courts will often let you ask that your harasser pay for any filing fees. You'll need the person's address if you want to serve them with a restraining order or press charges against them. The police can get this information from the harasser's postmaster if they need to.

6. **Protect Your Online Space.** Change your password frequently. Pay attention to your files, directories, and last logout information. Monitor information about yourself on the Net with Alta Vista (www.av.com) and other search engines.

7. **Protect your offline space.** Take all the precautions you would if an old boy/girl friend was acting crazy, especially if you think the person can find you at home or at work.

Security

As an increasing number of people learn about the power of communicating, shopping, and basically interacting with others over the Net, protecting personal and sensitive information is sometimes a concern. Many people don't fully understand the security risks they face when using the Internet, much less what they can do about them. Some may ask questions such as, "Is it safe to give my credit card number when making online purchases?" "Can someone intercept and read my communications?," and probably most worrisome, "Can someone get into my computer and steal my files?" The good news is that businesses stand to make a great deal of money by marketing to the expansive numbers of web users who enjoy the convenience of conducting communications and transactions over the Net. Such companies, along with other entrepreneurs, are spending a great deal of money to advance technologies that assure secure transactions, whether sending a confidential e-mail about a student or conducting a stock purchase. Most everyone today agrees that they have done a good job. All in all, many parts of the web set up for sensitive transactions are quite secure places to conduct business. The major credit card companies are so sure of this that, similar to offline transactions, many will absorb the cost of unauthorized or fraudulent transactions (except for the first $50 for some). Most companies will even absorb 100% of the cost in case of fraudulent transactions over the Net. Check your credit card company for their specific policy regarding online fraudulent transactions.

How often do you hand your credit card to a waiter in a restaurant or give out your account number over the telephone when ordering products? Such actions probably pose a greater security risk than charging items online — at least from trusted Web sites. There is a chance that a thief could intercept your credit card number as it travels from your computer to the Web site's server, but it's highly improbable. In fact, it's much more difficult to carry out such a scheme online than it is in the real world where your credit card number is printed on statements and receipts that are mailed, filed, or thrown away. Some sites may work with your browser to encrypt, or encode, your transaction information so that, if it's intercepted, it can't be read. Online banks and investment services use encryption to protect the information in your transactions. Before information leaves the Web site's server for your computer, or vice versa, it's turned into code. After it reaches the appropriate destination, it's decoded. While the information travels over the Internet — where it may be vulnerable to being intercepted by someone with malicious intentions — it's essentially gibberish.

Your web browser will let you know when encryption is in use by displaying an icon at the bottom that looks like a lock. Sites that are not secure either show the lock open or don't show one at all. Another way to determine whether a site is secure or not is by looking at the site's address. Secure sites which encrypt communications during transmission begin with https:// instead of http://. Regardless of safe transactions, you should know that many Web sites you visit can tell who and where your Internet service provider is, what site you were last at, what Web browser you're using, and what you do while you're at the site. By asking you to register, a site can collect additional information from you, such as your name, e-mail address, postal address, income level, and interests. It's up to you whether to provide this. Notwithstanding, if you're listed in the white pages of the telephone book, your name, address, and telephone number are probably in databases on the World Wide Web, available for others to search. For example, try looking yourself up in some of the more well known databases such as:

→ Whitepages. www.whitepages.com

→ Realpages. www.realpages.com

→ Bigfoot. www.bigfoot.com

→ Anywho Directories. www.anywho.com

→ And if you want to spend a little money, conduct a background check on yourself at www.knowx.com

---

Identity Theft

The U.S. Federal Trade Commission says that identity theft is its number one source of consumer complaints — 42 percent of all complaints, in 2001. This translates into a thief stealing someone's identity, opening accounts in the victim's name and going on a shopping spree every 79 seconds. How can someone steal your identity? According to the Federal Trade Commission (2003), by co-opting your name, Social Security number, credit card number, or some other piece of your personal information for their own use. The thief often uses the victim's personal information to open accounts, purchase vehicles, apply for loans, credit cards, social benefits, establish services with utility companies, rent apartments and more all in the victim's name without their knowledge. In short, identity theft occurs when someone appropriates your personal information without your knowledge to commit fraud or theft. According to the FTC, the following are some ways that identity thieves work:

→ They open a new credit card account, using your name, date of birth, and Social Security number. When they use the credit card and don't pay the bills, the delinquent account is reported on your credit report.

→ They call your credit card issuer and, pretending to be you, change the mailing address on your credit card account. Then, your imposter runs up charges on your account. Because your bills are being sent to the new address, you may not immediately realize there's a problem.

→ They establish cellular phone service in your name.

→ They open a bank account in your name and write bad checks on that account.

One of the most effective methods for minimizing your risk for identity theft is to order a copy of your credit report from each of the three major credit reporting agencies every year. Make sure it is accurate and includes only those activities you've authorized. The law allows credit bureaus to charge you up to $9.00 for a copy of your credit report. The three major credit reporting agencies are as follows:

Equifax — www.equifax.com

To order your report, call: 1-800-685-1111 or write: P.O. Box 740241, Atlanta, GA 30374-0241

To report fraud, call: 1-800-525-6285 and write: P.O. Box 740241, Atlanta, GA 30374-0241

Experian — www.experian.com

To order your report, call: 1-888-EXPERIAN (397-3742) or write: P.O. Box 2104, Allen TX 75013

To report fraud, call: 1-888-EXPERIAN (397-3742) and write: P.O. Box 9532, Allen TX 75013

TransUnion — www.transunion.com

To order your report, call: 800-916-8800 or write: P.O. Box 1000, Chester, PA 19022.

To report fraud, call: 1-800-680-7289 and write: Fraud Victim Assistance Division, P.O. Box 6790, Fullerton, CA 92834-6790

If you believe you have been the victim of identity theft, you may use the form available online at http://www.consumer.gov/idtheft to send a complaint to the Federal Trade Commission.

Viruses

A virus is a program or piece of code that is loaded onto your computer without your knowledge and runs against your wishes. All computer viruses are created by people and most can replicate themselves. A simple virus that can make a copy of itself over and over again is relatively easy to produce. Even such a simple virus is dangerous because it will quickly use all available memory and bring your system to a halt. An even more dangerous type of virus is one capable of transmitting itself across networks and bypassing security systems (Webopedia, 2003). To protect yourself from viruses on the Internet, don't download files from sources that may not be safe. Viruses are usually hidden in programs and activated when the programs run. They also can be attached to certain other types of executable files, such as special-action Web files and video files. Generally, when you're about to download a type of file that could contain a virus, your browser will display a warning and ask whether you want to open the file or save it to disk. If you're confident that the file comes from a trustworthy source, you may want to save it. If you're not sure, you may want to cancel your download. However, rather than practicing "download abstinence", you might continue and have a protected transaction by using an antivirus program. Immediately after downloading a file to your computer and before doing anything with it, have the file scanned for viruses by your antivirus program. There is still a chance that the file might contain a new and undocumented virus which will not be detected by antivirus software, although this chance is very small. If you don't have antivirus software loaded on your computer, you should get it right away. You might check out the following as starters:

➔ http://www.symantec.com

➔ http://www.mcafee.com

➔ http://www.trendmicro.com

➔ http://www.grisoft.com

The first two companies, Symantec and McAfee, also provide software that gives your computer what is known as firewall protection. A firewall is used to prevent unauthorized Internet users from accessing private networks connected to the Internet, especially intranets. All messages entering or leaving the intranet pass through the firewall, which examines each message and blocks those that do not meet the specified security criteria. In all likelihood, your school probably already has more than one type of firewall for the school network. You may need one, however, if you access the Internet using a different system such as from home. If you use a dial-up service and you are not online for extended periods of time, you are probably safe without one because dial-up services typically provide you with a random type of access which is difficult to trace to you. If you are accessing the Internet using a broadband or high speed connection, it is critical that you have a firewall installed on your computer. The reason for this is that broadband connections are "always on" even when your computer is not. It is much easier for hackers to find a security breach and gain access to your computer after you do turn on your computer.

One way that you can be confident against being infected is to practice "safe surfing." That is, you should consistently and periodically upgrade your antivirus and firewall programs with new updates as they are made available over the Internet, perhaps every couple of weeks. Programs such as Symantec Norton Antivirus© and Symantec Norton Personal Firewall (www.norton.com) makes this very simple because it includes a Live Update feature. This feature allows you to click on a button which has your computer connect with the company's database of known viruses, check to see if there are available any updates since the last check, download them, and then add or install them to your computer's list of known viruses (this can actually also be done automatically every time you boot up your computer). You should also know that such antivirus software will also check for any irregularities in your computer system's configuration upon turning it on and "booting up". Your operating system will usually keep an image of your system's configuration as it legitimately changes and checks against that image, especially memory, that may change because of a virus. Once detecting such a change, you are made aware of the variation and given the chance for the antivirus program to remove and innoculate against future occurrences.

A special kind of virus is one that attaches itself to documents and data files such as spreadsheets, usually in the form of a macro (a miniprogram usually used for conducting repetitive tasks). Malicious users can embed destructive instructions in a document they send to you (say, as an e-mail attachment). When you open the document, the virus moves into action. Microsoft Word and Microsoft Excel are particularly susceptible to these problems — known as "macro viruses". Microsoft has provided on their website (www.microsoft.com) "patches" to their programs which ward against such viruses. Also, many virus scanners now also detect such macro viruses, but their success rate is, however, lower than that for other viruses. Another type of virus is called a worm which is a program or algorithm that replicates itself over a computer network and usually performs malicious actions, such as using up the computer's resources and possibly shutting the system down (Webopedia, 2003).

Trojan Horses

A Trojan Horse program, like the legendary wooden creature after which it is named, offers you some apparent benefit (such as a pretty screen saver), encouraging you to install it and run it. After it gains your trust, it then has access to your machine to do whatever else it likes in the background. As an example, in December, 1997, two students wrote a software product that allowed users to customize their Internet software. It appeared to work as advertised, but also secretly e-mailed the user's password to the students. This action went undetected until March of 1998, when the students themselves revealed it to the press to demonstrate the security risks faced by Internet users. Trojan horses are another good reason to invest in an effective antivirus program.

Programming Bugs

Despite the best of intentions, many software products contain programming mistakes known as "bugs". In other words, a bug is an error or defect in software or hardware that causes a program to malfunction. According to folklore, the first computer bug was an actual bug. Discovered in 1945 at Harvard, a moth trapped between two electrical relays of the Mark II Aiken Relay Calculator caused the whole machine to shut down (Webopedia, 2003). Malicious users can exploit bugs to make the software behave in unintended ways. For example, researchers periodically discover serious bugs in some of the world's most popular e-mail software: Microsoft Outlook, Netscape Communicator and Eudora Pro. The bugs allow malicious users to worm their way into your computer and perform their own actions. After its detections, these e-mail software providers will develop patches to correct the problem. Another reason why it is critically important to keep your software up to date.

Cookies

A cookie is a small amount of information stored on your computer by a Web site that you have visited. The cookie typically includes information that your Web browser sends back to the site whenever you visit it again such as your password for the site or a customized view of the site that you have chosen. The reason that cookies are designed and planted on your computer is so that your browsing experience is more personal and simplified. For instance, cookies will help you bypass a site's password logon procedures because your password is simply entered from within your cookie. Then, you might receive a hearty and personalized welcome message. More intricate cookies keep track of the type of links you follow within a site, how much time you spend there, and what you do there (e.g., download a file) so that the site owners may begin to develop a profile for you that allows them to target new information that your profile indicates would probably be of interest to you. Some less than reputable sites use cookies to determine your originating e-mail address which they will use to send you unsolicited e-mails in the form of advertisements. Such online behavior is usually experienced as a violation and is an example of the dark side of cookie use. Consequently, cookies are the focus of debate among those who view them as a service or "the cost of doing business" and those who passionately protect their privacy and civil liberties.

In general though, cookies are common and usually harmless. They can't be used to take information about you or your computer that you have not provided (again, another reason to be very careful what you kind of information you give up at a site). But they can be used by certain services to create a profile of your interests based on the sites you visit. Then information on participating sites can be customized for you which can certainly be a time-saver.

Browsers such as Netscape or IE can help you better control cookies by alerting you whenever a server tries to give you a cookie. In Internet Explorer, click on the [Tools] menu, then click on [Internet Options]. On the Privacy tab, move the slider up for a higher level of privacy or down for a lower level of privacy (while reading the effect on processing cookies). To delete cookies from your system, simply find them on your computer, usually in a folder called "Cookies" and delete them. Or, in IE, click on [Tools], then [Internet Options], then [Delete Cookies]. At least a couple of drawbacks exist to denying or deleting cookies, however. One problem is that cookies are so prevalent that you may be constantly dealing with cookie alerts which will seriously inhibit you from timely and enjoyable web surfing. Also, a site may not allow you to download valuable and free utilities and updates without first accepting their cookie. For instance, if you want to download some utilities from Microsoft, and you have set up your browser to not accept cookies, the company's site will detect this and stop you from continuing. A message will appear on your screen that alerts you to this situation and instructs you to turn cookies back on if you still want to pursue your download.

ActiveX

Even if you do not intentionally download software from a Web site, elements of a site may download, run on your computer, and pose a potential security risk such as by unleashing a virus onto your system. For example, ActiveX technologies allow software to be distributed over the Internet. You'll encounter ActiveX in the form of controls, usually graphic items such as scrolling marquees, on Web sites. Think of them as small programs within the site that run on your computer. An ActiveX control is like a plug-in, but worse. It doesn't require any installation (so users will use them without thinking twice), leaves no trace afterwards, and gives the illusion of extra security. A famous example of a malicious ActiveX control occurred in early 1997 when a group of computer experts demonstrated to the German press how to use the personal financial software product Quicken to transfer money from your bank account to theirs while innocently browsing their Web site. Similar to ActiveX are VB or Visual Basic files (ending in .vb).

Java

Java is a computer language. Java-based mini-applications, also known as applets, can be downloaded from Web sites and run by Web browsers. Generally, these applets are limited in what they can do. However, there are some Java-related bugs. For instance, suppose you're browsing the Web and an error message pops up, saying you have been disconnected and asks for your user name and password again. Would you believe this message? Many people would, and faithfully follow the instructions. But this "error message" could be a JavaScript on the Web page you're viewing that takes your user name and password and forwards it to a malicious attacker. Indeed, in August of 1998, a computer expert demonstrated how to send an innocuous-looking e-mail message to HotMail users (HotMail is a popular free e-mail provider located at www.hotmail.com) that disguises itself as a HotMail system message and ask users for their password and then reports the password secretly to the attacker.

Spyware

In general, spyware is any technology that aids in gathering information about a person or organization without their knowledge. On the Internet, spyware is programming that is put in someone's computer to secretly gather information about the user and relay it to advertisers or other interested parties. Spyware can get in a computer as a software virus or as the result of installing a new program. Data collecting programs that are installed with the user's knowledge are not, properly speaking, spyware, if the user fully understands what data is being collected and with whom it is being shared (http://whatis.techtarget.com). Similar to spyware, adware is any software application in which advertising banners are displayed while the program is running. The authors of these applications include additional code that delivers the ads, which can be viewed through pop-up windows or through a bar that appears on a computer screen. The justification for adware is that it helps recover programming development cost and helps to hold down the cost for the user.

Adware has been criticized for occasionally including code that tracks a user's personal information and passes it on to third parties, without the user's authorization or knowledge. This practice has been dubbed spyware and has prompted an outcry from computer security and privacy advocates, including the Electronic Privacy Information Center.

One excellent (and free) piece of software that detects and removes spyware is Adaware which is available from www.lavasoftusa.com. This program comprehensively scans your memory, registry, hard, removable and optical drives for known data mining, aggressive advertising, and tracking components. In addition, Adaware comes with supporting software that "goes out" to the Net and checks for additional spyware components in its database. I run this program at least once per week and always detect new spyware.

I want to emphasize one more time that these type of threats are unlikely to effect you if you maintain your software and have installed on your computer notable (and up-to-date) antivirus protection, a firewall, and spyware detection programs.

Certificates

Digital certificates, granted by certifying authorities such as VeriSign and thawte, signify that a Web site or element of a Web site has been digitally signed by its creator. A certificate lets you know who is responsible for the site or element, and verifies that it is free from malicious components (such as viruses) and has not been tampered with since it was certified. When your browser is presented with a certificate, it checks its list of certifying authorities. If it finds a match, it allows your activity to continue. If your browser warns you that something is amiss about a certificate, your safest course is to cancel your activity.

In summary, you would not be too cautioned to invest in reputable antivirus and firewall programs, have your browser warn you of impending ActiveX, JavaScripts, and VB scripts and interact only with trusted sites. Your best defense, however, is probably to be somewhat distrustful of requests for sensitive information such as your password. For instance, in May, 1997, users of America OnLine (AOL) in the United States received e-mail — supposedly from AOL staff — asking them to re-enter their passwords and credit card details. Needless to say, it was a scam. In December of the same year, when Yahoo opened its free e-mail service, a similar scam surfaced, with Internet users receiving e-mail from an official-looking address at yahoo.com, informing them they had won a free modem, for which they had to pay the freight costs (by credit card, of course) to collect their prize. When in doubt, don't fulfill a seemingly legitimate request if it is at all out of the ordinary. Call the company making the request to verify the authenticity of the request.

CyberCounseling

To my surprise and amazement, I received the following unsolicited e-mail one day:

Hello.

I type to you tonight asking for your help. I carry a secret that I have never talked about openly to anyone before. I am a 24 year old divorced mother. Very successful and still going to college. My son and I are very active in the community we live in and to other people I am a normal person. To most I am an overachiever and extremist. God has blessed our lives, but no matter how hard I work and push myself, I'm finding that my past is always there. My over achieving has its reasons. I have never went to anyone for help. I am usually the person people come to for help. I am very understanding and my past has educated me enough in that I've been there. Tonight, for the first time on searching the net about child abuse, I see that I'm not alone and that I'm not strange. I feel the desire to talk to someone but, unfortunately, don't have a clue as to who to talk to. I suffered emotional and physical abuse from my family and sexual abuse from a nonfamily member as a child. This is my first asking for help like this. I came across your name on the web and thought maybe you would know of someone who could help. If not, I understand.

Signed,

First Name Only

Although I have kept knowledgeable of the cybercounseling (i.e., attempting counseling over the Internet) evolution, I had never quite become so directly involved. I was more an outside observer looking into this fascinating and curious development. As a result of this e-mail, the reality of cybercounseling became more vivid and personal for me. Suddenly, the ethical and legal considerations applied to me. What would I do with this message? Was this message real or a hoax? How old is the writer? I decided to reply and informed the author that I was not licenced in her state and therefore would not pursue providing her with professional counseling. Next, I wrote some highly facilitative sentences with the intent of instilling hope. Finally, I suggested how she might self-refer to a therapist which could fit her needs and move her toward healing. My reply arrived at this unknown person's address although I never received further communications from her (assuming she is female as indicated by her first name).

When you think of conducting counseling with your students, you probably envision you and your client(s) in your office, in the classroom, or perhaps even on a "walk and talk." However, others may also have a mental image of a counselor who sits in front of the computer and conducts counseling over the Internet. Cybercounseling is the attempt to provide counseling services in an Internet environment. The environment may include e-mail, chatrooms, or Internet video conferencing. For example, one site (http://www.metanoia.org/imhs) lets their users know that, *Now you can meet with a psychotherapist for personal counseling or advice, from the privacy of your own computer. Using the Internet, professional counselors are forming effective helping relationships with people like you.* The site also provides an impressive array of helpful suggestions when using this medium for counseling and includes characteristics of legitimate online therapists.

The practice of cybercounseling began slowly although is rapidly finding popularity among both counselors and cyberclients. Since the first edition of *SchoolCounselor.com*, these sites have proliferated into the hundreds, if not thousands. The practice has become so popular that there now exists online directories of e-therapists such as the one found at www.findingstone.com/find-a-therapist. Among counseling professionals, cybercounseling has created somewhat of a debate about the utility and effectiveness of this new medium. Moreover, those concerned about traditional ethical and legal issues in counseling are wondering how such matters relate to the Internet environment.

Sanders and Rosenfield (1998) noted that the world of social sciences in general, and counseling and psychotherapy in particular, have always had an uneasy relationship with telecommunications technology. Social scientists predicted the collapse of normal social relations after the invention of the telegraph, and even though the telephone has been with us for around 100 years, it still has difficulty being accepted into the everyday world of counseling and psychotherapy as a valid communications medium. Counseling by telephone has definitely been the poor relation compared with face-to-face counseling in terms of professional recognition. Since the advent of the Internet and the interest in computer as the new technology mediating telecommunications via e-mail, we might be forgiven for thinking that the telephone is dead.

In an attempt to determine the pervasiveness of counseling related activity on the Internet, Sampson, Kolodinsky, and Greeno, (1997) conducted an analysis in April 1996, using the WebCrawler search engine. Results of the analysis revealed that two thirds of the counseling-related home pages examined were that of groups, and fully 50% were groups advertising some type of counseling-related service. Only 15% were home pages placed by individuals. Of particular note were on-line services offered by groups or individuals for a fee, either as a reply to questions posed via e-mail or for interactive chat sessions. The credentials for practitioners involved a wide range, including M.D., Ph.D., M.A., and L.P.C. Many "counselors" identified no professional credentials at all. In fact, most home pages provided little information about the nature of qualifications of those providing services other than degree-level designation. For example, an individual with "M.A." listed after his or her name frequently did not disclose the subject area of the degree. In a separate nonrandom analysis of 401 sites from the same 3,764 home pages, 15 home pages were identified that offered direct on-line services. Offerings ranged from $15 charged for answering a question via e-mail to $65 for a 60-minute chat session. These on-line offerings ranged from single treatment interventions to an individual offering services in 35 different specialty areas.

The authors concluded that the results of their search can be used to encourage debate about counseling over the Internet. Based on the percentage of websites offering direct on-line services, they estimated that there were at least 275 practitioners offering direct counseling services across the Internet at the time. The estimate is no doubt much higher today and, consequently, has become an increasingly pressing issue. Instead of being a "potential" future event, online counseling and counseling-related activities are a "present" reality. Although these numbers are relatively small in comparison with the tens of thousands of counselors currently offering services through more traditional means, the annualized growth rate of the web indicates that increases in Internet counseling will occur. Future enhancements in technology are likely to only accelerate the availability of counseling services through networking.

The evolution of the Internet into the information highway offers many future possibilities and potential problems in the delivery of counseling services for your students. Following is an overview of each:

Possibilities

→ **Delivery of counseling services:** Walz (1996) noted that the information highway "allows counselors to overcome problems of distance and time to offer opportunities for networking and interacting not otherwise available" (p. 417; also see Robson, 2000). In addition, counseling over the Net may be a useful medium for those with physical disabilities whom may find even a short distance a significant obstacle. And yet for others whom are reticent in meeting with a counselor and/or self-disclosing, the Net may prove to be an interactive lubricant which may very well foster the counseling process.

→ **Delivery of information resources:** The Internet is a convenient and quick way to deliver important information. In cybercounseling, information might be in the form of a homework assignment between sessions or bibliocounseling.

→ **Assessment and evaluation:** Access to a wide variety of assessment, instructional, and information resources, in formats appropriate in a wide variety of ethnic, gender, and age contexts (Sampson, 1990; Sampson & Krumboltz, 1991; Solomon, 2001), could be accomplished via WWW and FTP sites.

→ **Communications:** Especially via e-mail, counselors and clients can exchange messages throughout the counseling process. Messages may inform both counselor and client of pertinent changes or progress. E-mail can provide an excellent forum for answering simple questions, providing social support, or to schedule actual or virtual meeting times.

→ **Marriage and family counseling:** If face-to-face interaction is not possible on a regular basis, marriage counseling might be delivered via video conferencing, in which each couple and the counselor (or counselors) are in different geographic locations. After independent use of multimedia based computer-assisted instruction on communication skills, spouses could use video conferencing to complete assigned homework (e.g., communication exercises; Jedlicka & Jennings, 2001; Jencius & Sager, 2001; Sampson, et al., 1997).

→ **Supervision:** Some evidence has shown that e-mail is an enhancing tool in the process of counselor supervision and consultation. It provides an immediate and ongoing channel of communication between and among as many people as chosen (Christie, 2002; Myrick & Sabella, 1995; Schnieders, 2002). Also, electronic file transfer of client records, including intake data, case notes (Casey, Bloom, & Moan, 1994), assessment reports, and selected key audio and video recordings of client sessions, could be used as preparation for individual supervision, group supervision, case conferences, and research (Sampson, et al., 1997).

Potential Problems

→ **Confidentiality:** Although encryption and security methods have become highly sophisticated, unauthorized access to online communications remains a possibility without attention to security measures. Counselors whom practice on the Net must ethically and legally protect their clients, their profession, and themselves by using all known and reasonable security measures.

→ **Computer competency:** Both the counselor and client must be adequately computer literate for the computer/network environment to be a viable interactive medium. From typing skills to electronic data transfer, both the counselor and client must be able to effectively harness the power and function of both hardware and software. Similar to face-to-face counseling, counselors must not attempt to perform services outside the limitations of their competence.

→ **Location-specific factors:** A potential lack of appreciation on the part of geographically remote counselors of location-specific conditions, events, and cultural issues that affect clients may limit counselor credibility or lead to inappropriate counseling interventions. For example, a geographically remote counselor may be unaware of traumatic recent local events that are exacerbating a client's reaction to work and family stressors. It may also be possible that differences in local or regional cultural norms between the client's and counselor's community could lead a counselor to misinterpret the thoughts, feelings, or behavior of the client. Counselors need to prepare for counseling a client in a remote location by becoming familiar with recent local events and local cultural norms. If a counselor encounters an unanticipated reaction on the part of the client, the counselor needs to proceed slowly, clarifying client perceptions of their thoughts, feelings, and behavior (Sampson, et al., 1997).

→ **Equity:** Does the cost of Internet access introduce yet another obstacle for obtaining counseling? Does cybercounseling further alienate potential clients whom might have the greatest need for counseling? Even when given access to the Net, could a client competently engage cybercounseling without possibly having ever had a computer experience? Cybercounseling seems to exacerbate equity issues already confronting live counseling.

→ **Credentialing:** How will certification and licensure laws apply to the Internet as state and national borders are crossed electronically? Will counselors be required to be credentialed in all states and countries where clients are located? Could cybercounseling actually be the impetus for a national credential recognized by all states? Will we need to move towards global credentialing? Who will monitor service complaints out-of-state or internationally?

→ **High tech v. High touch:** How can counselors foster the development of trusting, caring, and genuine working relationships in cyberspace? Until video transmission over the Web makes telecounseling a reality, cybercounseling relies on a process devoid of non-verbal or extraverbal behavior. Even if we were able to conduct real-time counseling over the Net via video, can this medium help us to communicate so as to foster the counseling core conditions? Further, Lago (1996) poses a key question: "Do the existing theories of psychotherapy continue to apply, or do we need a new theory of e-mail therapy? (p. 289)"' He then takes Rogers' (1957) work on the necessary and sufficient conditions for therapeutic change as his starting-point and lists the computer-mediated therapist competencies as: the ability to establish contact, the ability to establish relationship, the ability to communicate accurately with minimal loss or distortion, the ability to demonstrate understanding and frame empathic responses, and the capacity and resources to provide appropriate and supportive information. This proposal begs the question as to whether such relationship conditions as outlined by Rogers can be successfully transmitted and received via contemporary computer-mediated telecommunications media.

→ **Impersonation:** A famous cartoon circulated over the Net depicts a dog sitting in front of a computer. The caption says, "The nice thing about the Internet is that nobody knows you're a dog." Experienced Internet users can relate to the humor in this cartoon because they know that there are many people who hide behind the Net's veil of anonymity to communicate messages they ordinarily would not communicate in real life. Messages that convey unpopular sentiments and would ordinarily be met with castigation. Others rely on anonymity provided by the Net to play out fantasies or practical jokes. Who is your cyberclient, really? Does your client depict himself/herself as an adult and is actually a minor? Has the client disguised their gender, race, or other personal distinctions that may threaten the validity or integrity of your efforts.

→ **Ethics:** How do current ethical statements for counselors apply or adapt to situations encountered online? For the most part, counselors can make the leap into cyberspace and use current ethical guidelines to conduct themselves in an ethical fashion. However, problems exist. The future will inevitably see a change in what it means to be ethical as we learn the exact nature of counseling online.

→ **Crisis Management:** Difficulties in responding to crisis situations may arise both as a result of client anonymity and because the therapist may be unfamiliar with the local community resources available in the client's geographic region. In addition, local laws requiring mental health professionals to breech confidentiality and report a client's danger to self or others, or suspected incidents of child, elder, or spousal abuse, vary from one geographic jurisdiction to another. When the client resides in a different legal jurisdiction from the therapist, it is currently unclear which laws, those covering the therapists geographic region or those covering the client's geographic region, are applicable. This issue becomes more complex when differing nationalities are involved (Childress, 1998).

The Ethical Web Counselor

In 1995, the National Board for Certified Counselors (NBCC) appointed a cybercounseling task force to examine the practice of online counseling and to assess the possible existence of any regulatory issues NBCC might need to address. The task force established a listserv composed of more than 20 individuals who had specific knowledge, expertise, skills and opinions regarding the practice of what is herein referred to as cybercounseling. Soon it became apparent that counseling had a diverse presence on the Internet, from websites that simply promoted a counselor's home or office practice, to sites that provided information about counseling and others which actually claimed to offer therapeutic interventions either as an adjunct to face-to-face counseling or as a stand alone service. Some sites were poorly constructed, poorly edited and poorly presented. Others were run by anonymous individuals, individuals with no credentials or fraudulent credentials, and some sites were operated by individuals with appropriate credentials and years of professional experience. However these credentials were all based on education and experience gained in face-to-face counseling, and the relevance of these credentials to the practice of cybercounseling is unknown. No one knew if the lack of visual input made a difference in the outcome of the counseling process. No one knew about the legality of counseling across state or national boundaries. No one knew if there was any relevant research in any field of communication which could shed light on these questions (Bloom, 1997).

Next, the NBCC task force created a document entitled Standards for the Ethical Practice of Cybercounseling which is now called Standards for the Practice of Internet Counseling (available online at http://www.nbcc.org/ethics/webethics.htm). The relative newness of the use of the Internet for service and product delivery leaves authors of such standards at a loss when beginning to create ethical practices on the Internet. This document, like all codes of conduct, changes as information and circumstances not yet foreseen evolve. However, each version of this code of ethics is the current best standard of conduct passed by the NBCC Board of Directors (see http://www.nbcc.org/ Reprinted by Permission). As with any code, and especially with a code such as this, created for an evolving field of work, NBCC and CCE welcome comments and ideas for further discussion and inclusion.

NBCC Standards for the Practice of Internet Counseling

© 2001, NBCC. Reprinted by permission.

This document contains a statement of principles for guiding the evolving practice of Internet counseling. In order to provide a context for these principles, the following definition of Internet counseling, which is one element of technology-assisted distance counseling, is provided. The Internet counseling standards follow the definitions presented below.

A. Taxonomy for Defining Face-To-Face and Technology-Assisted Distance Counseling

The delivery of technology-assisted distance counseling continues to grow and evolve. Technology assistance in the form of computer-assisted assessment, computer-assisted information systems, and telephone counseling has been available and widely used for some time. The rapid development and use of the Internet to deliver information and foster communication has resulted in the creation of new forms of counseling. Developments have occurred so rapidly that it is difficult to communicate a common understanding of these new forms of counseling practice.

The purpose of this document is to create standard definitions of technology-assisted distance counseling that can be easily updated in response to evolutions in technology and practice. A definition of traditional face-to-face counseling is also presented to show similarities and differences with respect to various applications of technology in counseling. A taxonomy of forms of counseling is also presented to further clarify how technology relates to counseling practice.

Nature of Counseling

Counseling is the application of mental health, psychological, or human development principles, through cognitive, affective, behavioral or systemic intervention strategies, that address wellness, personal growth, or career development, as well as pathology.

Depending on the needs of the client and the availability of services, counseling may range from a few brief interactions in a short period of time, to numerous interactions over an extended period of time. Brief interventions, such as classroom discussions, workshop presentations, or assistance in using assessment, information, or instructional resources, may be sufficient to meet individual needs. Or, these brief interventions may lead to longer-term counseling interventions for individuals with more substantial needs. Counseling may be delivered by a single counselor, two counselors working collaboratively, or a single counselor with brief assistance from another counselor who has specialized expertise that is needed by the client.

Forms of Counseling

Counseling can be delivered in a variety of forms that share the definition presented above. Forms of counseling differ with respect to participants, delivery location, communication medium, and interaction process. Counseling participants can be individuals, couples, or groups. The location for counseling delivery can be face-to-face or at a distance with the assistance of technology. The communication medium for counseling can be what is read from text, what is heard from audio, or what is seen and heard in person or from video. The interaction process for counseling can be synchronous or asynchronous. Synchronous interaction occurs with little or no gap in time between the responses of the counselor and the client. Asynchronous interaction occurs with a gap in time between the responses of the counselor and the client.

The selection of a specific form of counseling is based on the needs and preferences of the client within the range of services available. Distance counseling supplements face-to-face counseling by providing increased access to counseling on the basis of necessity or convenience. Barriers, such as being a long distance from counseling services, geographic separation of a couple, or limited physical mobility as a result of having a disability, can make it necessary to provide counseling at a distance. Options, such as scheduling counseling sessions outside of traditional service delivery hours or delivering counseling services at a place of residence or employment, can make it more convenient to provide counseling at a distance.

A Taxonomy of Forms of Counseling Practice. Table 1 presents a taxonomy of currently available forms of counseling practice. This schema is intended to show the relationships among counseling forms.

Table 1

A Taxonomy of Face-To-Face and Technology-Assisted Distance Counseling

Counseling

→ Face-To-Face Counseling

→ Individual Counseling

→ Couple Counseling

→ Group Counseling

Technology-Assisted Distance Counseling

→ Telecounseling

   → Telephone-Based Individual Counseling

   → Telephone-Based Couple Counseling

   → Telephone-Based Group Counseling

→ Internet Counseling

   → E-Mail-Based Individual Counseling

   → Chat-Based Individual Counseling

   → Chat-Based Couple Counseling

   → Chat-Based Group Counseling

   → Video-Based Individual Counseling

   → Video-Based Couple Counseling

   → Video-Based Group Counseling

Definitions

Counseling is the application of mental health, psychological, or human development principles, through cognitive, affective, behavioral or systemic intervention strategies, that address wellness, personal growth, or career development, as well as pathology.

Face-to-face counseling for individuals, couples, and groups involves synchronous interaction between and among counselors and clients using what is seen and heard in person to communicate.

Technology-assisted distance counseling for individuals, couples, and groups involves the use of the telephone or the computer to enable counselors and clients to communicate at a distance when circumstances make this approach necessary or convenient.

Telecounseling involves synchronous distance interaction among counselors and clients using one-to-one or conferencing features of the telephone to communicate.

Telephone-based individual counseling involves synchronous distance interaction between a counselor and a client using what is heard via audio to communicate.

Telephone-based couple counseling involves synchronous distance interaction among a counselor or counselors and a couple using what is heard via audio to communicate.

Telephone-based group counseling involves synchronous distance interaction among counselors and clients using what is heard via audio to communicate.

Internet counseling involves asynchronous and synchronous distance interaction among counselors and clients using e-mail, chat, and videoconferencing features of the Internet to communicate.

E-mail-based individual Internet counseling involves asynchronous distance interaction between counselor and client using what is read via text to communicate.

Chat-based individual Internet counseling involves synchronous distance interaction between counselor and client using what is read via text to communicate.

Chat-based couple Internet counseling involves synchronous distance interaction among a counselor or counselors and a couple using what is read via text to communicate.

Chat-based group Internet counseling involves synchronous distance interaction among counselors and clients using what is read via text to communicate.

Video-based individual Internet counseling involves synchronous distance interaction between counselor and client using what is seen and heard via video to communicate.

Video-based couple Internet counseling involves synchronous distance interaction among a counselor or counselors and a couple using what is seen and heard via video to communicate.

Video-based group Internet counseling involves synchronous distance interaction among counselors and clients using what is seen and heard via video to communicate.

Standards for the Ethical Practice of Internet Counseling

These standards govern the practice of Internet counseling and are intended for use by counselors, clients, the public, counselor educators, and organizations that examine and deliver Internet counseling. These standards are intended to address practices that are unique to Internet counseling and Internet counselors and do not duplicate principles found in traditional codes of ethics.

These Internet counseling standards of practice are based upon the principles of ethical practice embodied in the NBCC Code of Ethics. Therefore, these standards should be used in conjunction with the most recent version of the NBCC ethical code. Related content in the NBCC Code are indicated in parentheses after each standard.

Recognizing that significant new technology emerges continuously, these standards should be reviewed frequently. It is also recognized that Internet counseling ethics cases should be reviewed in light of delivery systems existing at the moment rather than at the time the standards were adopted.

In addition to following the NBCC® Code of Ethics pertaining to the practice of professional counseling, Internet counselors shall observe the following standards of practice:

Internet Counseling Relationship

1. In situations where it is difficult to verify the identity of the Internet client, steps are taken to address impostor concerns, such as by using code words or numbers.

2. Internet counselors determine if a client is a minor and therefore in need of parental/ guardian consent. When parent/guardian consent is required to provide Internet counseling to minors, the identity of the consenting person is verified.

3. As part of the counseling orientation process, the Internet counselor explains to clients the procedures for contacting the Internet counselor when he or she is off-line and, in the case of asynchronous counseling, how often e-mail messages will be checked by the Internet counselor.

4. As part of the counseling orientation process, the Internet counselor explains to clients the possibility of technology failure and discusses alternative modes of communication, if that failure occurs.

5. As part of the counseling orientation process, the Internet counselor explains to clients how to cope with potential misunderstandings when visual cues do not exist.

6. As a part of the counseling orientation process, the Internet counselor collaborates with the Internet client to identify an appropriately trained professional who can provide local assistance, including crisis intervention, if needed. The Internet counselor and Internet client should also collaborate to determine the local crisis hotline telephone number and the local emergency telephone number.

7. The Internet counselor has an obligation, when appropriate, to make clients aware of free public access points to the Internet within the community for accessing Internet counseling or Web-based assessment, information, and instructional resources.

8. Within the limits of readily available technology, Internet counselors have an obligation to make their Web site a barrier-free environment to clients with disabilities.

9. Internet counselors are aware that some clients may communicate in different languages, live in different time zones, and have unique cultural perspectives. Internet counselors are also aware that local conditions and events may impact the client.

Confidentiality in Internet Counseling

10. The Internet counselor informs Internet clients of encryption methods being used to help insure the security of client/counselor/supervisor communications.

Encryption methods should be used whenever possible. If encryption is not made available to clients, clients must be informed of the potential hazards of unsecured communication on the Internet. Hazards may include unauthorized monitoring of transmissions and/or records of Internet counseling sessions.

11. The Internet counselor informs Internet clients if, how, and how long session data are being preserved.

Session data may include Internet counselor/Internet client e-mail, test results, audio/video session recordings, session notes, and counselor/supervisor communications. The likelihood of electronic sessions being preserved is greater because of the ease and decreased costs involved in recording. Thus, its potential use in supervision, research, and legal proceedings increases.

12. Internet counselors follow appropriate procedures regarding the release of information for sharing Internet client information with other electronic sources. Because of the relative ease with which e-mail messages can be forwarded to formal and casual referral sources, Internet counselors must work to insure the confidentiality of the Internet counseling relationship.

Legal Considerations, Licensure, and Certification

13. Internet counselors review pertinent legal and ethical codes for guidance on the practice of Internet counseling and supervision. Local, state, provincial, and national statutes as well as codes of professional membership organizations, professional certifying bodies, and state or provincial licensing boards need to be reviewed. Also, as varying state rules and opinions exist on questions pertaining to whether Internet counseling takes place in the Internet counselor's location or the Internet client's location, it is important to review codes in the counselor's home jurisdiction as well as the client's. Internet counselors also consider carefully local customs regarding age of consent and child abuse reporting, and liability insurance policies need to be reviewed to determine if the practice of Internet counseling is a covered activity.

14. The Internet counselor's Web site provides links to websites of all appropriate certification bodies and licensure boards to facilitate consumer protection.

Adopted November 3, 2001

http://www.nbcc.org/ethics/webethics.htm

The following links may also prove helpful for learning about cybercounseling ethics:

➔ http://ericcass.uncg.edu/digest/2000-03.html

➔ http://www.counseling.org/ctonline/sr598/lee498.htm

➔ http://www.counselingzone.com/members/chat/chat98martin.html

➔ http://www.libraries.wright.edu/libnet/subj/cou/cpmeta/mhc.html#ccati

➔ http://netpsych.com/Powell.htm

➔ http://jtc.colstate.edu/vol1_2/cyberpsych.htm

If the Internet really does herald a new age of user-friendly computer-mediated communication for the masses, will the world of counseling be left behind? E-mail, originally developed to help desk-bound students and workers in commercial organizations, was modeled on the office memorandum. If computer communications are to mediate properly and effectively in therapeutic relationships, we need to strive continually to identify the salient interpersonal processes unique to therapeutic relationships, not borrow second-hand technology designed for business organizations by computer scientists. There needs to be further collaboration between therapists, social scientists and computer scientists who together would identify therapy-salient processes, model them in terms of psycho-social communications theories, and finally design them into therapy-dedicated, computer-mediated communications systems. If we fail in this endeavor, we could find therapists in ten years' time still using technologies designed for corporate business communications or computer-banking as the means by which they conduct therapy with their clients at a distance (Sanders & Rosenfield, 1998).

In summary, the Internet, like any tool, is either helpful or harmful depending on the user's purpose, capability, and actions. Focusing on parts that are helpful and avoiding those which are not can be a difficult task because of the vastness and morphological nature of the Net. Issues of psychological health and overall well-being while using the Net for commendable ventures is enhanced by knowledge and skills which promote robust discovery.

Russell A. Sabella, Ph.D.

CHAPTER SEVEN

Counseling MegaLinks

This chapter provides you with a categorized list of 1200 (take or give a few) counseling related websites. The sites are those which I've reviewed, to some extent used, and recommended to others over the years. I have learned about the sites in various ways. For instance, I have discovered them:

1. As I have conducted research for my work at the university.

2. As other counselors have recommended them via listservs.

3. As other educators or similar professionals have recommended them in newsletters, listservs, or other communications.

4. As I have read about them in one or more of many technology related books, magazines, articles, etc.

5. After readers of the SchoolCounselor.com newsletter (www.schoolcounselor.com/ newsletter) have suggested them.

By no stretch of the imagination is this list exhaustive. In fact, in the first edition of this book, I believe I captured the majority of the available counseling related sites at the time, approximately 800 or so. Today, there are thousands, if not hundreds of thousands, of such sites which proved to be a much more daunting task. Therefore, consider the list of sites useful starting places which may spark your curiosity and help you to discover more "gems" out there to help you in your work. I encourage you to pay particular attention to the list of Internet/Technology Training Resources. These sites will help you conduct effective and efficient research on the Net and overall assist you in building upon your technological literacy and level of application. The other categories of websites listed here do not necessarily reflect any particular scheme, only one that I developed as I found the sites.

For instance, I am well aware that advocacy is a critical element of effective comprehensive school counseling programs and that I do not have a list of these kinds of websites. On the other hand, I found myself needing to add a few more categories such as Tools and Lessons which was not nearly as prevalent during the first edition. One thing that I intentionally did not want this book to be right now is a "Yellow Pages" of school counseling Websites. I am much more interested in helping you to learn appropriate skills so that you will not need such a resource.

If I may so myself, the process for presenting these sites to you was a marvelous demonstration of using technology to increase effectiveness and efficiency. Since 1995, I have used a piece of database software called *Internet Organizer* (http://www.primasoft.com) to manage the site information. Internet Organizer allows me to automatically detect the address for a site, include a description, categorize, see descriptive statistics of the sites, and much more. Unfortunately, the database does not have the capability to check the integrity of a site to determine if it is still valid after it is entered. To do this part, I exported the site information to a text file and analyzed them with another piece of software called *REL Link Checker Lite*, a free program available from http://www.relsoftware.com/rlc (I also highly recommend a similar program called Xenu found at http://home.snafu.de/tilman/ xenulink.html). Checking 1200 links by hand would have taken days, probably even weeks. Link Checker Lite accomplished the task in less than 20 minutes! Unfortunately, I found that approximately 300 of the original sites had incorrect addresses which greatly surprised me given that I chose carefully. As I researched them, I found it interesting to know that most of the sites had actually moved to a new address.

This was not surprising after all, given the much lower cost of owning, developing, and maintaining one's own website these days. K-12 schools and sites about peer helper programs and training were the primary culprits. To research what happened to the sites, of course, I used Google.com.

I suspect that, even though I have again included only what I believe to be reputable sites, some may be removed from the time of this publication. This is normal and even likely given the dynamic nature of the Web. Many times, however, a broken or unresponsive link may be caused by a server that is temporarily unresponsive or "down." In this instance, you should just try back later. In other instances, individual documents may have been moved within a web site rather than deleted, perhaps during the remodeling of a site. This can happen especially when the site goes beyond the root address. For example, if you are looking for the June 1999 issue of the SchoolCounselor.com newsletter at www.schoolcounselor.com/newsletter/june1999.htm and you receive an error, you should go to the root directory (www.schoolcounselor.com) and look for an apparent link to the site in question. If you still cannot find the link you want, you might then look for a search tool on the site that allows you to locate the resource. If none of thee methods work, and if you deem the resource valuable enough, you could try finding the document in a Web search engine such as Google.com in case the site has changed its name entirely or it was reproduced (a.k.a. mirrored) on another site. Another option might be to try to contact the author or webmaster.

I have included boxes next to each site for your convenience as a way to check off the sites you have visited. Once you visit a site you find especially beneficial to you, you may want to bookmark it in your own browser for easy access.

And now, I present, the MegaLinks:

Academic

❏ **CSS/Financial Aid PROFILE — Apply Online**
http://profileonline.collegeboard.com/index.jsp
The financial aid application service of the College Board.

❏ **FastWeb: Free Scholarship and College Searches Plus Financial Aid Tools and More**
http://www.fastweb.com
FastWEB is the largest online scholarship search available, with 600,000 scholarships representing over one billion in scholarship dollars. It provides students with accurate, regularly updated information on scholarships, grants, and fellowships suited to their goals and qualifications, all at no cost to the student. Students should be advised that FastWEB collects and sells student information (such as name, address, e-mail address, date of birth, gender, and country of citizenship) collected through their site.

❏ **How To Study**
http://www.how-to-study.com
This page is designed to help students do better in school.

❏ **Scholarship Scams**
http://www.finaid.org/scholarships/scams.phtml
Check this page to see how you can avoid being scammed on your way to college.

❏ **Student Gateway to the U.S. Government**
http://www.students.gov
Federal government interagency project that provides postsecondary students with easy access to all kinds of federal government information and services. Students of all ages, interests, and types have found it to be a valuable resource.

❏ **The Anne Ford Scholarship**
http://www.ld.org/awards/index.cfm

The Anne Ford Scholarship is a $10,000 award given to a high school senior with an identified learning disability (LD) who is pursuing an undergraduate degree.

❏ **US Universities**
http://www.usuniversities.com

Power search with comprehensive listings of state and private universities and colleges, community colleges, accredited institutes, and non-traditional programs. Search by state and/or major field of study.

Accountability

❏ **Action-Oriented Research: Promoting School Counselor Advocacy and Accountability**
http://ericae.net/db/edo/ED347477.htm

An article from the ERIC database.

❏ **Evidence-Based Education (EBE) Presentation**
http://www.ed.gov/offices/OESE/SASA/eb

Comprehensive documents and PowerPoints!

❏ **Free Online Surveys**
http://freeonlinesurveys.com

A user-friendly way to create and deploy surveys. The free version allows for up to 50 responses and the professional version is competitively priced. This site allows for basic multiple choice surveys to those that might include a rubric.

❏ **GraphCalc: Windows 2D/3D Graphing Calculator Software**
http://www.graphcalc.com

GraphCalc is ready to use out of the box. Don't bother reading the documentation. Just start the program and you'll see how easy it is to use.

❏ **Helping Families, Schools and Communities Understand and Improve Student Achievement**
http://www.ed.gov/offices/OESE/esea/testingforresults

An article from the US DOE.

❏ **Kathy Schrock's Guide for Educators — Assessment Rubrics**
http://school.discovery.com/schrockguide/assess.html

Here you will find a collection of assessment rubrics that may be helpful to you as you design your own.

❏ **Looking at Student Work**
http://www.lasw.org

Why look at student work? There are a range of purposes for looking at student work. These purposes include: professional development; accountability (determining the effectiveness of curriculum and instruction); setting standards; and reflecting on student learning and development.

❏ **Microsoft Education — Excel 97**
http://www.microsoft.com/education/default.asp?ID=Excel97Tutorial

Explore the powerful features of Microsoft Excel 97 to simplify data research and organization by using worksheets and charts. This page will allow you to download a complete book (in parts) designed in Microsoft Word!

❏ **NCES's Create a Graph**
http://nces.ed.gov/nceskids/graphing

Here you will find four different graphs and charts for you to consider. Maybe it will help explain what you are trying to show.

❏ **Resources for Data-Driven Decision-Making**
http://www.surfline.ne.jp/janetm/IT4L/lms.htm

Learning/Curriculum Management Systems and Student Information Systems: Resources from CoSN Compendium "No More Flying Blind: Using Data-Driven Decision-Making to Guide Student Learning."

❏ **Rubric, Rubrics, Teacher Rubric Makers**
http://teach-nology.com/web_tools/rubrics

The rubric generators below will allow you to make grading rubrics by filling out a simple form. The materials are made instantly and can be printed directly from your computer. Your creations are exclusive to you. If you would like to keep your creations, save them when you make them.

❏ **Rubrics**
http://www.odyssey.on.ca/~elaine.coxon/rubrics.htm

Lots and lots of them! Also includes a neat page about teaching with technology.

❏ **Rubrics and Evaluation Resources**
http://www.ncsu.edu/midlink/ho.html

❏ **The Teachers' Internet Use Guide**
http://www.rmcdenver.com/useguide/assessme/aindex.htm

Steps for developing, adapting, or adopting assessments that will tell you whether students have learned what you expect them to learn within any given lesson.

❏ **ToolBelt**
http://www.ncrel.org/toolbelt

This site includes information-gathering tools ranging from checklists to surveys. Some tools are designed for printing and circulating in paper form, while others are computer-based surveys or Web sites. These tools are designed to help educators collect data about their classroom, school, district, professional practice, or community. The information from these tools can be used to assess status and growth, plan for improvement, and make decisions based on facts rather than impressions or intuitions.

❏ **What Works Clearinghouse**
http://www.w-w-c.org

The What Works Clearinghouse, a project of the U.S. Department of Education's Institute of Education Sciences, was established to provide educators, policymakers, and the public with a central, independent, and trusted source of scientific evidence of what works in education. It is administered by the Department through a contract to a joint venture of the American Institutes for Research and the Campbell Collaboration.

Audio & Video

❏ **CNN Videoselect**
http://cnn.com/videoselect/netshow
Watch selected video streams of CNN updated throughout the day.

❏ **Corey Deitz & Jay Hamilton RealAudio Archive**
http://www.radioearth.com/corjay.htm
Entertaining!

❏ **DiscJockey.Com Internet Radio Station Network**
http://discjockey.com
Amazing selection, live too! Submit your requests.

❏ **Mike's Radio World Live Dance Music Radio**
http://www.mikesradioworld.com/ft_urban.html
A guide to radio stations broadcasting in Real Audio.

❏ **rightnow**
http://www.llangley.com/yoga/wisdom/rightnow%5B2%5D.htm
Truly inspirational message — carpe diem!

❏ **The American Hero Service-Learning Project**
http://www.4greyhounds.org/ahslp.html
Greyhound Heroes! The American Hero Service-Learning Project. "When we are teaching unconditional love nothing gets it across to the children like an animal."

❏ **The Internet Movie Database (IMDb).**
http://www.imdb.com
The Internet Movie Database is a free, searchable database of over 260,000 film and television productions made since 1892.

Career

❏ **Academic Employment Network**
http://www.academploy.com
If you are looking for a teaching job or other academic position, a national employment search is but a click away!

❏ **America's Job Bank**
http://www.ajb.dni.us
America's Talent Bank is a nationwide electronic resume system. To market their qualifications, job seekers enter resumes into this national network, which is then searched by employers for workers who meet their needs. Supported by the Department of Labor, America's Talent Bank (ATB) is a product of state employment service agencies and is provided as an additional service to the public.

❏ **An Interviewer's Handbook**
http://www.ssta.sk.ca/research/human_resources/148.htm
An Interviewer's Handbook by Judith Gibney. This handbook for interviewers was prepared for the lay person who becomes involved in teacher selection at the school level.

❏ **Career and Educational PoWWWer**
http://web.utk.edu/~powwwer
This site is for high school students, their parents, and professionals who work with high school students. It is a site for those who wish to use the vast resources that are available on the World Wide Web (WWW) for career and educational planning purposes.

❏ **CareerLab — 200 FREE Cover Letters**
http://www.careerlab.com/letters/default.htm
Very helpful.

❏ **CareerMosaic**
http://www.careermosaic.com
A HUGE site of helpful links, resources, databases, and links.

❏ **CareerWeb**
http://www.cweb.com

Many helpful articles, resources, online tests, and more for the job seeker.

❏ **Colleges and Universities in the United States**
http://www.clas.ufl.edu/CLAS/american-universities.html

As home pages are found for American Universities granting bachelor or advanced degrees, they are added here, one page per university.

❏ **DICE**
http://www.dice.com

Job search engine for full-time, permanent & contract computer consulting and programming employment opportunities. Also available are quite a few career related tools.

❏ **FlipDog.com**
http://www.flipdog.com/js/jobsearch-results.html?loc=world_US&srch=job&job=1
Contact thousands of recruiters.

❏ **Graduate School Guide Online**
http://www.schoolguides.com
Comprehensive and easy to use.

❏ **HireEd.net**
http://www.hireed.net/home.cfm

HireEd.net is an online job bank and resume posting service sponsored by the Association for Supervision and Curriculum Development (ASCD).

❏ **In The Long Run**
http://www.asd.k12.ak.us/Schools/West/Future.html

West High School's Planning for the Future page. A nice list of career related sites.

❏ **Interviewing Effectively**
http://depthome.brooklyn.cuny.edu/career/interhnd_5.htm

Links and an interview tool!

❏ **Job Shadowing Resources**
http://www.jobshadow.org

Groundhog Job Shadow Day is an initiative to engage students in the world of work. This site will help you get involved.

❏ **Occupational Outlook Handbook**
http://www.bls.gov/oco/home.htm

You can perform a keyword search on the Handbook, use the Index to the Handbook, or select from an occupational cluster ... and much more!

❏ **Peterson's Education Center**
http://www.petersons.com

Within these thousands of pages of easy-to-use, organized content, you will find a wealth of information on elementary and secondary schools, colleges and universities, professional degree programs, study abroad and distance learning opportunities, executive management programs, financial aid, internships, summer programs, career guidance, and more.

❏ **Pima/Santa Cruz Equity/School to Work Resources**
http://www.geocities.com/Athens/Delphi/7786

❏ **School-to-Work Web Sites**
http://ncrve.berkeley.edu/NetGain/NETGain15.html

Links to web sites dealing with school-to-work.

❏ **School-to-Work: Program Resources**
http://7-12educators.miningco.com/msub4.htm
Short but sweet.

❏ **Thayer Academy: College Counseling**
http://www.thayer.org/college

Useful links involving the entire college search and student success process.

❏ **The Bridges Initiatives Inc.**
http://www.bridges.com
The latest tool for career exploration among K-12 children and the adults who want them to succeed.

❏ **The Career Key: Choosing a Career — Career Guidance**
http://www.careerkey.org/english
The Career Key is among the nation's leading Internet centers for career decision making — receiving approximately 2000 visits per day, with total exceeding 500,000. Also in Chinese!

❏ **The Five O'Clock Club**
http://www.fiveoclockclub.com
Some tips and free articles.

❏ **The Florida School-to-Work Information Navigator**
http://www.flstw.fsu.edu
A true clearinghouse for the whole country.

❏ **THE MONSTER BOARD**
http://www.monster.com
A must see, first stop for career development.

❏ **Washington Post's What Color is Your Parachute?**
http://www.washingtonpost.com/parachute
The Net Guide to aid job hunters and career changers who want to use the Internet as part of their job search.

❏ **WELCOME TO YOUR FUTURE**
http://www.angelfire.com/nj/hsstudentresourcepgs
Bid as the high schoolers resource page, this site has many useful links to career and college exploration — quite comprehensive.

❏ **Work Zone**
http://www.workzone.net
Many fine and useful articles about career and job finding.

Children

❏ **Adventures From The Book Of Virtues Home Page**
http://www.pbs.org/adventures
From the Public Broadcasting System (PBS).

❏ **Arthur: The World's Most Famous Aardvark**
http://www.pbs.org/wgbh/arthur
Fun graphics, games, puzzles, coloring, and more... from PBS.

❏ **BJ's Homework Helper**
http://school.discovery.com/homeworkhelp/bjpinchbeck
B.J. Pinchbeck's Homework Helper is produced by B.J., and 11 year old, and his Dad. Quite extensive!

❏ **Children's Literature Web Guide**
http://www.acs.ucalgary.ca/~dkbrown
The Children's Literature Web Guide is an attempt to gather together and categorize the growing number of Internet resources related to books for Children and Young Adults. Much of the information that you can find through these pages is provided by others: fans, schools, libraries, and commercial enterprises involved in the book world.

❏ **CTW Family Workshop — Home of Sesame Street**
http://www.ctw.org/index/0
Tons of info!

❏ **Cyber-Seuss**
http://www.afn.org/~afn15301/drseuss.html
Fun!

❏ **Disney.com — The Web Site for Families**
http://www.disney.com
Lots of fun and things to do!

❏ **Focus Adolescent Services**
http://members.tripod.com/FocusStretch/Main.html

Description of services for programs, resources, and support for teen substance abusers.

❏ **Health Risk Factors for Adolescents**
http://www.educ.indiana.edu/cas/adol/conflict.html

A collection of electronic resources intended for parents, educators, researchers, health practitioners, and teens. Compiled by the Center for Adolescent Studies at Indiana University.

❏ **KIDS COUNT**
http://www.aecf.org/kidscount

KIDS COUNT, a project of the Annie E. Casey Foundation, is a national and state-by-state effort to track the status of children in the U.S.

❏ **Kids Games**
http://www.gameskidsplay.net

Looking for kids games? How about rules for playground games, verses for jump-rope rhymes, and much more? You have come to right place!

❏ **KidSource OnLine**
http://www.kidsource.com

The source for in depth and timely education and healthcare information that will make a difference in the lives of parents and their children.

❏ **KidsPeace — The National Center for Kids Overcoming Crisis**
http://www.kidspeace.org

KidsPeace is a private, not-for-profit organization, that endeavors to bring hope and healing to America's children through public awareness and treatment programs.

❏ **Lucie Walters ... Adolessons Online**
http://www.lucie.com

Lucie Walters, a La. newspaper columnist, offers advice to teens on subjects such as sexuality, depression, alcohol, pregnancy, romance, eating disorders and parents. Site contains an archive of past columns.

❏ **Play It Cyber Safe**
http://www.playitcybersafe.com

The goal of this Web site is to empower children, parents and teachers to prevent cyber crime through knowledge of the law, their rights and how to avoid misuse of the Internet.

❏ **The KIDS Report**
http://scout.cs.wisc.edu/scout/KIDS

The KIDS Report is a biweekly publication produced by K-12 students as a resource to other K-12 students. It is an ongoing, cooperative effort of 12 classrooms from around the United States. Teachers assist and provide support, however students select and annotate all resources included in every issue of the KIDS Report. The publication is supported by the Internet Scout Project.

❏ **Welcome to Straight Talk About School**
http://www.balancenet.org

Designed for teens, this site aims to provide advice and answers to frequently asked questions. It offers chat rooms for teens, new interactive monthly themes, and resources for parents and teachers.

College

❏ **College and University Rankings — Online Sites and Controversy**
http://www.library.uiuc.edu/edx/rankings.htm

The purpose of this page is to draw together and provide context to various college ranking services.

❏ **College Is Possible: American Council on Education**
http://www.collegeispossible.org

America's colleges and universities have prepared this site to guide you to the books, websites, and other resources that admissions and financial aid professionals consider most helpful.

❏ **CollegeNET**
http://www.collegenet.com

Take virtual tours of college campuses.

❏ **Colleges and Universities**
http://www.mit.edu/people/cdemello/univ-full.html

Quite the list!

❏ **collegesource.com**
http://www.collegesource.com

College source Online features over 10,900 College Catalogs in complete cover-to-cover original page format including 2-year, 4-year, graduate, and professional schools. Also available are close to 11,000 college catalogs in PDF format and full-text information about: assessment testing; career information; college application services; college guides; college planning sites; counseling; education related search engines; financial aid information.

❏ **College view**
http://www.collegeview.com

Examine more than 3,800 schools to find the college that's right for you. Take a virtual campus tour, apply online, and more.

❏ **FAFSA on the Web — U.S. Department of Education**
http://www.fafsa.ed.gov

FAFSA opens the door to the federal aid process. Every step you can take gets you closer to achieving your education goals.

❏ **FinAid: The Financial Aid Information Page**
http://www.finaid.org

This page provides a free, comprehensive, independent, and objective guide to student financial aid. It was created by Mark Kantrowitz, author of The Prentice Hall Guide to Scholarships and Fellowships for Math and Science Students.

❏ **GI Bill Web Site**
http://www.gibill.va.gov

❏ **IPEDS College Opportunities On-Line**
http://nces.ed.gov/ipeds/cool

IPEDS College Opportunities On-Line is your direct link to over 9,000 colleges and universities in the United States.

❏ **KeyColleges.Com**
http://www.keycolleges.com

This site is designed to assist you in making college and career choices, learning about scholarships and financial aid, even where to find bargains in campus housing.

❏ **NewsDirectory: College Locator**
http://www.ecola.com/college

Extensive set of links to colleges and college newspapers.

❏ **Preparing Your Child For College: 2000 Edition**
http://www.ed.gov/pubs/Prepare/

This resource book is designed to assist parents help their children, with the help of teachers and counselors — plan ahead to ensure they are prepared academically for the rigors of college and to save now and plan financially for the costs of a college education.

❏ **Princeton Review Counselor-O-Matic**
http://www.princetonreview.com/college/research/advsearch/match.asp

How does this work? The Counselor-O-Matic starts by guiding you through a review of your course selection, grades, test scores, and extracurricular record. Using the information you provide, Counselor-O-Matic calculates an admissions rating for you that gives you an estimate of what your chances of admission are at most colleges. In fact, the process is very similar to the approach used by many colleges to evaluate applications.

❏ **ScholarAid**
http://www.scholaraid.com/

ScholarAid.com is a free, online scholarship directory with a database of over 500,000 national, state and local level sources of student financial aid.

❏ **Scholarship Search and Financial Aid Resource — Find Money for College**
http://scholarships.brokescholar.com/

BrokeScholar is a free scholarship search engine connecting students and parents with financial aid and college scholarships.

❏ **StudentAffairs.com**
http://www.studentaffairs.com

Your guide to the Internet for college student affairs.

❏ **U.S. Two-Year Colleges**
http://cset.sp.utoledo.edu/twoyrcol.html

One of the most complete list available: Over 1,000 U.S. two-year campus links.

❏ **AATBS Home Page**
http://www.aatbs.com/Home.HTM

Official site of the Association for Advanced Training in the Behavioral Sciences (AATBS).

❏ **Art Therapy**
http://www.vickyb.demon.co.uk/

This page may answer some questions you may have about Art Therapy, what exactly it is and who may be able to benefit from it.

❏ **Art therapy links**
http://www.uofl.edu/sahs/et/otherurl.htm

❏ **Behavior Analysis, Inc.**
http://www.behavioranalysis.com/

This site is dedicated to providing useful and current information for practitioners and consumers of behavior analysis.

❏ **Behavior Home Page**
http://www.state.ky.us/agencies/behave/homepage.html

❏ **Bill O'Hanlon's PossibilityLand**
http://brieftherapy.com/

Access to information on psychotherapy, Brief Therapy, Solution-Oriented Brief Therapy, Solution-Focused Therapy, therapeutic hypnosis, and of course, Possibility Therapy.

❏ **C. G. Jung, Analytical Psychology, and Culture**
http://www.cgjung.com/cgjung/

Highly resourceful and professional.

❏ **Center For Creative Play Home Page**
http://www.center4creativeplay.org/

The Center is a toy and technology lending library with over 1000 toys, a fully equipped computer lab, a child-friendly play area, and a parent resource center. The Center was started by parents and continues to run on parent voices.

❏ **Classical Adlerian Psychology Home Page**
http://ourworld.compuserve.com/
homepages/hstein/
Readings, demonstrations, and more.

❏ **Creative Arts Therapy Links**
http://www.mmbmusic.com/cat_links.html

❏ **Cross-Cultural Communication**
http://www.nwrel.org/cnorse/booklets/
ccc/

❏ **Gestalt Therapy: An Introduction**
http://www.gestalt.org/yontef.htm

❏ **Institute for Reality Therapy in Ireland**
http://indigo.ie/~irti/irti.htm
*Description of the theory and many useful
related resources.*

❏ **Kid Power Play Therapy, Counseling, and
Training**
http://www.snowcrest.net/kidpower/
*The Kid Power web site is dedicated to
empowering people with resources and
information concerning play therapy, children, parenting, and adult counseling.*

❏ **Mister Rogers' Neighborhood**
http://www.pbs.org/rogers/
Useful for teaching play counseling.

❏ **Person-Centered International**
http://www.negia.net/~1234/pci.htm
*Person-Centered International is a multi-
faceted network organization dedicated to
the promotion and application of person-
centered principles. Members are dedicated
to research, education, clinical application,
and societal influence of the principles and
philosophy hypothesized by Carl R. Rogers.*

❏ **Psychology Tutorials and Demonstrations**
http://psych.hanover.edu/Krantz/
tutor.html
*This is a page that will contain links to
hypertext tutorials in psychology as they
become available.*

❏ **psychotherapy-center.com**
http://www.psychotherapy-center.com/
A link to free articles.

❏ **Re-evaluation Counseling**
http://www.rc.org/
*Re-evaluation Counseling is a process
whereby people of all ages and of all backgrounds can learn how to exchange effective
help with each other in order to free themselves from the effects of past distress experiences.*

❏ **Reality Therapy**
http://www.kathycurtissco.com/
dr.htm#Quotes
*Another site bringing information and
resources about Reality Therapy.*

❏ **Sigmund Freud Museum**
http://freud.t0.or.at/
*The father of psychoanalysis receives an
excellent and authoritative treatment about
his life and activities at this Web site, sponsored by the Sigmund Freud Museum that is
located in Vienna.*

❏ **The Case of Felix Ungar**
http://home.earthlink.net/~andyda/psych/
cases/felixindex.html
*Explore Felix from the viewpoint of various
counseling approaches.*

❏ **The National Association Of Cognitive-
Behavioral Therapists (NACBT)**
http://www.nacbt.org/
*Information and resources about cogni-
tive-behavior therapy.*

❏ **Types of Therapy**
http://www.findingstone.com/services/
typesoftherapy.htm
Covers quite a few.

Counselor Education

❑ **Academic Info: Psychology**
http://www.academicinfo.net/psych.html

This site contains an annotated directory of Web sites devoted to the study of psychology.

❑ **ACES Technology Interest Network**
http://www.acesonline.net/leadership.htm

ACES Technology Interest Network is a group of counselor educators interested in the use of technology in the fields of counselor education and counseling.

❑ **Andy's Psychology Pages**
http://home.earthlink.net/~andyda/psych/psych.html

Andy says, "This page is the gateway to my psychology pages. In these pages I will try to entertain and inform. A number of these pages are research papers, notes and research materials I used while in graduate school."

❑ **Arkansas-Little Rock: College of Education Online**
http://www.ualr.edu/~coedept/

A page dedicated to the most useful information gateway and guide to the best resources available on the Internet for teachers.

❑ **Ask the Dream Doctor**
http://www.dreamdoctor.com/

Dream analysis sorted by category and a daily tip for healthy sleep habits are featured.

❑ **British Journal of Guidance and Counselling**
http://www.carfax.co.uk/bjg-ad.htm

❑ **Crisis, Grief, and Healing: Men and Women (Tom Golden LCSW)**
http://www.webhealing.com/

According to the author, "This page is meant to be a place men and women can browse to understand and honor the many different paths to heal strong emotions." The site provides many useful links to grief and healing informational resources.

❑ **DAS Online**
http://nces.ed.gov/dasol/

The Data Analysis System (DAS) is a software application that allows you to produce tables and correlation matrices from NCES data sets, mainly postsecondary data. There is a separate DAS for each data set, but all have a consistent interface and command structure.

❑ **Dr. Gerler's Online Group Counseling Course**
http://www.genesislight.com/539a

Nicely done. Other courses also available at this site.

❑ **EDUCATION POLICY ANALYSIS ARCHIVES**
http://olam.ed.asu.edu/epaa/

An electronic journal.

❑ **Effective Presentations**
http://www.kumc.edu/SAH/OTEd/jradel/effective.html

Tutorials intended to aid in developing an effective oral presentation, designing effective visual aids for presentations, and creating an effective poster presentation.

❑ **Electronic Journals and Periodicals in Psychology and Related Fields**
http://psych.hanover.edu/Krantz/journal.html

This site attempts to maintain a relatively complete index of psychologically related electronic journals, conference proceedings, and other periodicals.

❏ **Ethics Updates**
http://ethics.acusd.edu

Ethics Updates is designed primarily to be used by ethics instructors and their students. It is intended to provide updates on current literature, both popular and professional, that relates to ethics.

❏ **Exhibits Collection — Personality**
http://www.learner.org/exhibits/personality

A well done exhibit about personality.

❏ **Fenichel's CURRENT TOPICS IN PSYCHOLOGY**
http://www.fenichel.com/Current.shtml

As described by the author, this site provides useful general references for both professionals and the general public. It is not intended as a substitute for individualized professional evaluation or treatment. There are many good resources here, including information, support groups, and clinical treatment providers.

❏ **Goals 2000: Reforming Education to Improve Student Achievement**
http://www.ed.gov/pubs/G2KReforming/
Document available also in PDF.

❏ **Higher Education Jobs**
http://www.higheredjobs.com/

HigherEdJobs.com was founded in 1996 to list open positions at colleges and universities.

❏ **IJET International Journal of Educational Technology**
http://www.outreach.uiuc.edu/ijet

The International Journal of Educational Technology (IJET) is an internationally refereed journal in the field of educational technology, sponsored by The Graduate School of Education at the University of Western Australia and the College of Education at the University of Illinois at Urbana-Champaign.

❏ **Journal of Technology Education**
http://scholar.lib.vt.edu/ejournals/JTE/

The Journal of Technology Education provides a forum for scholarly discussion on topics relating to technology education. Manuscripts should focus on technology education research, philosophy, theory, or practice. In addition, the Journal publishes book reviews, editorials, guest articles, comprehensive literature reviews, and reactions to previously published articles. Past issues are available both in HTML and PDF formats.

❏ **MERLOT**
http://www.merlot.org/Home.po

MERLOT is a free and open resource designed primarily for faculty and students of higher education. Links to online learning materials are collected here along with annotations such as peer reviews and assignments.

❏ **National Program for Transforming School Counseling**
http://www.edtrust.org/main/main/index.asp

Summary of work being undertaken by the Education Trust for the school counseling initiative.

❏ **Online Dictionary of Mental Health**
http://www.shef.ac.uk/~psysc/psychotherapy/
Comprehensive.

❏ **Personality and IQ Tests**
http://www.davideck.com/online-tests.html

Includes personality, IQ, and other.

❏ **PrePrac98**
http://www.coe.ufl.edu/faculty/myrick/preprac98/preprac98.html

Another depiction of a counseling student class experience.

❏ **PrePracExp — University of Florida**
http://www.coe.ufl.edu/faculty/myrick/
preprac/theproject.html

   An example of displaying on the web, description and photos, of a classroom experience.

❏ **Psychology of Cyberspace — Computer and Cyberspace Addiction**
http://www.shpm.com/articles/internet/
cybaddict.html

   A link from the Self-Help and Psychology Magazine website, this paper begins, "A heated debate is rising among psychologists. With the explosion of excitement about the Internet, some people seem to be a bit too excited. Some people spend way too much time there. Is this yet ANOTHER type of addiction that has invaded the human psyche?"

❏ **Psychotherapy, Education, and the Movies**
http://www.hesley.com/

   Although this web site was designed with professionals in mind, almost anybody can benefit from watching movies with more awareness. This web site depicts popular movies that are placed at the service of therapy and education, a process described in the recently published, Rent Two Films and Let's Talk in the Morning. Through highlighting new movies, video releases, and classics, this site hopes to help clinicians, teachers and consultants harness the motivating power of films.

❏ **Raymond Perry, Jr., Ph.D., University of Wisconsin Oshkosh**
http://www.coehs.uwosh.edu/faculty/
perry/

   A compendium of useful links.

❏ **SALMON: Study and Learning Materials ON-line**
http://salmon.psy.plym.ac.uk/year1/
bbb.htm

   Award winning site covering psychological topics such as Biological Basis of Behavior, Physiological Psychology, Perception, Psychological Research Techniques, and lots more.

❏ **School Counsellors Position Paper**
http://www.nswppa.org.au/counsel.html

   From the NSW Primary Principals' Association.

❏ **Smoother Sailing — Information & Research**
http://www.des-moines.k12.ia.us/pro-
grams/10smoother-index.htm

   Smoother Sailing, Des Moines' unique elementary counseling program, helps children cope with the "rough seas" of growing up. Praised nationally as a model of excellence among elementary counseling programs, Smoother Sailing affects the lives of more than 15,343 children in the 42 elementary schools of the Des Moines Public School District.

❏ **Test Junkie**
http://www.queendom.com/
test_col.html#career

   More fun and funny online tests.

❏ **The American School Board Journal**
http://www.asbj.com/

   The award-winning, editorially independent education magazine published by the National School Boards Association.

❏ **The Company Therapist**
http://www.thetherapist.com/

   A fictional site composed of therapist notes, actions, etc. Useful for learning via case studies.

❏ **The Institute for Psychohistory**
http://www.psychohistory.com/

The Institute for Psychohistory is a scholarly research and publication institute chartered by the State of New York as a not-for-profit educational corporation, the Association for Psychohistory, Inc. This website contains extensive material reproduced from The Journal of Psychohistory and from the book in process by Lloyd deMause, "Childhood and History." In addition, it contains links to the Institute branches, the International Psychohistorical Association and PSYCHOHISTORY, a discussion list and chat room, with archives.

❏ **The Specialized Scholarly Monograph in Crisis**
http://www.arl.org/scomm/epub/papers

This site represents the first time that three organizations—the American Council of Learned Societies, the Association of American University Presses, and the Association of Research Libraries—have formally joined together to address in concert a whole raft of issues surrounding the publication of specialized scholarship.

❏ **The World Lecture Hall**
http://www.utexas.edu/world/lecture/

The World Lecture Hall (WLH) contains links to pages created by faculty worldwide who are using the Web to deliver class materials.

❏ **The World-Wide Web Virtual Library: Electronic Journals**
http://www.e-journals.org/

This is the WWW Virtual Library Electronic Journals Catalog. Entries in this catalog are added and maintained through WILMA (Web Information-List Maintenance Agent).

❏ **Theory**
http://www.hwi.com/tygger/edpsych/default.html

Informative site which includes info and slide presentations about developmental, cognitive, information processing, and behavioral theories.

❏ **Third Annual TCC Online Conference**
http://leahi.kcc.hawaii.edu/org/tcon98/

A virtual conference (the Third Annual Teaching in Community Colleges Conference, Online Instruction: Trends & Issues II) with posted papers.

❏ **Welcome to the Resource Station — Education Articles**
http://www.classroom.com/resource/articles/

Especially for information about the Internet.

❏ **World-Wide Graduate School Directory**
http://www.gradschools.com/welcome.html

Quite a comprehensive source of online graduate school/program information.

Crisis

❑ **APA HelpCenter: Get the Facts: How Therapy Helps: Managing Traumatic Stress**
http://helping.apa.org/daily/traumaticstress.html

Managing Traumatic Stress: Tips for Recovering From Disasters and Other Traumatic Events

❑ **Athealth.com: PTSD Resourses**
http://www.athealth.com/Practitioner/Newsletter/FPN_5_19.html

Mental Health Information — Vol. 5 Issue 19. Focus on PTSD.

❑ **Children and Trauma: Reactions to the WTC Attack Sept 11, 2001**
http://www.psychservices.com/hope.shtml

A wonderful list of links to trauma resources.

❑ **Children, Stress, and Natural Disasters**
http://www.wplc.org/remember911/children_dealing_with_disasters.cfm

❑ **Connect For Kids: The Aftershocks of National Tragedy: One Year Later**
http://www.connectforkids.org/usr_doc/CopingWithGrief.htm

Connect for Kids has compiled some of the Web's strongest resources for parents, teachers and community members, to help all of our nation's children work through the tragic and unprecedented events of September 11, 2001.

❑ **Crisis Guides Home Page from the NEA**
http://www.nea.org/crisis/

Includes dealing with crisis before, during, and after a crisis and respective tools.

❑ **Crisis Management Institute**
http://cmionline.org/

An array of crisis response and violence prevention. This group also provides other school services and consultation in this area.

❑ **David Baldwin's Trauma Information Pages**
http://www.trauma-pages.com/

A variety of resources and links.

❑ **Early Warning, Timely Response: A Guide to Safe Schools**
http://www.ed.gov/offices/OSERS/OSEP/Products/earlywrn.html

Early Warning, Timely Response: A Guide to Safe Schools offers research-based practices designed to assist school communities identify these warning signs early and develop prevention, intervention and crisis response plans.

❑ **Helping Children After a Disaster — AACAP Facts For Families # 36**
http://www.aacap.org/publications/factsfam/disaster.htm

Article with helpful links.

❑ **Helping Children and Adolescents Cope with Violence and Disasters**
http://www.nimh.nih.gov/publicat/violence.cfm

"The National Institute of Mental Health and other Federal agencies are working to address the issue of assisting children and adolescents who have been victims of or witnesses to violent and/or catastrophic events. The purpose of this fact sheet is to tell what is known about the impact of violence and disasters on children and adolescents and suggest steps to minimize long-term emotional harm. "

❑ **Helping Children Understand the Terrorist Attacks — U.S. Department of Education**
http://www.ed.gov/inits/september11

Info and resources.

❑ **Hope Morrow's Trauma Central**
http://home.earthlink.net/~hopefull/home/home_contents.htm

Handouts and other articles.

❏ **Links to Advice on Supporting and Communicating With Children After September 11**
http://www.gse.harvard.edu/~hfrp/advice.html

Advice for parents, teachers, and community members.

❏ **National Center for PTSD**
http://www.ncptsd.org/

This organization is dedicated to "To advance the clinical care and social welfare of America's veterans through research, education, and training in the science, diagnosis, and treatment of PTSD and stress-related disorders. This website is provided as an educational resource concerning PTSD and other enduring consequences of traumatic stress."

❏ **National School Safety Center**
http://www.nssc1.org/

The Center will identify and promote strategies, promising practices and programs that support safe schools for all students as part of the total academic mission.

❏ **National Youth Violence Prevention Resource Center**
http://www.safeyouth.org/

Lots of news and focus on hot topics in this area.

❏ **PBS: Coverage of Events of Tuesday, September 11, 2001**
http://www.pbs.org/americaresponds/

"America Responds" is a snapshot of PBS's coverage of the September 11, 2001 terrorist attacks. This Web site was maintained in the months immediately following the attacks, and now serves as an archive of related resources, analysis and discussion from that moment in time.

❏ **PsychWorks, Inc: PTSD response**
http://www.psychworks.com/PTSD%20response.htm

Includes answers to the following questions: 1. What happens to people after a disaster or other traumatic event? 2. How do people respond differently over time? 3. How should I help myself and my family? 4. How do I take care of children's special needs? 5. When should I seek professional help? 6. Resource links ?

❏ **Sesame Workshop — Tragic Times, Healing Words**
http://www.sesameworkshop.org/parents/advice/article.php?contentId=49560

Includes an age appropriate table. Also available in Spanish!

❏ **Talking To Children About Violence**
http://www.esrnational.org/guide.htm

"Growing up has never been easy. It's especially difficult for young people in times of crisis. We owe it to our children to listen to what is on their minds, and in their hearts, and give them the best of our understanding and our guidance. Educators for Social Responsibility has prepared this guide for adults who are concerned about how to communicate with young people about difficult issues in their wider world. "

❏ **Terrorism and Children: Talking with Children about Terrorism**
http://www.ces.purdue.edu/terrorism/children/terrorism.html

Judith Myers-Walls, a Purdue University Extension specialist in child development and family studies, has researched children's reactions to wars and disasters and offers advice for parents and others on how to help children cope with the terrorist attacks at the World Trade Centers and Pentagon.

❑ **The CHILD SURVIVOR of Traumatic Stress**
http://users.umassmed.edu/
Kenneth.Fletcher/kidsurv.html
Articles and references.

❑ **UCLA School Mental Health Project**
http://smhp.psych.ucla.edu/
Go to the Center Response section and scroll to "Crisis Prevention and Response." One of the things you will find cited is our resource aid "Responding to a Crisis at a School" which contains specific guidelines for responding and follow-up in the weeks to come. You can download this with a click and print off the relevant materials.

❑ **United States Secret Service: National Threat Assessment Center (NTAC)**
http://www.ustreas.gov/usss/ntac_ssi.shtml

❑ **University of Miami: Keeping Children Safe**
http://www.keepingchildrensafe.com/
A FREE downloadable book, "Keeping Children Safe" is a prevention/intervention program that was developed to examine the effects of exposure to community violence and it's association with symptoms of posttraumatic stress in children.

Diversity

❑ **America's Stirfry Multicultural Books K12 Gifts Toys Jewelry Games Cards**
http://www.americas-stirfry.com/
America's Stir-fry offers a broad variety of educational products, including over 75 popular children's book and video titles published in many of the languages of the world, including English, Japanese, Chinese, Vietnamese, Korean, Spanish and Hawaiian.

❑ **Asian-Nation: The Landscape of Asian America**
http://www.asian-nation.org

❑ **Atlanta 1906: A Race Riot**
http://www.wpba.org/
atlantariot1906.html
Produced by Public Broadcasting Atlanta, in conjunction with the PBS series "The Rise and Fall of Jim Crow," this visual history of the 1906 Atlanta Race Riot is a useful education tool that offers an introduction to this traumatically violent event in the city's not-so distant past.

❑ **Beyond Prejudice**
http://www.eburg.com/beyond.prejudice/
Beyond Prejudice is an extensive and flexible multimedia program that teaches participants how to identify and alter prejudicial behavior. This unique approach provides the guidance and the structure for taking positive action against the prejudices that divide us.

❏ **Bridging Cultures in Our Schools — Welcome**
http://web.wested.org/online_pubs/bridging/welcome.shtml

This knowledge brief provides a framework for understanding how teachers' culturally driven — and often unconsciously held — values influence classroom practice and expectations, and, when in conflict with the values of immigrant and other parents from more collectivistic societies, can interfere with parent-teacher communication. The brief looks at some specific sources of cross-culture conflicts and illustrates some strategies for resolving them.

❏ **Cartes Virtuelles SOURD-PRISE !! E-Cards**
http://www.cvm.qc.ca/dcb/carte

Send an electronic greeting card with pictures related to deafness, deaf, sign language, etc.

❏ **Center for Multicultural Education**
http://depts.washington.edu/~centerme/home.htm

The Center for Multicultural Education at the University of Washington, Seattle WA, focuses on research projects and activities designed to improve practice related to equity issues, intergroup relations, and the achievement of students of color. The Center also engages in services and teaching related to its research mission.

❏ **Clearinghouse for Multicultural/Bilingual Education**
http://departments.weber.edu/mbe/HTMLs/MBE.html

The purpose of this website is to provide educators, from pre-kindergarten to higher education, with commercial and non-commercial sources for multicultural and bilingual/ESL information, materials, and resources.

❏ **Diversity Database, University of Maryland**
http://www.inform.umd.edu/EdRes/Topic/Diversity/

The University of Maryland's Diversity Database is a comprehensive index of multicultural and diversity resources.

❏ **Diversity Job Bank**
http://www.imdiversity.com/

Find a job with a diversity sensitive employer

❏ **Diversity Leadership Forum (DLF) Online**
http://www.diversityleadershipforum.org/

The Diversity Leadership Forum is a national non-profit professional association, providing the arena for a multidisciplinary collaboration of diversity practitioners to shape the development of the Diversity Field. Focusing solely on diversity practitioners, DLF offers the networking, dialogue, best practices, skill enhancement, cutting edge research, strategic planning and renewal resources critical to the success of the profession and to the health of our society.

❏ **Diversity OnLine**
http://www.geocities.com/WestHollywood/Village/2428/

A monthly newspaper published by The Community Center, a non-profit GLBT service organization in Boise, Idaho.

❏ **DiversityInc.com**
http://www.diversityinc.com/

The leading source for daily diversity news.

❏ **Improving Ethnic and Racial Relations in the Schools.**
http://www.ed.gov/databases/ERIC_Digests/ed414113.html

Improving Ethnic and Racial Relations in the Schools, an ERIC digest.

❏ **Education First: Black History Activities**
http://www.kn.pacbell.com/wired/BHM/AfroAm.html

Black History consists of a six web sites: Hotlist, Subject Sampler, Treasure Hunt, and WebQuests.

❏ **ENC: Equity and Diversity**
http://www.enc.org/topics/equity/

A resource for educators concerned about creating equitable conditions in which every child can succeed. These equity materials can help teachers and administrators acknowledge children's diverse strengths, identify inequities, and improve the ways they serve students with varied needs.

❏ **ERASE: Resources for Parents, Teachers, & Students**
http://www.arc.org/erase/pts.html

The ERASE Initiative provides these pages as a resource to education activists: students, parents, teachers or concerned community members. We want to support local work that helps overcome racial injustice in the schools and that promotes a vision of racial equity.

❏ **Intercultural E-Mail Classroom Connections**
http://www.stolaf.edu/network/iecc/

The IECC (Intercultural E-Mail Classroom Connections) mailing lists are provided by St. Olaf College as a free service to help teachers and classes link with partners in other countries and cultures for e-mail classroom penpal and project exchanges.

❏ **KIDPROJ's Multi-Cultural Calendar**
http://www.kidlink.org/KIDPROJ/MCC/

"KIDLINK students and KIDLEADERs have made this calendar possible. Included in the files you will find the unique ways our KIDLINK kids are celebrating their country's holidays and festivals. The entries might contain recipes for holiday foods, historical background, significance of the holidays and the special ways in which these days are observed. Our calendar entries are rich in local customs that perhaps cannot be found in books."

❏ **Multicultural Education**
http://curry.edschool.virginia.edu/go/multicultural/teachers.html

A multicultural lesson toolbox!

❏ **Multicultural Education and Ethnic Groups: Selected Internet Sources**
http://wwwlibrary.csustan.edu/lboyer/multicultural/main.htm

Here is an introduction to the resources on the Web concerning multicultural education and diversity.

❏ **Multicultural Education Resources**
http://www.education.gsw.edu/johnson/MulticulturalEducation.htm

Tons of resourceful links.

❏ **Multicultural Education Supersite**
http://www.mhhe.com/socscience/education/multi/

The McGraw-Hill Multicultural Supersite attempts to narrow the gap between multicultural education theory and practice through a collection of information and original resources for in-service teachers, preservice teachers, and teacher educators.

❏ **Myth of the Melting Pot America's Racial and Ethnic Divides**
http://www.washingtonpost.com/wp-srv/national/longterm/meltingpot/melt0222.htm

A three part series.

❏ **National MultiCultural Institute (NMCI)**
http://www.nmci.org/

The National MultiCultural Institute (NMCI) was founded in 1983 in response to our nation's growing need for new services, knowledge, and skills in diversity. Since then, we have had over 16,000 participants attending our conferences and workshops. NMCI is proud to be one of the most experienced organizations in the field of diversity training.

❏ **National Society of Black Engineers Online**
http://www.nsbe.org/

Engineers create everything from rockets to Mars to the fun Super Soaker, a high-powered water gun invented by African-American engineer Lonnie Johnson of the Jet Propulsion Labs! For Black History Month why not learn more abut engineering.

❏ **Pathways: Asian and Pacific Islander**
http://eric-web.tc.columbia.edu/pathways/asian_pacific/

This pathway is designed to inform educators, administrators, parents, and community leaders about the Asian Pacific American student population and its educational and cultural characteristics.

❏ **Race Relations at About.com**
http://racerelations.about.com/mbody.htm

❏ **REACH: Teaching Children to Resist Bias**
http://www.uua.org/re/reach/parenting/children_resist_bias.html

Teaching Children To Resist Bias: What Parents Can Do ... Research tells us that between ages 2 and 5, children become aware of gender, race, ethnicity, and disabilities. They also become sensitive to both the positive attitudes and negative biases attached to these four key aspects of identity by their family and by society in general.

❏ **The Civil Rights Project Harvard University**
http://www.civilrightsproject.harvard.edu

"Our mission is to help renew the civil rights movement by bridging the worlds of ideas and action, and by becoming a preeminent source of intellectual capital and a forum for building consensus within that movement."

❏ **Through the Lens of Time: Images of African Americans from the Cook Collection**
http://www.library.vcu.edu/jbc/speccoll/cook/

Search or browse nearly 300 images of African Americans dating from the nineteenth and early twentieth century from the Cook Collection of Photographs.

❏ **Tolerance.org: Teaching Tolerance Home**
http://www.tolerance.org/teach/index.jsp

A Web project of the Southern Poverty Law Center, Tolerance.org encourages people from all walks of life to "fight hate and promote tolerance."

❏ **Two Faces of the Nation (PBS)**
http://www.pbs.org/wgbh/pages/frontline/shows/race

Frontline discussion of race relations in America.

❏ **Voice of the Shuttle: Minority Studies Page**
http://vos.ucsb.edu/

Education

❑ **Best Practices in Education**
http://www.bestpraceduc.org/
A not-for-profit organization dedicated to working with American teachers to find effective educational practices from other countries to adapt and apply in United States schools.

❑ **Cornell Youth and Work Program**
http://www.human.cornell.edu/youthwork/
The Cornell Youth and Work Program fosters the transition of youth to adulthood through research and development on school-to-work opportunities.

❑ **Council for Basic Education — Standards (US and International)**
http://www.c-b-e.org/
Many articles, kits, and publications.

❑ **ED Initiatives**
http://www.ed.gov/pubs/EDInitiatives/
A biweekly look at progress on the Secretary of Education's priorities.

❑ **ED's Oasis: Teacher Support for Classroom Internet Use**
http://www.edsoasis.org/
ED's Oasis' primary purpose is to make the Internet easier and more rewarding to use with students. ED's Oasis provides links to what educators around the country recommend as the most engaging student-centered web sites, and examples demonstrating effective classroom Internet use from successful teachers.

❑ **Education Review- A Journal of Book Reviews**
http://www.ed.asu.edu/edrev/
Education Review (ER) publishes review articles of recently published books in education. ER contains sixteen departments covering the range of educational scholarship, and is intended to promote wider understanding of the latest and best research in the field.

❑ **Education World**
http://www.education-world.com/
Highly resourceful site that includes lesson plans, news, educational site ratings, and much more.

❑ **EDUFAX-Educational Resources for Consultants/Parents/Students.**
http://www.edufax.com/
EDUFAX provides individualized counseling for educational placement from preschool through graduate school, for re-entry and adult learners, and for the American and international student. We facilitate the perfect match by evaluating the academic, social, and personal needs of each student. This site is chock full of information including newsletters and links to colleges and universities.

❑ **Evalutech**
http://www.sret.sreb.org/
EvaluTech is a searchable database of curriculum related instructional materials specifically designed for kindergarten through grade 12.

❑ **Filamentality 2**
http://www.kn.pacbell.com/wired/fil/
According to the site, Filamentality is a fill-in-the-blank interactive Web site that guides you through picking a topic, searching the Web, gathering good Internet sites, and turning Web resources into activities appropriate for learners. So it helps you combine the Filaments of the Web with a learner's mentality (get it?).

❑ **Indiana Department of Education**
http://ideanet.doe.state.in.us/
Highly informative for all educators.

❏ **Kathy Schrock's Guide for Educators**
http://www.capecod.net/schrockguide/

Kathy Schrock's Guide for Educators is a classified list of sites on the Internet found to be useful for enhancing curriculum and teacher professional growth. It is updated daily to keep up with the tremendous number of new World Wide Web sites.

❏ **LETSNet Home Page**
http://commtechlab.msu.edu/sites/letsnet/

This website is dedicated to helping teachers experience the potential value of the World Wide Web (Web) in the classroom by providing actual examples of real teachers who are using the Internet today.

❏ **Meridian- Middle School Computer Technologies Journal**
http://www.ncsu.edu/meridian/

Full-text articles and resourceful links.

❏ **National Archives: The Digital Classroom**
http://www.nara.gov/education/classrm.html

Primary sources, activities, and training for educators and students.

❏ **National Foundation for the Improvement of Education**
http://www.nfie.org/

❏ **Online Innovation Institute**
http://oii.org/

The Online Innovation Institute (OII) is a results driven organization, which offers professional development workshops to help students and teachers improve classroom achievement.

❏ **Rethinking Schools Online**
http://www.rethinkingschools.org/

The Rethinking Schools Web site is chock full of information related to school choice, in addition to educational reform, social justice, and equity issues.

❏ **Teacher Magazine**
http://www.teachermagazine.org/

Online page for the magazine.

❏ **Teachnet.com**
http://www.teachnet.com/

Teachnet includes a free e-mail newsletter and over 1,000 regular users on their Postings mailing list.

❏ **The Children's Book Council**
http://www.cbcbooks.org/

CBC Online is the website of the Children's Book Council—encouraging reading since 1945. This guide is intended for the use of teachers and librarians, who authors, illustrators, parents, and booksellers. Some pages may only be accessed by members.

❏ **U.S. DEPARTMENT OF EDUCATION TOPICS SEARCH**
http://www.ed.gov/topicsaz/

To further assist you in finding education topics and information.

❏ **U.S. Government Documents Ready Reference Collection**
http://www.columbia.edu/cu/libraries/indiv/dsc/readyref.html

U.S. Government Documents Ready Reference Collection from Columbia University Libraries.

❏ **Youth Resources**
http://www.uscharterschools.org/

This site, developed as a joint project by the U.S. Department of Education, California State University's Charter Schools Project, and the Policy Support and Studies Program at WestEd, was created to promote the sharing of information and innovations by the people running local charter schools. The site gives detailed information on state charter school policies, charter schools profiles, and information related to starting and running a charter school.

Family and Parents

❏ **Children Now**
http://www.dnai.com/%7Echildren/
Children Now uses research and mass communications to make the well being of children a top priority across the nation.

❏ **Disney's Family Page**
http://familyfun.go.com/
Lots of activities and fun things to do.

❏ **Family**
http://family.go.com/
A Disney Site, this one offers a variety of resources for families.

❏ **Kidtools Home Page**
http://www.kidtools.com/
Information and product reviews on educational products for kids. Learn about the latest information on educational books, toys, software, audio and video products.

❏ **National Family Partnership**
http://www.nfp.org/
At its foundation, National Family Partnership is a network of parents who care about their kids and want to keep them safe from drugs. These parents, from different geographic areas, occupations and lifestyles, are united in one understanding: that prevention-keeping kids from ever using drugs-is far better than salvaging the health and well-being of kids abused by drugs.

❏ **National Parent Information Network**
http://npin.org/
The purpose of NPIN is to provide information to parents and those who work with parents and to foster the exchange of parenting materials.

❏ **Parents for Improved Education — Fairfax County Public Schools**
http://www.geocities.com/CapitolHill/9155/
The authors of the site explain: "We are parents of students being educated in Fairfax County Public Schools (Virginia) who have become increasingly concerned that despite the high ranking of standardized test scores, our children are not being properly educated in the core subjects." One link goes to a parent whom does not agree with the role of school counselors.

❏ **Parents Guide to the Internet**
http://www.ed.gov/pubs/parents/internet/
Viewable and downloadable!

❏ **PEP Parents, Educators, and Publishers**
http://www.microweb.com/pepsite/
The PEP site is an informational resource for Parents, Educators, and children's software Publishers. The content of this site has been developed in response to the interests and needs of these three audiences.

❏ **Stepfamily Network**
http://www.stepfamily.net/
Educating stepparents, parents, family professionals, and stepchildren.

❏ **The Children's Partnership**
http://www.childrenspartnership.org/
A national, nonpartisan organization that provides timely information to leaders and the public about the needs of Americas 70 million children—and promotes ways to engage all Americans to benefit children.

❏ **The F.U.N. Place — Families United on the Net**
http://www.thefunplace.com/
Packed with articles, games, chatrooms, resources — truly fun for the whole family.

❏ **The Future of Children**
http://www.futureofchildren.org/

The primary purpose of The Future of Children is to disseminate timely information on major issues related to children's well-being, with special emphasis on providing objective analysis and evaluation, translating existing knowledge into effective programs and polices, and promoting constructive institutional change.

❏ **The You Can Handle Them All Web Site**
http://www.disciplinehelp.com/

Excellent site which contains a great deal of information and resources about this topic.

Government

❏ **Bureau of Justice Statistics Crime & Justice Electronic Data Abstracts**
http://www.ojp.usdoj.gov/bjs/dtdata.htm

❏ **Institute for Intergovernmental Research (IIR)**
http://www.iir.com/

The Institute for Intergovernmental Research (IIR) is a research organization specializing in law enforcement, juvenile justice, and criminal justice issues.

❏ **Office of Justice Programs**
http://www.ojp.usdoj.gov/

Dedicated to comprehensive approaches, OJP's mission is to provide federal leadership in developing the nation's capacity to prevent and control crime, administer justice and assist crime victims.

❏ **Office of Juvenile Justice and Delin-quency Prevention**
http://ojjdp.ncjrs.org/

OJJDP provides Federal leadership, through a comprehensive, coordinated approach, to prevent and control juvenile crime and improve the juvenile justice system.

❏ **Project EASI ... Easy Access for Students and Institutions**
http://easi.ed.gov/

Project EASI (Easy Access for Students and Institutions) is a collaborative effort among a diverse group of government, business and education leaders to reengineer the country's postsecondary financial aid delivery system.

Grant Information

❏ **AERA Grants Program**
http://www.aera.net/grantsprogram/
Online information and applications for various grants.

❏ **Education Grants & Funding, Technology Products and Services, K-12 Lesson Plans**
http://www.eschoolnews.com/resources/funding/
Information on up-to-the-minute grant programs, funding sources, and technology funding.

❏ **Grants & Contracts — U.S. Department of Education**
http://www.ed.gov/topics/topics.jsp?&top=Grants+%26+Contracts
Lots of money out there!

❏ **Grants and Fund-raising Portal**
http://www.fundsnetservices.com/
A comprehensive website dedicated to providing nonprofit organizations, colleges, and Universities with information on financial resources available on the Internet.

❏ **GuideStar: What Grantmakers Want Applicants to Know**
http://www.guidestar.org/news/features/grantadvice.stm
Fifteen recommendations for obtaining grants with links.

❏ **NIH: Office of Extramural Research Grants Home Page**
http://grants2.nih.gov/grants/oer.htm

❏ **School Grants**
http://www.schoolgrants.org
A collection of resources and tips to help K-12 educators apply for and obtain special grants for a variety of projects.

❏ **Technology Grants**
http://www.globalclassroom.org/grants.html
A list of links for technology grant resources.

❏ **Technology Innovation Challenge Grant Projects**
http://www.ed.gov/Technology/challenge/grants1.html
Links to schools receiving the grant.

❏ **The Foundation Center — Finding Funders**
http://fdncenter.org/funders/
K-12 Funding opportunities with links to grant seeking for teachers, learning technology, and more.

❏ **The Scholastic Network Grant Seminar**
http://teacher.scholastic.com/professional/grants/scholgrantseminar.htm
Dr. Gary Carnow's FREE online seminar on grant-writing.

❏ **Writing Your First Successful Grant Application**
http://teachersplanet.com/grantart.shtml
An article written by Stanley Levenson, Ph.D.

Handhelds

❏ **Blue Nomad Software: WordSmith**
http://www.bluenomad.com/ws/
prod_wordsmith_details.html

WordSmith, co-developed by Blue Nomad and Quik Sense Software, LLC is an intuitive and full-featured word processor, document viewer and enhanced memo pad available for the Palm and compatible organizers.

❏ **FreewarePalm**
http://www.freewarepalm.com/

❏ **Handango**
http://www.handango.com/

Huge!

❏ **Handheld Computing**
https://www.pdabuzz.com/
SubscriberCenter/index.php

PDABuzz.com has been recognized as a leading news and information source by the Wall Street Journal, Washington Post, Pocket PC Magazine, and other major publications both online and in print.

❏ **K12Handhelds**
http://www.k12handhelds.com/

Handheld solutions for educators.

❏ **MemoWare — Thousands of Free Ebooks and PDA Documents!**
http://www.memoware.com/

❏ **My Palm Guide — Guiding Your Mobile Computing Experience**
http://mypalmguide.150m.com/

The purpose of this site is to help both new and old PalmOS PDA user to master their PDA applications and functions. Not just master built-in applications, we will also introduce you to many useful applications!

❏ **Palm TipSheet**
http://www.palmtipsheet.com

The Palm Tipsheet is a free monthly newsletter providing relevant news and practical tips for Palm handheld users. Each issue includes a list of notable links to newsworthy items from the past month, an indepth feature article on ways to more effectively use a Palm handheld and an interview with an international Palm handheld user.

❏ **PalmGear.com**
http://www.palmgear.com/

Tons of stuff for handhelds!

❏ **PalmGear.com**
http://palmgear.com/

❏ **PalmPilotArchives.com**
http://www.palmpilotarchives.com/

❏ **PDA Buzz / Tips & Tricks**
http://www.pdabuzz.com/Tips/

❏ **Pocket PC magazine**
http://www.pocketpcmag.com/

Free newsletters, tips, tricks, and more.

❏ **Pocket PC software**
http://www.ipaqsoft.net/

❏ **PocketGear**
http://www.pocketgear.com/

Tons of resources for handheld computers.

❏ **pocketnow.com**
http://www.pocketnow.com/

❏ **Tucows PDA — Download software, shareware, and freeware for Palm Pilot and other**
http://www.pilotzone.com/

❏ **Vasilenok's Birthday Notifier!**
http://www.vasilenok.com/products/
vbirthday.html

VBirthday scans your contacts for all Birthday/Anniversary events, sorts it and shows to you. You may sort by Name, by Age or by Next event.

Humor, Inspiration, and Fun

❑ **Chicken Soup for the Soul**
http://www.chickensoup.com/

The official Chicken Soup for the Soul website, this one contains helpful links to submit your story, contact speakers, and highlights soup stories. Through this site, you may also subscribe to a listserv and have delivered via e-mail a daily dose of chicken soup for the soul.

❑ **Coffee Break Arcade — Free Internet Games**
http://www.coffeebreakarcade.com

❑ **Counseling.com's Humor page**
http://www.counseling.com/Ccom/chumor.html

Funny!

❑ **Dumb Warnings**
http://www.dumbwarnings.com/

An index of — you guessed it — dumb warnings. Dumb warnings are divided into categories, including drinks, electronics, household, and Web. You can rate warnings, leave comments on warnings, or submit your own warnings.

❑ **E-greetings**
http://www.egreetings.com

Another e-greeting site.

❑ **Jerry King — Technology Cartoons**
http://www.jerryking.com/toons/technology/

❑ **Mental Health Humor**
http://www.bouldertherapist.com/html/humor/Humor.html

Lots of fun stuff.

❑ **Mental Health Humor**
http://dmoz.org/Health/Mental_Health/Humor/

❑ **PAML — CoHu: Counseling & Psychology Humor**
http://paml.alastra.com/groupsC/cohu.html

A bi-weekly newsletter with counseling and psychology related humor.

❑ **PopCap Games**
http://www.popcap.com/

❑ **Quoteland**
http://www.quoteland.com/

❑ **The Daily Motivator**
http://greatday.com/motivate/dmsummary

Add an inspirational message to your website that's automatically updated each day. You may also get one via e-mail.

❑ **The Impact of Humor...**
http://www.humormatters.com/articles/therapy2.htm

The Impact of Humor in the Counseling Relationship by Steven M. Sultanoff, Ph.D. with lots of resourceful links!

❑ **The Positive Press: Good News Every Day**
http://www.positivepress.com/

❑ **World Database of Happiness**
http://www.eur.nl/fsw/research/happiness/

The World Database of Happiness is an ongoing register of scientific research on subjective appreciation of life.

IT Literacy Resources

❏ **A Beginner's Guide to Effective E-mail**
http://www.webfoot.com/advice/e-mail.top.html

❏ **A Cost Performance Model for Assessing WWW**
http://www.ctg.albany.edu/projects/inettb/SpreadSheets.html

According to the site, The A Cost Performance Model for Assessing WWW Service Investments is a set of tools designed to assist organizations in estimating the likely costs and benefits of developing a Web-based service."

❏ **Acadia's PowerPoint Resource Center**
http://aitt.acadiau.ca/resources/ppt/

Lots of How-To's, sounds, clipart, and more.

❏ **Assessment Tools for the Basic and Advanced Technology Competencies**
http://www.dpi.state.nc.us/tap/assess.htm

This sample assessment tool was developed by NC technology educators in cooperation with the Instructional Technology Division of NCDPI. It contains supporting skills to mastering the required technology competencies and aligns the technology competencies with the student.

❏ **Beginners' Central, a Users Guide to the Internet**
http://northernwebs.com/bc/

This site is dedicated to helping people learn to use that information in a coherent manner. Beginners' Central is based on a chapter by chapter structure, you may skip to any chapter you're interested in, or if you wish, you can start at the beginning and work your way forward.

❏ **Bibliography for Educator's Introduction to the Internet**
http://www.monroe.lib.in.us/~lchampel/netedbib.html

❏ **Bibliography on Evaluating Internet Resources**
http://www.lib.vt.edu/research/evaluate/evalbiblio.html

According to the author, Nicole Auer, this bibliography has grown with the increasing number of documents which address the problems and issues related to teaching and using critical thinking skills to evaluate Internet resources.

❏ **Blue Web'n Applications**
http://www.kn.pacbell.com/cgi-bin/listApps.pl?Education&(Counseling)

Blue Web'n is a searchable database of outstanding Internet learning sites categorized by subject area, audience, and type (lessons, activities, projects, resources, references, & tools). Blue Web'n does not attempt to catalog all educational sites, but only the most useful sites — especially online activities targeted at learners. The address cited here will take you directly to the counseling subject area.

❏ **Bob Cozby's Computer Links**
http://howdyyall.com/surf/computer.htm

Highly resourceful, including links to many search engines, history of the Net, HTML tools/utilities, Plug-Ins and Filters, Computer Companies, jobs, operating systems, and more.

❏ **BPL Kids Page- Netiquette**
http://www.bpl.org/kids/Netiquette.htm

The Boston Public Library offers these practical guidelines in down to earth language that children can understand. There are also links to more sophisticated explanations, including a techno-ten commandments, a Usenet guide and an extensive examination of netiquette for older students by Arlene Rinaldi.

❏ **BUILDER**
http://www.builder.com/Authoring/Html/

Tips and tricks about Web development.

❑ **CAST Bobby**
http://bobby.watchfire.com/bobby

Bobby is a web-based public service offered by CAST that analyzes web pages for their accessibility to people with disabilities as well as their compatibility with various browsers.

❑ **CIT Information newsletter from IANR Communications and Information Technology,**
http://cit.information.unl.edu/

Covers communications and information technology, providing "how-to" articles to help you better manage your work time and news articles to keep you up-to-date on IT issues.

❑ **ClassZone — Web Research Guide**
http://www.classzone.com/

Learn the ins and outs of doing research on the Web by exploring the tutorials and activities in Web Research Guide.

❑ **Common Internet File Formats**
http://www.matisse.net/files/formats.html

❑ **Creating A Homepage**
http://members.aol.com/teachemath/create.htm

Helpful place for beginning web authors.

❑ **Disney Online — Activity Center**
http://disney.go.com/surfswell

Disney has several offerings to educate kids on the Internet, but this seemed the most appropriate for younger children. This Flash-based site includes three games on privacy, viruses and netiquette. The Challenge of Doom quiz then tests what students have learned. You can even learn more about your wireless device while on the Island!

❑ **Dummies Daily**
http://www.dummiesdaily.com/

Want to get more out of your computer? Here's the fun and easy way to learn about computers and the Internet! Sign up with this site and every business day you'll get a clear, informative computer tip, delivered directly to your e-mail box.

❑ **Educational Technology for Schools**
http://fromnowon.org/

An educational technology journal with full-text articles.

❑ **E-mail Tips and Techniques Archive**
http://www.ibiztips.com/e-mail_archive.htm

❑ **ERIC-EECE Electronic Discussion Groups**
http://ericeece.org/listserv.html

ERIC sponsored electronic discussion groups.

❑ **ESD Training Materials**
http://www.yamhillesd.k12.or.us/ESDPage/handouts/handouts.html

An extensive collection of training handouts, many of which are available on-line. These handouts have been developed over the last several years and are primarily for Macintosh applications, but handouts for Windows will soon be available.

❑ **Evaluating Web Resources**
http://www.science.widener.edu/~withers/webeval.htm

Teaching modules for effectively evaluating web resources.

❑ **Finding Information on the Internet- A TUTORIAL**
http://www.lib.berkeley.edu/TeachingLib/Guides/Internet/FindInfo.html

Brought to us by the library folks at the University of California, Berkeley, this is a most excellent free resource.

❏ **Frank Condron's World O'Windows**

http://www.conitech.com/windows

Frank Condron's World O'Windows is a collection of useful news, resources, and tips about Microsoft's current and future versions of Windows, including Windows 95, Windows 98, and Windows NT.

❏ **GVU's 8th WWW Survey Results**

http://www.gvu.gatech.edu/user_surveys/survey-1997-10/

This is the main document for the Graphic, Visualization, & Usability Center's (GVU) 8th WWW User Survey. GVU runs the Surveys as public service and as such, all results are available online (subject to certain terms and conditions).

❏ **IETF-TERENA Training Materials Catalogue**

http://www.trainmat.ietf.org/catalogue.html

❏ **Index to Web Guides**

http://www.monroe.lib.in.us/~lchampel/

List of Internet related topics with instruction and handouts from Lisa Champelli.

❏ **Institute for the Transfer of Technology to Education**

http://www.nsba.org/itte/

ITTE—the Institute for the Transfer of Technology to Education—is a program of the National School Boards Association. ITTE works actively with school districts across North America that are exploring creative ways to teach and learn with technology. Our district participants are large and small, are in cities, small towns and rural areas, and are economically diverse.

❏ **Integrating the Internet**

http://seamonkey.ed.asu.edu/~hixson/index/index5.html

Use this page to find primary resources, projects, a weekly newsletter, units of study, and a tutorial to help you plan projects and class homepages.

❏ **International Society for Technology in Education**

http://www.iste.org/

The International Society for Technology in Education (ISTE) is the largest teacher-based, nonprofit organization in the field of educational technology. Its mission is to help K-12 classroom teachers and administrators share effective methods for enhancing student learning through the use of new classroom technologies.

❏ **Internet 101: The Internet guide for teachers and parents**

http://www.horizon.nmsu.edu/101/

Also for counselors, this site helps educators deal with the Internet in their classrooms, and to helping parents guide their children as they explore the world wide web. Gathered here are many resources, helpful hints, and valuable explanations that can help ease your transition to online education, including straight talk about dealing with Internet pornography and copyright issues. Look around, learn much, and tell your colleagues about this site.

❏ **Internet Literacy**

http://www.udel.edu/interlit/

Contains online resources for the Internet Literacy textbook by Fred T. Hofstetter.

❏ **Internet World: The Voice of E-Business and Internet Technology**

http://www.internetworld.com/

A great place to start for learning about the Internet and Net related events/information.

❏ **Interpersonal Computing and Technology Journal**

http://www.helsinki.fi/science/optek/

The Interpersonal Computing and Technology Journal (IPCT-J) is a scholarly, peer-reviewed journal, published four times a year. The journal's focus is on computer-mediated communication, and the pedagogical issues surrounding the use of computers and technology in educational settings.

❏ **Jo Cool or Jo Fool: An Online Game about Savvy Surfing**
http://www.media-awareness.ca/eng/webaware/2joes/johome.htm
Comes with a teachers manual.

❏ **LangaList**
http://www.langa.com/
Make the most of your hardware, software, and time online with the LangaList— a free and lively, award winning, twice-a-week e-newsletter from noted computer author and editor Fred Langa. Each issue is packed with tips, tricks, and other useful and interesting information!

❏ **Life on the Internet Young, Smart and On Line**
http://www.pbs.org/internet/stories/ng

❏ **Microsoft Education — In & Out of the Classroom Tutorials**
http://www.microsoft.com/education/?ID=IOCTutorials
Free downloadable manuals for all your favorite Microsoft products.

❏ **Microsoft FrontPage Tips and Tricks**
http://www.microsoftfrontpage.com/content/TipsAndTricks/TipsAndTricks.htm

❏ **Netiquette Home Page**
http://www.albion.com/netiquette
"Netiquette" is network etiquette, the do's and don'ts of online communication. Netiquette covers both common courtesy online and the informal "rules of the road" of cyberspace. This page provides links to both summary and detail information about Netiquette for your browsing pleasure.

❏ **PBS Kids: t e c h k n o w**
http://www.pbs.org/kids/techknow/
Kids can take a WebLicence exam which demonstrates safe navigation skills.

❏ **PC Webopedia**
http://www.pcwebopaedia.com/
Online encyclopedia and search engine dedicated to computer technology.

❏ **Schools in Cyberspace**
http://homepages.strath.ac.uk/~cjbs17/Cyberspace
The Schools in Cyberspace site is a collection of pages with links, hints and tips to help schools get the most of the Internet as a resource to support learning and teaching.

❏ **Search Tips and Tricks**
http://www.imaginarylandscape.com/helpweb/www/seek.html
Informative and practical.

❏ **Take a Walk on the Wired Side- Information Literacy**
http://www.lib.utexas.edu/Exhibits/wired/case1.html
The authors of this site want us to know that, "Although we do not have to wholeheartedly embrace all new technologies, we should recognize the need to objectively assess the merits and failings of these resources to succeed in our information society—a society which demands that we learn skills necessary to locate reliable resources, efficiently search for answers, and carefully evaluate the answers we find."

❏ **Tech Tips for Teachers**
http://www.essdack.org./tips
A collage of topics and tips including electronic portfolios.

❏ **Technology @ Your Fingertips**
http://nces.ed.gov/pubs98/tech/index.asp
Technology @ Your Fingertips describes a process for getting the best possible technology solution for your organization. In this book you will find the steps you should take to identify your technology needs, consider your options, acquire the technology, and implement a technology solution that will serve you today and provide a foundation for your organization's technology in the future.

❏ **Technology Competencies**
http://ced.ncsu.edu/techcomps/

The goal of this site is to provide Internet resources for the technology competencies (in North Carolina) as well as practice quizzes for each competency. There is even a "Portfolio Suggestions" section which provides tips for creating portfolio items reflecting the Advanced Competencies.

❏ **TechTV**
http://www.techtv.com/techtv/
Mega computer help!

❏ **The HTML Goodies Home Page**
http://www.htmlgoodies.com/

HTML Goodies has won extensive industry recognition and more than 75 awards for its quality and comprehensive coverage. Created by Dr. Joe Burns, Ph.D., HTML Goodies contains hundreds of unique tutorials for HTML, XML, SGML and DHTML as well as one of the Web's most comprehensive repositories for JavaScript and other scripting languages. HTML Goodies is updated weekly by Dr. Burns and will soon be accepting audience resource submissions for inclusion in the site.

❏ **The Internet TOURBUS — free stuff, viruses, hoaxes, urban legends, search engine**
http://www.tourbus.com/

Learn how to avoid the pitfalls of the Web, master the search engines, debunk urban legends, and more. Net gurus Bob Rankin and Patrick Crispen (a.k.a. the "Click & Clack" of the online world) explain Internet technology in plain English with a dash of humor, in a FREE twice weekly e-mail newsletter.

❏ **THE MS WORD TO WEB PAGE**
http://www.archiva.net/
mstutorial3web.htm
Quite helpful.

❏ **The NetSmartz Workshop**
http://www.netsmartz.org/

The NetSmartz Workshop is an educational resource for children of all ages, parents and teachers on how to stay safer on the Internet.

❏ **Tips, Tricks and Secrets for Managing Your E-mail with Outlook Express**
http://e-mail.about.com/cs/oetipstricks
Learn how to handle your e-mail like a pro with Outlook Express with these tips and tricks.

❏ **Using and Understanding the Internet**
http://www.pbs.org/uti

According to the site by PBS, you'll find more than 300 links to quickly get you on your way, organized by topics, in our Beginners Guide to the Internet. After exploring the Guide and learning about 'Net applications, you can qualify for our "seasoned user certificate" by testing your knowledge in our Understanding & Using The Internet Quiz. If you're unfamiliar with some of the operating conventions of your web browser (such as using the back command), there's a special page with QuickTips. For beginners and seasoned veterans alike, we've created a one-page menu for easy access to the latest versions of major helper applications.

❏ **Using the Internet, for teachers, schools, students; an introduction**
http://www.geocities.com/Athens/4610
Full-text, user-friendly article.

❏ **WebReference.com**
http://www.webreference.com/
index2.html
Highly resourceful — on of my favorite.

❏ **WebReference.com (sm) — The Webmaster's Reference Library**
http://www.webreference.com
A must see for the school counseling webmaster.

❏ **Welcome to the Web**
http://www.teachingideas.co.uk/welcome

Combining bigger-than-life graphics, straightforward step-by-step directions and html-formatted worksheets, Mark Warner has created a colorful introduction for upper elementary and middle school students. Topics covered include Internet uses, guest books, browsers, and search and researching skills. It culminates in the Welcome to the Web Challenge!

❏ **Welcome to webTeacher**
http://www.webteacher.org/winexp/welcome.html

E-mail, video conferencing, chat rooms, Web page design, Internet safety, and curriculum searches. This site a self-paced Internet Tutorial that puts both basic and in-depth information about the World Wide Web at your fingertips.

K-12 Schools

❏ **Anacortes HS Guidance and Counseling Services**
http://www.cnw.com/~deets/guidance.htm

Describes their comprehensive guidance program.

❏ **Arrowhead Guidance Department**
http://www.methacton.k12.pa.us/arrowhead/default.htm

Lots of valuable resources and fun photos!

❏ **Block Island School Homepage**
http://www.bi.k12.ri.us/

Links include study skills, financial aid information, kids stuff, college/work, peer/mentor resources, teachers, parents, and social/environmental Responsibility. This site is searchable.

❏ **Bob Turba's CyberGuidance Office**
http://cyberguidance.net/

This site calls itself a virtual high school guidance office created by Bob Turba, Chairman of Guidance Services at Stanton College Preparatory School located in Duval County, Jacksonville, Florida. The site contains links to information about college, scholarship, financial aid, career, homework, and tutoring. I consider it a model school counseling site.

❏ **Cave Spring Junior High School-Roanoke, Virginia**
http://www.rcs.k12.va.us/csjh/

❏ **College Resource Center**
http://www.district125.k12.il.us/crc/

The CRC contains a wide variety of informational resources such as college pamphlets, videos, catalogs, and reference books that will assist and guide one through the college selection process.

❏ **Community High School Guidance & Counseling — Resources**
http://communityhigh.org/counseling/resources.html

❏ **Guidance Curriculum for the Comprehensive School Counseling Program (North Carolina)**
http://www.dpi.state.nc.us/curriculum/
Guidance

❏ **Hollywood Elementary School Counseling Page**
http://www.smcps.k12.md.us/hes/
counseling.htm

❏ **Millard South Counseling Center**
http://www.esu3.k12.ne.us/districts/
millard/south/guid/msguid.html

❏ **Monson High School Guidance Department**
http://www.monsonschools.com/Guidance/indexGuidance.html

❏ **Nebraska Comprehensive Guidance and Counseling Standards**
http://www.nde.state.ne.us/CARED/
standards.html
Nebraska School Counseling Program with lots of tools/forms.

❏ **Springfield High School Counseling Center**
http://www.springfield.k12.vt.us/schools/
shs/guidance/

❏ **St. Gertrude Guidance and Counseling**
http://www.saintgertrude.org/schoolinfo/
guidance.htm

❏ **Stonewall Jackson Senior High School Guidance**
http://www.pwcs.edu/sjhs/guidance.htm

❏ **UHS Guidance and Counseling**
http://www.cmi.k12.il.us/~furrersa/
guid_couns.html

❏ **Urbana High School Guidance and Counseling**
http://www.cmi.k12.il.us/~furrersa/

❏ **Vandercook Lake High School Counselors Page**
http://scnc.vandy.k12.mi.us/counsel.htm

❏ **West Springfield High School Career Center**
http://www.wshs.fcps.k12.va.us/career/
career.htm
According to the site, the purposes of the Career Center web page is to provide links to a variety of web sites that pertain to career and college related information.

❏ **Windsor H.S. Guidance**
http://www.windsor.k12.mo.us/hsguide/

❏ **WWW.AHS-COUNSELING.ORG**
http://ahs-counseling.org

Lesson Plans

❏ **A Class Citizenship Tree for Elementary Students**
http://www.askeric.org/cgi-bin/
printlessons.cgi/Virtual/Lessons/
Social_Studies/Civics/CIV0014.html

The purpose of this lesson plan is to present to elementary students the characteristics that define a socially healthy citizen. There are two objectives for learners: 1. Each student will identify two or three specific actions he or she can accomplish to practice good citizenship; and 2. Each student will verbally contract to accomplish one social health action before the end of the 9-week period.

❏ **Addiction—Health/Human Body lesson plan (grades 6-8)—DiscoverySchool.com**
http://school.discovery.com/lessonplans/
programs/addiction/

This lesson will help students to (a) Understand how families and peers influence their decision making; and (b) Examine the cycle of addiction to drugs and what can be done to prevent it. The site contains materials, procedures, discussion, questions, evaluation, extensions, suggested readings, vocabulary, and academic standards.

❏ **AIDS: Who's at Risk?—Health/Human Body lesson plan (grades 9-12)**
http://school.discovery.com/lessonplans/
programs/aidsrisk/

This lesson helps students to (a) analyze facts about who gets AIDS, how those populations have changed in the past few decades, and how AIDS is contracted; and (b) advocate for AIDS awareness and prevention.

❏ **All About Groups, Community (5 parts)**
http://www.lessonplanspage.com/
SSMDGroupsCommunity1-
ImportanceOfGroups2.htm

Upon successful completion of this lesson, students will be able to: Discuss the importance of groups in daily tasks; Identify how animals work together to fulfill group needs; Recognize their own need to be in a group in daily life activities; Report necessary information to their group in order for the group to successfully complete a task; Take turns sharing information; Listen to others in their group.

❏ **An AskERIC Write-A-Lesson Plan Guide**
http://www.askeric.org/Virtual/Lessons/
Guide.shtml

❏ **Apple Lesson Menu**
http://henson.austin.apple.com/edres/
lessonmenu.shtml

❏ **AskERIC Lesson Plans**
http://www.askeric.org/Virtual/Lessons/

❏ **Bag It — An AskERIC Lesson Plan**
http://www.askeric.org/cgi-bin/
printlessons.cgi/Virtual/Lessons/Health/
Mental_Health/MEH0007.html

This lesson is designed to make each child aware that stress has a major affect on his/ her feelings.

❏ **Being Brave and Dealing with Fear — An AskERIC Lesson Plan**
http://www.askeric.org/cgi-bin/
printlessons.cgi/Virtual/Lessons/Health/
Mental_Health/MEH0201.html

To help students learn how to be brave when dealing with fear.

❏ **Beyond September 11, 2001: Lesson Plans for coping with September 11**
http://www.teachervision.com/lesson-
plans/lesson-6807.html

❏ **Black History Treasure Hunt & Quiz**
http://www.kn.pacbell.com/wired/BHM/
bh_hunt_quiz.html

Students get to read through online questions while receiving hints from a resource list. After responding, immediate feedback is given.

❏ **Building a community Social Studies Lesson Plan, Thematic Unit, Activity, Workshop**
http://www.lessonplanspage.com/
SSOBuildingAClassroomCommunity12.htm

Objectives of this lesson includes: A. The students will become comfortable working with each other in an academic and social atmosphere; B. The students will explore the concept of making maps by becoming familiar with their classroom and the rest of their school and engaging in the actual building of a school map; and C. The students will discuss the concept of community and how it applies to their classroom.

❏ **CanTeach: Classroom Management: discipline & organization**
http://www.canteach.ca/elementary/
classman.html

❏ **Careers in Health—Health lesson plan (grades 6-8)—DiscoverySchool.com**
http://school.discovery.com/lessonplans/
programs/healthcareers/

Students will: 1. Identify several professions in the healthcare field; 2. Identify characteristics of effective healthcare providers; 3. Consider if any of the occupations covered in class are appropriate paths for them

❏ **Careers Lesson PLans from Ask Eric**
http://www.askeric.org/cgi-bin/lessons.cgi/
Vocational_Education/Careers

❏ **Chain of Compliments — An AskERIC Lesson Plan**
http://www.askeric.org/cgi-bin/
printlessons.cgi/Virtual/Lessons/Health/
Mental_Health/MEH0001.html

This is an activity in which students can enhance their classmates' esteem and promote cooperation in the classroom.

❏ **Changes of Puberty—Human Body/ Health lesson plan (grades 6-8)— DiscoverySchool.**
http://school.discovery.com/lessonplans/
programs/puberty/

Students will do the following: 1. Learn about the changes of puberty for boys and girls; and 2. Make a presentation about significant changes that take place during puberty.

❏ **Class Culture — An AskERIC Lesson Plan**
http://www.askeric.org/cgi-bin/
printlessons.cgi/Virtual/Lessons/
Social_Studies/Multicultural_Education/
MUL0004.html

The object of this lesson is to show that even within the class there are many different cultures — that every person has his/her own culture, but within the class there are a few things that everyone can agree on and those ideas make up the class culture.

❏ **Class Reunion — An AskERIC Lesson Plan**
http://www.askeric.org/cgi-bin/
printlessons.cgi/Virtual/Lessons/
Social_Studies/Psychology/PSY0001.html

Lesson prepared in an effort to make students ruminate about their future and preparation for life beyond high school. Painlessly requires students to begin the process of decision making regarding their own goals and objectives.

❏ **Classical Conditioning Experiment — An AskERIC Lesson Plan**
http://www.askeric.org/cgi-bin/
printlessons.cgi/Virtual/Lessons/
Social_Studies/Psychology/PSY0002.html

The learner will see the effect of classical conditioning in their everyday life.

❏ **Classroom Heart — An AskERIC Lesson Plan**
http://www.askeric.org/cgi-bin/
printlessons.cgi/Virtual/Lessons/Interdisci-
plinary/First_Day_of_School/FDA0208.html

This activity gives young children a visual description of how feelings can be damaged by remarks from others. Teachers are encouraged to use this lesson during the first week of school.

❏ **Comparing Cultures — An AskERIC Lesson Plan**
http://www.askeric.org/cgi-bin/
printlessons.cgi/Virtual/Lessons/
Social_Studies/Multicultural_Education/
MUL0005.html

This lesson will encourage students to use the higher level thinking skills and will help them learn to better cooperate with their peers. It will also help students develop a respect for cultures different from their own.

❏ **Conflict Management Techniques — An AskERIC Lesson Plan**
http://www.askeric.org/cgi-bin/
printlessons.cgi/Virtual/Lessons/
Social_Studies/Psychology/PSY0003.html

The purpose of this lesson is to help students identify personal management style(s), develop an awareness of strategies used in each conflict management style.

❏ **Considering Parenting Styles — An AskERIC Lesson Plan**
http://www.askeric.org/cgi-bin/
printlessons.cgi/Virtual/Lessons/Health/
Family_Life/FAL0200.html

The purpose of this lesson is to contrast three common parenting styles and consider the advantages and disadvantages of each. Students will discuss effective child guidance techniques.

❏ **Cruel Schools—Health lesson plan (grades 6-8)—DiscoverySchool.com**
http://school.discovery.com/lessonplans/
programs/cruelschools/

❏ **Cultural Acceptance — An AskERIC Lesson Plan**
http://www.askeric.org/cgi-bin/
printlessons.cgi/Virtual/Lessons/
Social_Studies/Sociology/SOC0001.html

To be able to experience how it feels to be a minority.

❏ **Cultural Awareness/Sharing Traditions — An AskERIC Lesson Plan**
http://www.askeric.org/cgi-bin/
printlessons.cgi/Virtual/Lessons/Health/
Family_Life/FAL0001.html

The purpose of the activity is to have students within a small team get to know each other by sharing cultural traditions which make their families unique. It shows that all families are different, and it's okay to be different.

❏ **Cultural Spaces — An AskERIC Lesson Plan**
http://www.askeric.org/cgi-bin/
printlessons.cgi/Virtual/Lessons/
Social_Studies/Sociology/SOC0006.html

Many students assume only their cultural and traditional practices are worldly accepted and practiced. As a result of this activity, the students will (a) identify cultural differences in relationship to personal "space;" and (b) experience discomfort with alien cultural practices.

❏ **Cultures of our Nation — An AskERIC Lesson Plan**
http://www.askeric.org/cgi-bin/
printlessons.cgi/Virtual/Lessons/
Social_Studies/Multicultural_Education/
MUL0006.html

The purpose of this activity is to build self-esteem and allow students to become more aware of their rich cultures. It also allows for students to realize how their cultures have contributed to making America what it is today.

❏ **Cyber Knowledge and Emotion**
http://www.cyke.com/

CYKE is a multimedia company dedicated to improving the emotional and physical health of children.

❏ **Dealing with Bullies**
http://www.coled.mnsu.edu/departments/
csp/Resources/School/
guidance%20lessons/
Dealing%20with%20Bullies.htm

The guidance lesson was developed to assist incoming 6th grade students in dealing with the situations that might arise as they enter the middle school setting. The lesson is presented in a fifty-five (55) minute classroom environment and is adopted from several different guidance curricula, including Sunburst staff development and Current Health magazine.

❏ **Decision Making — An AskERIC Lesson Plan**
http://www.askeric.org/cgi-bin/
printlessons.cgi/Virtual/Lessons/
Social_Studies/Psychology/PSY0004.html

This lesson encourages students to think of different ways in which they may solve their problems. The traditional "My father can beat up your father" or "I'll see you in court" are old-fashioned approaches to problem solving. Students will identify the problem, the choices and the consequences both positive and negative. The students will work together to make a group decision.

❏ **Defining Substance Abuse and Misuse — An AskERIC Lesson Plan**
http://www.askeric.org/cgi-bin/
printlessons.cgi/Virtual/Lessons/Health/
Substance_Abuse_Prevention/
SBA0001.html

The students will understand the difference between substance use, misuse, and abuse.

❏ **Developing Relationships with Older People — An AskERIC Lesson Plan**
http://www.askeric.org/cgi-bin/
printlessons.cgi/Virtual/Lessons/
Social_Studies/Sociology/SOC0002.html

This lesson is designed to help elementary age students develop relationships with older people.

❏ **Education Center Activity: Convince Me!**
http://www.eduplace.com/rdg/gen_act/
view/convince.html

Your students may be aware of the techniques used by advertisers to sell products and services. They may be less conscious of the purposes and intents of advertisements that try to shape their opinions and affect their behavior. In this activity, they look for and analyze examples of those ads.

❏ **Education Center Activity: Honor Special People**
http://www.eduplace.com/ss/act/
specpeo.html

Students design a postage stamp to honor a special person. Students identify people who have made a difference, analyze why people commemorate others, and describe ways individuals can help others.

❏ **Education Center Activity: Mirror, Mirror on the Wall**
http://www.eduplace.com/rdg/gen_act/view/mirror.html

The following mirror exercises will help students develop their observational skills so that they learn how to catch nuances of body movements and facial clues from their partners and respond to them. This collaborative effort can then translate into creative expression.

❏ **Education Place Activity: A Letter to Myself**
http://www.eduplace.com/activity/letter.html

Children set goals for the future and think about how they will achieve them.

❏ **Education Place Activity: Back From the Future**
http://www.eduplace.com/activity/future.html

Students examine their school community and culture from the point of view of someone from the future.

❏ **Education Place Activity: Cultural Show and Tell**
http://www.eduplace.com/activity/3_2_act1.html

Students will research their own cultural heritage and share it with the class in a Show and Tell presentation.

❏ **Education Place Activity: Finding Common Ground**
http://www.eduplace.com/activity/comground.html

Students will work in groups to find "win-win" solutions to common middle school problems. Includes a worksheet.

❏ **Education Place Activity: Jobs on File**
http://www.eduplace.com/activity/jobs.html

Students gather information about how people in their community make a living through surveys and interviews, and then organize that data. Includes downloads!

❏ **Education Place Activity: Teamwork**
http://www.eduplace.com/activity/team.html

Students identify what kinds of attitudes and behaviors are productive in a cooperative setting.

❏ **Education Place Activity: We Can Work It Out**
http://www.eduplace.com/activity/work.html

Students will learn how to consider alternatives before reacting to a conflict.

❏ **Education World: Curriculum: Back-to-School Letters and Survival Kits**
http://www.educationworld.com/a_curr/curr358.shtml

Examples of survival kits for students and teachers.

❏ **Education World: Lesson Planning Center: Archives: Special Ed & Guidance**
http://www.education-world.com/a_lesson/archives/spec_ed.shtml

❏ **Eisenhower Network: Lesson Plans & Activities: Math Topics**
http://www.enc.org/weblinks/lessonplans/math/

❏ **Eisenhower Network: Lesson Plans & Activities: Science Topics**
http://www.enc.org/weblinks/lessonplans/science/

❏ **Emotional Puppets — An AskERIC Lesson Plan**

http://www.askeric.org/cgi-bin/
printlessons.cgi/Virtual/Lessons/Health/
Mental_Health/MEH0002.html

To give students the opportunity to explore emotions. This lesson will allow the students to make hand puppets to fit the emotion he or she has chosen.

❏ **ESL Life Skills 101 — Job Interview — An AskERIC Lesson Plan**

http://www.askeric.org/cgi-bin/
printlessons.cgi/Virtual/Lessons/
Vocational_Education/Careers/
CAE0001.html

Without insight into the American cultural expectations of an applicant at a job interview, ESL students will find it difficult to succeed in this area. This activity gives students the chance to practice formal register and to learn what information and questions are often contained in an interview. The students will also experience both sides of the process to help provide greater insight into the perspective of a potential employer.

❏ **Examining Ideas about Body Image — An AskERIC Lesson Plan**

http://www.askeric.org/cgi-bin/
printlessons.cgi/Virtual/Lessons/Health/
Chronic_Conditions/CHR0200.html

The purpose of this lesson is to (a) assist students in realistically assessing their body image and weight management practices as part of school health education classes; and (b) dispel myths of "ideal body types." This instruction should be part of a planned, coordinated school health program.

❏ **Exceptional Apples — An AskERIC Lesson Plan**

http://www.askeric.org/cgi-bin/
printlessons.cgi/Virtual/Lessons/
Social_Studies/Multicultural_Education/
MUL0001.html

Similarities and differences among apples, and also among students. Also, the importance of these similarities and differences.

❏ **Expanding Pre-conceived Beliefs About Sex Roles — An AskERIC Lesson Plan**

http://www.askeric.org/cgi-bin/
printlessons.cgi/Virtual/Lessons/
Social_Studies/Gender_Studies/
GEN0200.html

Children look at the daily activities of their parents to determine if some jobs are for "women only" and "men only," or if most activities can be performed by both men and women.

❏ **Family Sculpture Demonstration — An AskERIC Lesson Plan**

http://www.askeric.org/cgi-bin/
printlessons.cgi/Virtual/Lessons/Health/
Family_Life/FAL0003.html

In an average class of 25 students, between 4 and 6 are Children of Alcoholics (COAs). There will also be children from homes disrupted by other family dysfunctions who have much in common with COAs. In these families, members tend to adjust their behaviors and take on certain roles to cope with the family problem. These survival roles frequently become compulsive, self-destructive and without choices. The purpose of this lesson is to empower participants by giving them some tools to examine their lives, and not to tell them that the way they are behaving is dysfunctional or based strictly on dysfunction.

❏ **Fire and Fire Prevention: A Thematic Unit Plan — An AskERIC Lesson Plan**

http://www.askeric.org/cgi-bin/
printlessons.cgi/Virtual/Lessons/Health/
Safety/SFY0012.html

The purpose of this interdisciplinary unit is to educate students about fire, fire prevention, and to provide them with the essential skills they will need if a fire actually occurs.

❏ **Fire Fighters at Work — An AskERIC Lesson Plan**
http://www.askeric.org/cgi-bin/printlessons.cgi/Virtual/Lessons/Social_Studies/Civics/CIV0019.html

This lesson is about fire fighters at work. The students will learn how fire fighters fight fires in the city, country, forest, and on the waterfront. They will also learn about the equipment used to fight fires.

❏ **Friendship Flowers**
http://www.lessonplanspage.com/SSOFriendshipFlowers-TeachFriendship13.htm

This lesson facilitates a discussion about friends and the good qualities that a friend should posses.

❏ **Get Into It!**
http://www.specialolympics.org/getintoit/

Special Olympics Get Into It is a FREE curriculum that celebrates giftedness — the giftedness of every student whatever his or her ability.

❏ **Getting to Know Me**
http://www.lessonplanspage.com/SSPersonalTimeline23.htm

The student will construct a dated timeline of their life using photos and magazine cutouts to display information.

❏ **Getting to Know You — An AskERIC Lesson Plan**
http://www.askeric.org/cgi-bin/printlessons.cgi/Virtual/Lessons/Interdisciplinary/First_Day_of_School/FDA0202.html

To help children quickly get to know one another and set up an atmosphere for learning.

❏ **Go Away, Bad Dreams! — An AskERIC Lesson Plan**
http://www.askeric.org/cgi-bin/printlessons.cgi/Virtual/Lessons/Health/Mental_Health/MEH0010.html

By reading the story "Go Away, Bad Dreams", the children will see that bad situations can turn into good ones and that they can control those situations. A link to Amazon.com for purchasing the book is included.

❏ **Good Apples — An AskERIC Lesson Plan**
http://www.askeric.org/cgi-bin/printlessons.cgi/Virtual/Lessons/Social_Studies/Multicultural_Education/MUL0007.html

The purpose of this lesson, used during the early part of the school year, is to introduce the concept that everyone is the same in some ways and different in others.

❏ **Group Rope Squares — An AskERIC Lesson Plan**
http://www.askeric.org/cgi-bin/printlessons.cgi/Virtual/Lessons/Health/Substance_Abuse_Prevention/SBA0002.html

This lesson will further reinforce group cohesion and communication skills as well as problem solving and cooperation. In teaching a drug prevention program, it is important to introduce activities like this that illustrate to students that Together they can help solve each other's problems, depend on one another, and communicate their needs to others.

❏ **Guidance Resources**
http://208.183.128.8/guidance/

❏ **Hands Without Guns, a Positive Lesson of Non-Violence — An AskERIC Lesson Plan**
http://www.askeric.org/cgi-bin/printlessons.cgi/Virtual/Lessons/Social_Studies/Current_Events/CUR0200.html

Students will produce creative positive responses in various forms: written, spoken, musical, or visual expression, to the issue of violence and gun violence.

❏ **Health — Lesson Plans and Webquests**
http://www.edhelper.com/cat55.htm

❏ **I Believe in Me Books — An AskERIC Lesson Plan**
http://www.askeric.org/cgi-bin/printlessons.cgi/Virtual/Lessons/Vocational_Education/Careers/CAE0003.html

Images of people in various careers suitable for coloring. Based on the above career and motivational book series designed for grade k-3. Includes links to books!

❏ **Who Will Wear the Hats and Who Will Use the Tools?**
http://www.ricw.state.ri.us/lessons/1.htm

❏ **KNE WebQuest | School Safety**
http://www.kn.pacbell.com/wired/nonviolence/

❏ **Learning to Respect Each Other — An AskERIC Lesson Plan**
http://www.askeric.org/cgi-bin/printlessons.cgi/Virtual/Lessons/Social_Studies/Sociology/SOC0010.html

The number of minorities in the U.S. increases each year; some Americans distrust those who appear to be different. This is often due to limited shared experiences. Schools and families can educate children about race relations. The goals of this lesson are that students will describe the relationships between Americans of different racial and ethnic groups.

❏ **Lesson plans at Teachnet.com**
http://www.teachnet.com/lesson/

❏ **Looking at Different Cultures — An AskERIC Lesson Plan**
http://www.askeric.org/cgi-bin/printlessons.cgi/Virtual/Lessons/Social_Studies/Multicultural_Education/MUL0008.html

To examine different cultures of the world.

❏ **Looking Into the Mirror — An AskERIC Lesson Plan**
http://www.askeric.org/cgi-bin/printlessons.cgi/Virtual/Lessons/Social_Studies/Sociology/SOC0003.html

Students often fail to feel and understand the impact of racial, cultural, and/or socio-economic intolerance in their own lives in relation to other individuals. For this reason, this lesson is intended to deliver a vivid portrayal of intolerance and inequality as well as provoke a response to the various types of intolerance that exist in our multicultural society.

❏ **Magic Bullets — An AskERIC Lesson Plan**
http://www.askeric.org/cgi-bin/printlessons.cgi/Virtual/Lessons/Health/Substance_Abuse_Prevention/SBA0200.html

Students will improve their understanding of the dangers of addiction in its various forms. Students will internalize values of the folk tale, including: magical thinking (drug use) does not work in real life; our mistakes hurt ourselves and others; achieving an important goal requires time and hard work; self-mastery is the real challenge of life; and adults give up power if teens prove ready.

❏ **Mannequin — An AskERIC Lesson Plan**
http://www.askeric.org/cgi-bin/printlessons.cgi/Virtual/Lessons/Interdisciplinary/First_Day_of_School/FDA0206.html

This activity is designed to stimulate creative thinking, encourage cooperation, and help students get acquainted.

❑ **Members in Our Community — An AskERIC Lesson Plan**
http://www.askeric.org/cgi-bin/printlessons.cgi/Virtual/Lessons/Social_Studies/Civics/CIV0200.html

This lesson is a great way to teach students about the different members and professions in each community, so students can see how important it is to be a good and helpful community member.

❑ **Mental Health Lesson Plans from Ask Eric**
http://www.askeric.org/cgi-bin/lessons.cgi/Health/Mental_Health

❑ **Middle School Net**
http://www.middleschool.net/

❑ **Monsters Are Make Believe — An AskERIC Lesson Plan**
http://www.askeric.org/cgi-bin/printlessons.cgi/Virtual/Lessons/Health/Mental_Health/MEH0009.html

The learner will be able to demonstrate that Monsters are created in our imagination and they are not real living beings.

❑ **Multicultural Community — My Home! — An AskERIC Lesson Plan**
http://www.askeric.org/cgi-bin/printlessons.cgi/Virtual/Lessons/Social_Studies/Multicultural_Education/MUL0003.html

Students are engaged in a study of the multicultural character of the local community. Community resources, e.g., people, places, things, and events, are incorporated into the classroom/field-based investigation

❑ **Multicultural Fair — An AskEric Lesson Plan**
http://www.askeric.org/cgi-bin/printlessons.cgi/Virtual/Lessons/Social_Studies/Multicultural_Education/MUL0009.html

This Multicultural Fair is designed to both create an interest in, as well as educate the students involved in the different cultures, and how they can benefit through the knowledge gained through this study.

❑ **Native American Interdisciplinary Educational Unit — An AskERIC Lesson Plan**
http://www.askeric.org/cgi-bin/printlessons.cgi/Virtual/Lessons/Interdisciplinary/INT0046.html

The Native American has for hundreds of years been stereotyped. This lesson will help children understand that what they see in movies and television is not always historically accurate.

❑ **No-Bullying Proposal Webquest**
http://www.gecdsb.on.ca/d&g/nobullying

❑ **Our Music Festival — An AskERIC Lesson Plan**
http://www.askeric.org/cgi-bin/printlessons.cgi/Virtual/Lessons/Social_Studies/Multicultural_Education/MUL0002.html

To investigate the diversity of cultures represented in the class

❑ **Outta Ray's Head English Lesson Plans**
http://home.cogeco.ca/~rayser3/

A collection of lesson plans with handouts by Ray Saitz and many contributors; all of the lessons have been used and refined in the classroom. Any handouts can be used by teachers without any fee; however, you should e-mail him or the original author to let me, or him, or her, know that you did.

❑ **Paper Clip Game for Learning the Value of Rules — An AskERIC Lesson Plan**
http://www.askeric.org/cgi-bin/printlessons.cgi/Virtual/Lessons/Social_Studies/Civics/CIV0023.html

The paper clip game serves as a good devices for discussing the need for and importance of rules in society. It acts as a springboard for developing a working definition of law and understanding the importance of law. It serves to overcome an often negative perception of law.

❏ **Parenting — Discipline and Guidance — An AskERIC Lesson Plan**
http://www.askeric.org/cgi-bin/
printlessons.cgi/Virtual/Lessons/Health/
Family_Life/FAL0004.html

Students will understand the role of discipline and guidance in their own lives and become better able to appropriately guide and discipline young children.

❏ **PBS Kids: It's My Life — Middle School Transition**
http://pbskids.org/itsmylife/school/
middleschool

Lots of info, links, interactive games, and catchy graphics.

❏ **Peace Begins With You — An AskERIC Lesson Plan**
http://www.askeric.org/cgi-bin/
printlessons.cgi/Virtual/Lessons/Interdisci-
plinary/INT0053.html

To increase students awareness of skills needed to live peacefully in society. These skills include listening to each other, problem-solving, cooperating, mediating problems, decision-making, and communication. Students will recognize and explore aspects of peace both at home and throughout the world. Peace must begin in ones own back-yard.

❏ **Planning for Study Time**
http://www.askeric.org/cgi-bin/
printlessons.cgi/Virtual/Lessons/Interdisci-
plinary/Study_Skills/STD0205.html

This lesson will help the student to iden-tify suitable study times and analyze the motivation for studying.

❏ **Preparation of an Application Letter and Resume — An AskERIC Lesson Plan**
http://www.askeric.org/cgi-bin/
printlessons.cgi/Virtual/Lessons/
Vocational_Education/Careers/
CAE0002.html

To be able to write and format an appli-cation letter and resume in preparation for a successful job search. Includes a resume worksheet!

❏ **Problem Solving — A Part of Everyday Thinking — An AskERIC Lesson Plan**
http://www.askeric.org/cgi-bin/
printlessons.cgi/Virtual/Lessons/Interdisci-
plinary/INT0057.html

The purpose of this activity, is to help students master the process of applying critical thinking to each and every problem/ task that confronts them in their daily under-takings. Further, this activity can serve as a base reference and model for every problem/ task assigned or any problem that a student or students might bring up.

❏ **Puberty—Human Body lesson plan (grades 6-8)—DiscoverySchool.com**
http://school.discovery.com/lessonplans/
programs/ragingteens/

Students will understand the following: 1. People can track body changes during pu-berty by close observation and accurate record keeping.

❏ **Put-ups & Put-downs (Warm Fuzzies & Cold Pricklies)**
http://www.coled.mnsu.edu/departments/
csp/Resources/School/
guidance%20lessons/
Put%20Ups%20and%20Put%20Downs.htm

The following classroom guidance lesson was developed at Kennedy Elementary School by Candy Bell (Professional School Counselor) and Abigail J. Ostby (School Counseling Intern). This lesson was designed to help young children (Kindergarten and Grade 1) learn the difference between put-ups and put-downs as well as their effects on people's feelings.

❑ **Rain — An AskERIC Lesson Plan**
http://www.askeric.org/cgi-bin/
printlessons.cgi/Virtual/Lessons/
Social_Studies/Multicultural_Education/
MUL0012.html

The author writes, "The children find this lesson both interesting and thought provoking. They like it because it is a game, and it is easy. I like it because it helps show children what games were like for early Native Americans, how to use the environment around them, and how to "think on their feet" and relate to others. They learn cooperation, which is very much the "Indian Way"."

❑ **Reach for Your Dreams**
http://www.coled.mnsu.edu/departments/
csp/Resources/School/
guidance%20lessons/
Reach%20for%20Your%20Dreams.htm

Reach for Your Dreams is a serious of activities geared for use with elementary age children and their families. Reach for Your Dreams is a family activity book that contains a story line with corresponding activities. This program is designed to assist student recognition and development of their gifts, talents, dreams, and increase self-esteem. The thirty-six activities, along with the story line, provide opportunities for students to explore the areas of: self-discovery, communication skills, getting along, choices, exploring emotions, and recognizing dreams. Many of the activities are adaptable to be used within the classroom, small group settings, or in one-on-one meetings. Other activities require family involvement and include the parents in supporting their son or daughter's growth.

❑ **Resolving Conflicts—Health lesson plan (grades 6-8)—DiscoverySchool.com**
http://school.discovery.com/lessonplans/
programs/resolvingconflicts/

Students will do the following: 1. Examine different kinds of hurtful behavior; 2. Develop strategies for dealing with hurtful behavior; 3. Work with their peers to create an environment in which students treat each other respectfully.

❑ **Responding to Social Crises — An AskERIC Lesson Plan**
http://www.askeric.org/cgi-bin/
printlessons.cgi/Virtual/Lessons/Health/
Mental_Health/MEH0200.html

The purposes of this mental health activity are to assist students in processing their reactions, obtaining support from others, and offering peer support in response to social crises. This lesson is compatible with the National Health Education Standards (JCNHES, 1995).

❑ **Safety Lesson Plans from ERIC**
http://www.askeric.org/cgi-bin/lessons.cgi/
Health/Safety

A variety of fire safety lessons.

❑ **Sailing Through The Storm**
http://www.coled.mnsu.edu/departments/
csp/Resources/School/
guidance%20lessons/
Sailing%20Through%20the%20Storm.htm

"Sailing Through The Storm To The Ocean Of Peace," is a classroom guidance lesson developed by Cheryl Biegler, along with other Lakeville area elementary counselors, to assist elementary students (grades 2-3) in identifying different kinds of violence/bullying and the feelings that often accompany violence/bullying. Students also learn methods to cope with and resolve violent situations.

❑ **Screaming Emotions — An AskERIC Lesson Plan**
http://www.askeric.org/cgi-bin/
printlessons.cgi/Virtual/Lessons/Health/
Mental_Health/MEH0202.html

The objectives of this lesson include that students will be able to (a) write a short story about an emotion; (b) illustrate their stories to aid comprehension; and (c) present their stories to the rest of the class, incorporating good eye contact, volume, and posture.

❏ **Self-Esteem Activity**
http://www.col-ed.org/cur/misc/misc09.txt

This strategy, used at the beginning of the day, can increase the positive feelings of each student and the classroom atmosphere as well.

❏ **Self-Esteem—Health lesson plan (grades 6-8)—DiscoverySchool.com**
http://school.discovery.com/lessonplans/programs/selfesteem/

Students will do the following: 1. Explore the concept of self-esteem; 2. Analyze their personal strengths and weaknesses; 3. Consider the role self-esteem plays in a healthy life.

❏ **Sexual Harassment—Health lesson plan (grades 9-12)—DiscoverySchool.com**
http://school.discovery.com/lessonplans/programs/sexualharassment/

Students will do the following: 1. Define the term sexual harassment; 2. Identify examples of sexual harassment; 3. Consider appropriate responses to sexual harassment

❏ **Sexual Pressures—Health lesson plan (grades 6-8)—DiscoverySchool.com**
http://school.discovery.com/lessonplans/programs/sexualpressures/

By the end of these lessons, students will be able to: 1. Demonstrate an understanding of the sexual pressures among teen youth; 2. Create personal approaches to questions addressing sexual behavior; 3. Practice skills in speaking and listening as tools for learning; and 4. Apply basic skills of logic and reasoning.

❏ **Silly Quiz — An AskERIC Lesson Plan**
http://www.askeric.org/cgi-bin/printlessons.cgi/Virtual/Lessons/Interdisciplinary/INT0068.html

This activity is used to introduce students to creative thinking by giving them a fun and unusual test. Usually after the first questions, students realize that they may have to think about what the question is asking

❏ **Skill Growth — An AskERIC Lesson Plan**
http://www.askeric.org/cgi-bin/printlessons.cgi/Virtual/Lessons/Health/Mental_Health/MEH0005.html

Students are not as prepared for school as they or their parents think they are. Many are ready to tackle skills much to hard for them. Others are afraid to admit that they do not have a skill mastered. This lesson is designed to help students realize that everyone develops skills at their own speed.

❏ **Social Studies Lesson Plans**
http://www.theteachersguide.com/socialstudies.html

❏ **Socialstudies Psychology — Lesson Plans Webquests**
http://www.edhelper.com/cat275.htm

❏ **Stories of AIDS—Health/Human Body lesson plan (grades 9-12)—DiscoverySchool.co**
http://school.discovery.com/lessonplans/programs/storiesofaids/

Students will do the following: 1. Examine the physical effects of AIDS; and 2. Study the plight of people living with AIDS and the effects on their families and friends

❏ **Study Skills Unit Plan — An AskERIC Lesson Plan**
http://www.askeric.org/cgi-bin/printlessons.cgi/Virtual/Lessons/Interdisciplinary/Study_Skills/STD0204.html

Students will participate in a week-long unit designed to help improve their study and test-taking skills. Lots of Internet resources!

❏ **Substance Abuse Influences — An AskERIC Lesson Plan**
http://www.askeric.org/cgi-bin/printlessons.cgi/Virtual/Lessons/Health/Substance_Abuse_Prevention/SBA0003.html

There is no other area in the schools today that commands more public attention than that of substance use and abuse. This particular activity shows that substance abuse education is more effective if it focuses on processes of decision making rather than problems.

❏ **Summer Safety Safari**
http://www.lessonplanspage.com/PESSOSummerSafetySafari-Posters1.htm

First grade students will demonstrate their understanding of summer safety by creating guidelines for Summer Safety posters.

❏ **SunSmart — An AskERIC Lesson Plan**
http://www.askeric.org/cgi-bin/printlessons.cgi/Virtual/Lessons/Health/Safety/SFY0200.html

In this lesson, students learn how to protect themselves from the dangers of the sun. Although aimed at students living in Australia, this activity can be adapted by teachers worldwide.

❏ **Talking About Family Changes — An AskERIC Lesson Plan**
http://www.askeric.org/cgi-bin/printlessons.cgi/Virtual/Lessons/Health/Family_Life/FAL0005.html

Students coming from single-parent and divorced families ,and even students who live in traditional families, face major changes in the family. Divorce, illness, death, birth and remarriage can cause stress and confusing feelings. Encouraging children to talk to trusted adults and friends about feelings and worries can help assuage fears and work out problems. This activity shows students how hard it can be to accomplish a common goal (such as a healthy family) without communication. The goal of this lesson is to understand relationships within the family.

❏ **Teacher Talk Forum: Lesson Plans**
http://education.indiana.edu/cas/ttforum/lesson.html

❏ **TeachersFirst Content Matrix**
http://www.teachersfirst.com/matrix.htm

❏ **Teaching Values: Self-Determination**
http://www.askeric.org/cgi-bin/printlessons.cgi/Virtual/Lessons/Health/Mental_Health/MEH0008.html

This lesson will help students understand the value of self-determination. It demonstrates this value through role play.

❏ **Teen Pregnancy—Health/Human Body lesson plan (grades 6-8)—DiscoverySchool.com**
http://school.discovery.com/lessonplans/programs/teenpregnancy/

Students will do the following: 1. Consider the short- and long-term consequences of teenagers having babies; 2. Recognize the responsibilities associated with being pregnant and having a newborn; 3. Become familiar with the resources available in their community for pregnant teenagers

❏ **Teen-Matters.com**
http://www.teen-matters.com/home.htm
Helping teens discuss serious matters.

❏ **The Chalkboard: k-12/k12 Education, Classroom Teacher**
http://www.thechalkboard.com/

The Chalkboard provides educators with lesson plans, related links for science, language, k-12, math, special education, school-to-work, and more! Classroom resources, including curriculum units for students, are offered free from corporations, as well as educational-related news, grants and other opportunities.

❏ **The Gateway to Educational Materials**
http://www.thegateway.org/

❏ **The Gingerbread Man Trail — An AskERIC Lesson Plan**
http://www.askeric.org/cgi-bin/
printlessons.cgi/Virtual/Lessons/Interdisci-
plinary/First_Day_of_School/FDA0203.html

The purpose of this lesson is to present a fun, memorable way for children to learn where the secretary, principal, nurse, janitor, cafeteria, playground, and other grade levels are located and at the same time matching a face and job with each of these locations and its importance to the functioning of the school.

❏ **The Lesson Plans Page**
http://www.lessonplanspage.com

❏ **The Use of \"Substitution\" As A Creative Thinking — An AskERIC Lesson Plan**
http://www.askeric.org/cgi-bin/
printlessons.cgi/Virtual/Lessons/Interdisci-
plinary/INT0079.html

The following is part of a six week unit designed to teach the seven creative thinking techniques represented by the acronym, "SCAMPER." SCAMPER provides students with a mini "toolbox" of techniques to use in virtually any situation requiring the production of creative ideas.

❏ **Tobacco/Smoking Resistance**
http://www.lessonplanspage.com/PEArt-
TobaccoSmoking-
EffectsAndRolePlayPeerPressWithPuppetsK3.htm

The student will be able to 1. Recall the detrimental effects of smoking; 2. Role play a peer pressure situation of smoking.

❏ **Traits Needed for Effective Group Process — An AskERIC Lesson Plan**
http://www.askeric.org/cgi-bin/
printlessons.cgi/Virtual/Lessons/Interdisci-
plinary/INT0074.html

Students are assisted to (a) compile a list of 10 desirable traits for working with others; (b) learn to evaluate which traits are needed for specific jobs; (c) describe these traits in work settings; (d) make plans for developing them; and (e) seek parental involvement.

❏ **Triangles Are Not Bad! — An AskERIC Lesson Plan**
http://www.askeric.org/cgi-bin/
printlessons.cgi/Virtual/Lessons/
Social_Studies/Multicultural_Education/
MUL0011.html

We must teach people how to operate in a world that is diverse and pluralistic. Schooling is not effective if it doesn't have a multicultural component. This is true now and will be even more so in the future. By 2000 AD, 1 in 3 will be minorities. 80% of the labor force will be women and minorities. By 2010 AD, 1 in 2 will be minorities. By not recognizing and teaching diversity, minority cultures are devalued with the implication that they are less significant. The message becomes "You are not okay if you are different from the majority culture members".

❏ **Truth and Lies Game — An AskERIC Lesson Plan**
http://www.askeric.org/cgi-bin/
printlessons.cgi/Virtual/Lessons/Interdisci-
plinary/First_Day_of_School/FDA0201.html

This is a fun, get-acquainted activity. Used in the beginning of the school year, during a class party, or at the end of the year.

❏ **Turn on Inventiveness- Potato Possibilities — An AskERIC Lesson Plan**
http://www.askeric.org/cgi-bin/
printlessons.cgi/Virtual/Lessons/Interdisci-
plinary/INT0076.html

The purpose of this lesson is to promote creative right hemispheric thinking by incorporating visual thinking, inventive thinking and humor in learning

❏ **Understanding the Concept of Empathy**
http://www.lessonplanspage.com/
SSOTerrorism-
UnderstandingEmpathy57.htm

After completing this activity, students will have an understanding of one of the concepts we refer to frequently during the year — the concept of empathy.

❏ **Unit Plan on Cooperation, Trust, Problem-Solving — An AskERIC Lesson Plan**
http://www.askeric.org/cgi-bin/
printlessons.cgi/Virtual/Lessons/Interdisciplinary/INT0135.html

The purpose of this unit is to provide opportunities for 5th grade students to learn to work cooperatively and develop trust with classmates. These lessons are designed to help the students understand the importance of a positive self-concept, interpersonal relationships and problem-solving skills to the development of wellness.

❏ **Wants and Needs**
http://www.lessonplanspage.com/
SSOWantsAndNeeds-
WithMagazinePics12.htm

Students will cooperatively sort magazine pictures into Wants and Needs. They will glue the pictures onto the correctly labeled posterboard in an effort to develop an appreciation of the difference between the two.

❏ **Web Worksheet Wizard v3.0 Home**
http://wizard.hprtec.org/

❏ **Who am I Collage — An AskERIC Lesson Plan**
http://www.askeric.org/cgi-bin/
printlessons.cgi/Virtual/Lessons/Health/
Mental_Health/MEH0006.html

In order for students to build self esteem they need to know who they are and what is important and unique to themselves personally. Students also need to have a concrete way in which to express this. Students can become resident 'experts' in the classroom and this is one way of finding out what the range of knowledge is among a group of students.

❏ **Who am I? — An AskERIC Lesson Plan**
http://www.askeric.org/cgi-bin/
printlessons.cgi/Virtual/Lessons/Interdisciplinary/First_Day_of_School/FDA0209.html

This lesson is to be completed at the beginning of the school year, as a way for students to introduce themselves to their fellow classmates.

❏ **Who's in the Bag? — An AskERIC Lesson Plan**
http://www.askeric.org/cgi-bin/
printlessons.cgi/Virtual/Lessons/Health/
Mental_Health/MEH0004.html

Many students do not know how to develop relationships. Their negative social attitudes and low self-esteem hinder interaction. Use this exercise in the beginning of the year or group activities for the purpose of introducing the teacher and students to one another.

❏ **Winter Survival — An AskERIC Lesson Plan**
http://www.askeric.org/cgi-bin/
printlessons.cgi/Virtual/Lessons/Health/
Safety/SFY0011.html

In this lesson plan the students will learn what to do when stranded in a car during the middle of winter. From this experience, students will also learn how to construct a winter survival kit for their parents car.

❏ **Your Own Classroom Court — An AskERIC Lesson Plan**
http://www.askeric.org/cgi-bin/
printlessons.cgi/Virtual/Lessons/
Social_Studies/Civics/CIV0024.html

This activity is meant for teachers who would like to allow their students to have a more active role in setting classroom rules, in decision-making, and as a means of settling differences.

Listserv

❏ **Counseling Discussion Groups**
http://www.csun.edu/~hfedp001/
counseling_listservs.html
Provides links to over 20 discussion groups.

❏ **International Counselor Network (ICN)**
http://listserv.utk.edu/archives/icn.html
According to the author and listowner, Ellen Rust, The International Counselor Network (ICN) was started in order to cut down on the isolation felt by many counselors who do not have enough time or opportunity to connect with their colleagues in person. The network has grown to over 1000 members since it began in February, 1993. Members are from several countries and all U.S. states and include counselors, counselor educators, graduate students, and others interested in counseling issues. ICN members collaborate by sharing ideas, resources, and discussions about mental health issues. They share articles or papers they have written and ask for comments or reactions. Those who are more familiar with the Internet guide newcomers to useful WWW sites, other mailing lists, and counseling resources. Instructions for subscribing are included.

❏ **Counselor Education and Supervision Network**
http://listserv.kent.edu/scripts/
wa.exe?SUBED1=cesnet-l&A=1

❏ **ListFish**
http://www.listfish.com/
A directory of e-mail publications and discussion lists.

❏ **Mailing List Archives**
http://www.askeric.org/Virtual/
Listserv_Archives/
Archives of several education-related mailing lists are maintained by the AskERIC Virtual Library.

❏ **Succeeding in School**
http://genesislight.com/web%20files/
The program "Succeeding in School" is designed to help students focus on behaviors, attitudes, and human relations skills that lead to improved academic achievement.

❏ **Topica**
http://www.topica.com/
Start a free online newsletter today.

❏ **Welcome to FreeLists — Free, No-hassle Mailing Lists**
http://www.freelists.org/

❏ **Yahoo! Groups**
http://groups.yahoo.com/
Also share photos & files, plan events, send a newsletter, and more.

Mental Health Resources

❑ **Behavior OnLine: The Mental Health and Behavioral Science Meeting Place**
http://www.behavior.net

According to the site, Behavior OnLine aspires to be the premier World Wide Web gathering place for mental health professionals and applied behavioral scientists—a place where professionals of every discipline can feel at home. Behavior OnLine will thrive only if many people and organizations participate and help to shape it. Behavior OnLine is a registered trademark of Behavior OnLine, Inc.

❑ **Bright Futures in Practice: Mental Health**
http://www.brightfutures.org/mentalhealth/pdf/

A FREE downloadable book. Also links to Volume 2.

❑ **Computers in Mental Health**
http://www.ex.ac.uk/cimh/

The site aims to encourage the development of useful computing applications in the field of mental health. There is an associated discussion list which is open to professionals with an interest in computing and mental health. To join that list send e-mail in the text write 'subscribe cimh' lastname firstname. You will then be sent an application form.

❑ **Counseling Resources on the Net**
http://www.csun.edu/%7Ehfedp001/links.html

Highly resourceful site with many links brought to us by the department of Educational Psychology and Counseling, California State University at Northridge.

❑ **Internet Mental Health**
http://www.mentalhealth.com/

The goal of this site is to, "Our goal is to improve understanding, diagnosis, and treatment of mental illness throughout the world." Internet Mental Health is a free encyclopedia of mental health information. It was designed by a Canadian psychiatrist, Dr. Phillip Long, and programmed by his col-

league, Brian Chow. Information about the 50 most common mental disorders is available. Contains many links and a search engine!

❑ **Mental Health Counseling**
http://www.libraries.wright.edu/libnet/subj/cou/cpmeta/mhc.html

A megalist of links.

❑ **Mental Health InfoSource**
http://www.mhsource.com/

This is an interactive megasite which includes many links, resources, opportunities to ask questions, and earn CEU's.

❑ **Mental Health Net**
http://www.cmhc.com/

Mental Health Net is an award-winning guide to mental health, psychology, and psychiatry online. The site currently indexes over 7,500 refereed resources and is home to over 9,000 regular members.

❑ **NAMI (National Alliance for the Mentally Ill)**
http://www.nami.org/

A grassroots, self-help, support, education, and advocacy organization of people with serious mental illnesses and their families and friends. MAMI's mission is to eradicate mental illnesses and to improve the quality of life for those who suffer from these no-fault brain disorders.

❑ **National Mental Illness Screening Project**
http://www.mentalhealthscreening.org/

A nonprofit organization developed to coordinate nationwide mental health screening programs and to ensure cooperation, professionalism, and accountability in mental illness screenings.

❑ **NIMH — Child and Adolescent Mental Health**
http://www.nimh.nih.gov/publicat/childmenu.cfm

Booklets, fact sheets, web pages on the mental health problems and disorders affecting children and adolescents and treatments.

❏ **Prep Test NCE Licensure Exam Links**
http://www.counselingexam.com/
Review for the NCE and the NCMHCE.

❏ **Psych Central: Dr. John GROHOL's Mental Health Page**
http://www.grohol.com/
The site titled Psych Central: Dr. John Grohol's Mental Health Page, is boasted as a personalized one-stop index for psychology, support, and mental health issues, resources, and people on the Internet. This site has been reviewed by The Wall Street Journal, Newsweek, U.S. News & World Report, the Washington Post, USA Today, The Village Voice, Business Week and dozens of other publications!

❏ **SAMHSA's National Mental Health Information Center**
http://www.mentalhealth.org/
This site was created to advance understanding and respect for people suffering from mental illness. This site contains resources and information for individuals and family seeking help and information related to improving mental health for all people.

❏ **Self Improvement Online**
http://www.selfgrowth.com/
Billed as the definitive web guide to personal growth, self improvement, self-help and personal power. This site is designed to be an organized directory referencing information in other Web Sites on the World Wide Web.

❏ **Tarleton Student Counseling Center Self-Help**
http://www.tarleton.edu/~counseling/
Has both self-help information, links, and counseling resources.

News

❏ **BUSINESS WEEK ONLINE**
http://www.businessweek.com/
Lots of information and resources.

❏ **CNN Interactive**
http://www.cnn.com/

❏ **College News Online**
http://www.collegenews.com/
College News Online is a free campus newswire and student service dedicated to meeting the Internet needs of students, graduates and others interested in higher education.

❏ **ED Review**
http://www.ed.gov/offices/OIIA/OIA/edreview/
A bi-weekly e-mail update on U.S. Department of Education activities relevant to the Intergovernmental and Corporate community and other stakeholders.

❏ **Education Week on the Web**
http://www.edweek.org/
Archived full-text articles, products and services, magazines, daily news, and special reports.

❏ **eSchoolNews.com**
http://www.eschoolnews.org/
K-12 school technology newspaper including info about technology funding opportunities and plenty of news. I visit here all the time.

❏ **Fox News**
http://foxnews.com
Information, video, and audio from the FOX News Channel.

❏ **Google News**
http://news.google.com

Topics are updated continuously through-out the day, so you will see new stories each time you check the page. Google has developed an automated grouping process for Google News that pulls together related headlines and photos from thousands of sources worldwide — enabling you to see how different news organizations are reporting the same story. You pick the item that interests you, then go directly to the site which published the account you wish to read.

❏ **IFILM — Super Bowl**
http://superbowl.ifilm.com/superbowl/
Superbowl commercials!

❏ **Mercury Center**
http://www.mercurycenter.com/

❏ **NewsDirectory: Newspapers and Media**
http://www.ecola.com/
Magazines and television too.

❏ **Online Newspapers**
http://onlinenewspapers.com/
Thousands of newspapers on the Net.

❏ **Public Education Network**
http://www.publiceducation.org/news/signup.htm
The PEN Weekly NewsBlast provides tens of thousands of readers a free, unbiased selection of education headlines every week.

❏ **San Francisco Chronicle on The Gate**
http://www.sfgate.com/cgi-bin/chronicle/list-sections.cgi

❏ **Slashdot: News for nerds, stuff that matters**
http://slashdot.org/

❏ **The Chronicle of Higher Education**
http://chronicle.com/

This World-Wide Web site is a service of The Chronicle of Higher Education. Published weekly, The Chronicle is the No. 1 news source for college and university faculty members and administrators. A subscription to The Chronicle includes free access to all of this Web site and to daily electronic-mail updates.

❏ **The Nando Times**
http://www.nando.net/

❏ **Top Breaking News Headlines From 1stHeadlines**
http://www.1stheadlines.com/
Headlines from around the world.

❏ **USA TODAY**
http://www.usatoday.com/

❏ **USA TODAY Latest news (Education)**
http://www.usatoday.com/educate/body.htm
An online gateway to the world of education by the folks at USA Today.

❏ **What's New — Government Resources on the Web**
http://www.lib.umich.edu/govdocs/whatsnew.html
Kept current.

Organizations

❑ **AAMFT**

http://www.aamft.org/

The American Association for Marriage and Family Therapy (AAMFT) is the professional association for the field of marriage and family therapy. According to the organization, they represent the professional interests of more than 23,000 marriage and family therapists throughout the United States, Canada and abroad.

❑ **Advocates for Youth Home Page**

http://www.advocatesforyouth.org/

Advocates for Youth (formerly Center for Population Options) is dedicated to creating programs and promoting policies which help young people make informed and responsible decisions about their sexual and reproductive health. We provide information, training, and advocacy to youth-serving organizations, policy makers, and the media in the U.S. and internationally.

❑ **AMCD ONLINE**

http://www.bgsu.edu/colleges/edhd/
programs/AMCD/

The mission of the Association for Multicultural Counseling and Development (AMCD) is to provide global leadership, research, training and development of multicultural counseling professionals with a focus on racial and ethnic issues. Presented is information about services, standards of training, and membership.

❑ **American Association of Pastoral Counselors**

http://www.aapc.org/

Association of Pastoral Counselors (AAPC) represents and sets professional standards for over 3,200 Pastoral Counselors and more than 100 pastoral counseling centers in the United States.

❑ **American Association of School Administrators**

http://www.aasa.org/

Links including Front Burner Issues, Membership, Conferences/Free Workshops, the Education Marketplace, Legislative Alerts, Job Bulletin, Publications, Programs, State Associations, Hot Links, and a Search Engine.

❑ **American College Personnel Association**

http://www.acpa.nche.edu/

❑ **American Council For Drug Education**

http://www.acde.org/

Learn how you can help the American Council for Drug Education in its quest to diminish substance abuse and its impact. Become an individual or corporate member of ACDE.

❑ **American Counseling Association**

http://www.counseling.org/

❑ **American Dance Therapy Association**

http://www.adta.org/

The ADTA site educates users about dance therapy and provides useful links including: "Contacts for Regional and Local Activities, Research Committee, Membership, Credentials, and Education."

❑ **American Hospice Foundation**

http://www.americanhospice.org/

Informative.

❑ **American Psychological Association**

http://www.apa.org/

❏ **American School Counselor Association**
http://www.schoolcounselor.org/

The American School Counselor Association (ASCA) is a worldwide nonprofit organization based in Alexandria, Va. Founded in 1952, ASCA supports school counselors' efforts to help students focus on academic, personal/social and career development so they not only achieve success in school but are prepared to lead fulfilling lives as responsible members of society. The association provides professional development, publications and other resources, research and advocacy to more than 13,000 professional school counselors around the globe.

❏ **American School Health Association**
http://www.ashaweb.org/

The Association, a multidisciplinary organization of administrators, counselors, dentists, health educators, physical educators, school nurses and school physicians, advocates high-quality school health instruction, health services and a healthful school environment.

❏ **American Vocational Association**
http://www.avaonline.org/

The American Vocational Association is a professional organization of 38,000 teachers, counselors, school administrators, teacher educators and business/industry partners. Based in Alexandria, Virginia, AVA carries out a diverse array of programs that advance vocational-technical and school-to-careers education. Helpful links including legislation information, products, school-to-career, and publications.

❏ **Association for Counselor Education and Supervision**
http://www.acesonline.net/

The Association for Counselor Education and Supervision is one of seventeen (17) divisions of the American Counseling Association. ACA, the umbrella organization, is a scientific, educational organization serving members and the public by fostering the advancement of counseling and human development in all settings. This site contains information about the organization, leadership, conference, position announcements, research awards, and other American Counseling Association divisions.

❏ **Association for Death Education and Counseling**
http://www.adec.org/

The Association for Death Education and Counseling is a multidisciplinary professional organization dedicated to promoting excellence in death education, bereavement counseling and care of the dying. Based on theory and quality research, ADEC provides information, support and resources to its multicultural membership and, through them, to the public.

❏ **Association for Specialists in Groupwork**
http://asgw.educ.kent.edu/

❏ **Association for Supervision and Curriculum Development**
http://www.ascd.org/

❏ **Attention Deficit Disorder Association**
http://www.add.org/

ADDA's mission is to help people with AD/HD lead happier, more successful lives through education, research, and public advocacy.

❏ **Benton Foundation**
http://www.benton.org/

The Benton Foundation works to realize the social benefits made possible by the public interest use of communications. Bridging the worlds of philanthropy, public policy, and community action, Benton seeks to shape the emerging communications environment and to demonstrate the value of communications for solving social problems. Through demonstration projects, media production and publishing, research, conferences, and grantmaking, Benton probes relationships between the public, corporate, and nonprofit sectors to address the critical questions for democracy in the information age.

❏ **Board on Children, Youth, and Families**
http://www.bocyf.org

The Board on Children, Youth, and Families addresses a variety of policy-relevant issues related to the health and development of children, youth, and families. It does so by convening experts to weigh in on matters from the perspective of the behavioral, social, and health sciences. The Board's Committee on Adolescent Health and Development focuses attention on critical national issues of importance to youth and their families.

❏ **CACREP**
http://www.counseling.org/CACREP/

The Council for Accreditation of Counseling and Related Educational Programs (CACREP) was formed in 1981. This site contains access to a Directory of CACREP accredited programs, a student's guide to accreditation, the 2001 standards revision process, and the CACREP Board of Directors.

❏ **CHARACTER COUNTS!**
http://www.charactercounts.org/

CHARACTER COUNTS! is a nonprofit, nonpartisan, nonsectarian coalition of schools, communities and nonprofit organizations working to advance character education by teaching the Six Pillars of Character: trustworthiness, respect, responsibility, fairness, caring and citizenship.

❏ **Chi Sigma Iota**
http://www.csi-net.org/

The International Counseling Academic and Professional Honor Society.

❏ **Children and Adults with Attention Deficit Disorder**
http://www.chadd.org/

Through its professional advisory board, and other leaders in the field of ADHD, CH.A.D.D. brings you accurate, current information on medical, scientific, educational and advocacy issues.

❏ **College Parents of America**
http://www.collegeparents.org/

❏ **Creative Partnerships for Prevention**
http://www.cpprev.org/contents.htm

According to the site, the goal of this national initiative is to provide current information, ideas, and resources on how to use the arts and humanities to enhance drug and violence prevention programming, foster resiliency in youth, and implement collaborations within communities to strengthen prevention programs for youth. The materials developed for this initiative have been designed with the guidance of educators, prevention specialists, youth workers, and professionals from cultural institutions (arts and humanities organizations, museums, libraries, etc.). This site includes demonstrations, profiles of existing programs, a "community center", and links to other resources.

❏ **Directory of Electronic Journals and Newsletters**
http://www.arl.org/scomm/edir

ARL is a not-for-profit membership organization comprising the libraries of North American research institutions and operates as a forum for the exchange of ideas and as an agent for collective action. Membership in ARL is institutional. There are currently 121 members. ARL Membership Meetings are held twice a year; proceedings are available.

❏ **Education (Social Sciences)**
http://galaxy.einet.net/galaxy/Social-Sciences/Education.html

This is the professionals guide to a world of information — contains many links. This site is searchable.

❏ **Educators for Social Responsibility**
http://esrnational.org/

ESR's mission is to make teaching social responsibility a core practice in education so that young people develop the convictions and skills needed to shape a safe, sustainable, democratic, and just world.

❏ **Family Education Network's Today's Features**
http://familyeducation.com/community.asp

Helpful content for teachers, parents, and kids. Users may vote in opinion polls, visit a "community center," and take part in various topical "channels."

❏ **Financial Aid/NYSFAAA**
http://www.nysfaaa.org/

Includes a section especially for school counselors.

❏ **Florida School Counselor Association**
http://www.webcoast.com/fsca/

❏ **Gift From Within**
http://www.giftfromwithin.org

An international organization for survivors of trauma and victimization.

❏ **Health Action Information Network**
http://www.hain.org/

The Health Action Information Network (HAIN) is a non-profit non-government organization established in 1985 based in Quezon City, the Philippines. It is involved in health education and research and mainly works with community-based organizations involved in health and development.

❏ **International Association of Marriage and Family Counselors**
http://familycounselors.org/

❏ **Kids Can Make A Difference**
http://www.kidscanmakeadifference.org

Kids Can Make a difference (KIDS), an educational program for middle- and high school students, focuses on the root causes of hunger and poverty, the people most affected, solutions, and how students can help. The major goal is to stimulate the students to take some definite follow-up actions as they begin to realize that one person can make a difference.

❏ **Leading provider of Character Education Curriculum**
http://www.characterbuilders.org/

National Center for Youth Issues is a national, non-profit organization that creates and supplies character education materials and training for schools, youth organizations, parents and community groups.

❏ **NAADAC**
http://www.naadac.org/

Official website for the National Association of Alcoholism and Drug Abuse Counselors, this site contains information about NAADAC'S mission and facts, their national conference, subscribing to the Counselor's Magazine, certification, government relations, publications, liability insurance, and membership.

❏ **NASSP — Education Leaders in Middle & High Schools**
http://www.nassp.org/

❏ **National Association of Social Workers**
http://www.socialworkers.org/

❏ **National Middle School Association**
http://www.nmsa.org/

Established in 1973, National Middle School Association (NMSA) serves as a voice for professionals, parents, and others interested in the educational and developmental needs of young adolescents (youth 10-15 years of age). NMSA is the only national educational association exclusively devoted to improving the educational experiences of young adolescents.

❏ **National Association for College Admission Counseling**
http://www.nacac.com

The National Association for College Admission Counseling is an education association of secondary school counselors, college and university admission officers and counselors and related individuals who work with students as they make the transition from high school to postsecondary education.

❏ **National Association for Self-Esteem**
http://www.self-esteem-nase.org/

The purpose of the NASE is to fully integrate self-esteem into the fabric of American society so that every individual, no matter what their age or background, experiences personal worth and happiness. This site is highly resourceful by providing useful links, contacts, educational programming information, and a whole lot more.

❏ **National Association of Elementary School Principals**
http://www.naesp.org/

❏ **National Board for Certified Counselors, Inc. (NBCC)**
http://www.nbcc.org

❏ **National Career Development Association (NCDA)**
http://ncda.org/

❏ **National Center for Injury Prevention and Control**
http://www.cdc.gov/ncipc/ncipchm.htm

The Centers for Disease Control and Prevention (CDC) began studying home and recreational injuries in the early 1970s and violence prevention in 1983. From these early activities grew a national program to reduce injury, disability, death, and costs associated with injuries outside the workplace. In June 1992, CDC established the National Center for Injury Prevention and Control (NCIPC). As the lead federal agency for injury prevention, NCIPC works closely with other federal agencies; national, state, and local organizations; state and local health departments; and research institutions. This site contains updates, reports, and grant information.

❏ **National Clearinghouse for Alcohol and Drug Information**
http://www.health.org/

The National Clearinghouse for Alcohol and Drug Information (NCADI) is the information service of the Center for Substance Abuse Prevention of the Substance Abuse and Mental Health Services Administration in the U.S. Department of Health & Human Services. NCADI is the world's largest resource for current information and materials concerning substance abuse.

❏ **National Committee to Prevent Child Abuse**
http://www.childabuse.org/

Chock full of information, resources, statistics, chapter contact information, and advocacy tips, this site is a must see.

❏ **National Crime Prevention Council On-Line Resource Center**
http://www.ncpc.org/

The National Crime Prevention Council (NCPC) is a private, nonprofit, tax-exempt organization whose mission is to prevent crime and build safer, more caring communities. The site contains useful information about crime prevention, community building, comprehensive planning, and even fun stuff for kids.

❏ **National Depressive and Manic-Depressive Association — Depression and Bipolar Di**
http://www.ndmda.org/

❏ **National Educational Service (NES)**
http://www.nes.org/

❏ **National Employment Counseling Association**
http://www.geocities.com/Athens/Acropolis/6491/neca.html

❏ **National Families in Action**
http://www.emory.edu/NFIA/

National Families in Action is a national drug education, prevention, and policy center based in Atlanta, Georgia. The organization was founded in 1977. Its mission is to help families and communities prevent drug abuse among children by promoting policies based on science.

❏ **National Institute of Mental Health Web Site**
http://www.nimh.nih.gov

Useful information about publications, grants, news/events, and research activities.

❏ **National Opportunity NOCs**
http://www.opportunitynocs.org/

This site is a database of national not-for-profit organizations which can be useful to work with in the school setting.

❏ **National Peer Helper Association**
http://www.peerhelping.org

The National Peer Helpers Association equips individuals to help others by promoting standards of excellence in peer programs.

❏ **National PTA**
http://www.pta.org

A searchable site with headings that include information about PTA's, membership, news/events, programming, legislative activity, conventions, bulletin boards, and contacts.

❏ **National Victim Center**
http://www.nvc.org/

The National Victim Center, established in 1985, endeavors to meet the needs and protect the rights of victims of violent crime.

❏ **North Carolina Peer Helper Association**
http://members.aol.com/ncpha/
Resources, membership info, and more.

❏ **OCRE: Organization Concerned about Rural Education**
http://www.ruralschools.org/
Highly resourceful and informative site.

❏ **Ohio Counseling Association**
http://www.ohiocounselingassoc.com
The Ohio Counseling Association's Official web site.

❏ **Ontario School Counsellors' Association (OSCA)**
http://osca.ouac.on.ca/
OSCA is the professional organization which represents teacher-counsellors in the elementary and secondary schools of Ontario.

❏ **Operation Respect**
http://www.dontlaugh.org/
Founded by Peter Yarrow of the folk group Peter, Paul & Mary, the organization disseminates educational resources that are designed to establish a climate that reduces the emotional and physical cruelty some children inflict upon each other by behaviors such as ridicule, bullying and-in extreme cases-violence. It is a unique organization that provides a gateway to broad scale adoption of school-based character education as well as social and emotional learning (SEL) programs.

❏ **Points of Light Foundation**
http://www.pointsoflight.org/
The Foundation's mission is to engage more people more effectively in volunteer community service to help solve serious social problems. This site should be your starting place for volunteering and similar activities.

❏ **Sandplay Therapists of America**
http://www.sandplayusa.org/

Sandplay Therapists of America (STA) is a nonprofit organization established to train, support, and promote professional development in sandplay therapy in the tradition of Dora Kalff as based on the theories of C.G. Jung.

❏ **Six Seconds- Resources Emotional Intelligence**
http://www.6seconds.org

A nonprofit organization to support EQ for individuals, families, schools & communities. The group provides training and materials that transform current research into effective practice.

❏ **The Council of Chief State School Officers**
http://www.ccsso.org/

The Council of Chief State School Officers (CCSSO) is a nationwide, nonprofit organization composed of the public officials who head departments of elementary and secondary education in the states, the District of Columbia, the Department of Defense Education .

❏ **The George Lucas Educational Foundation**
http://www.glef.org/

GLEF is a nonprofit organization that documents and disseminates stories about exemplary practices in K-12 public education.

❏ **The National Center for Charitable Statistics at The Urban Institute**
http://nccs.urban.org/

The National Center for Charitable Statistics (NCCS) is the national repository of data on the nonprofit sector in the United States. Its mission is to develop and disseminate high quality data on nonprofit organizations and their activities. Links to documents, state profiles, resources on nonprofits and philanthropy, fact sheets, and more.

❏ **The National Fair Access Coalition on Testing**
http://www.fairaccess.org/

To protect fair access to psychological and educational tests by properly trained professionals to better serve the public.

❏ **The National Organization of Parents Of Murdered Children, Inc. (POMC)**
http://www.pomc.com/

To provide support and assistance to all survivors of homicide victims while working to create a world free of murder.

❏ **The National Self-Help Clearinghouse**
http://www.selfhelpweb.org/

The National Self-Help Clearinghouse is a not-for-profit organization that was founded in 1976 to facilitate access to self-help groups and increase the awareness of the importance of mutual support.

❏ **Welcome to NEA!**
http://www.nea.org/

❏ **What Kids Can Do**
http://whatkidscando.org

What Kids Can Do is a national nonprofit organization founded in the winter of 2001. We document the value of young people working with teachers and other adults on projects that combine powerful learning with public purpose for an audience of educators and policy makers, journalists, community members, and students.

❏ **Wisconsin Education Association**
http://www.weac.org/

WEAC represents the public policy, labor and professional interests of 86,500 education professionals in Wisconsin.

❏ **YWCA of the USA**
http://www.ywca.org/

The largest and oldest women's organization in the United States. The mission of the YWCA is to empower women and girls and to work to eliminate racism. Includes a downloadable action kit for combating racism and many more highly resourceful links.

Parenting

❑ **Guidance for Effective Discipline**
http://www.aap.org/policy/re9740.html

From the American Academy of Pediatrics Committee on Psychosocial Aspects of Child and Family Health.

❑ **Handouts for Parents**
http://henson.austin.apple.com/edres/
parents/parentmenu.shtml

Wonderful topics brought to us by Apple computers.

❑ **Helping Your Child Series**
http://www.ed.gov/pubs/parents/hyc.html

The FREE Helping Your Child publication series aims to provide parents with the tools and information necessary to help their children succeed in school and life. These booklets feature practical lessons and activities to help their school aged and preschool children master reading, understand the value of homework and develop the skills necessary to achieve.

❑ **Helping Your Child Through Early Adolescence — Helping Your Child Series**
http://www.ed.gov/pubs/parents/adolescence

This is a guide that helps parents of 10- to 14-year-olds answer questions that include: How will my child change between the ages of 10 & 14? How much independence should I give my child? How can I help my child form good friendships & resist harmful peer pressure? How can I keep my child motivated to learn & do well, both in & out of school? What can I do to help my child develop good values? How can I tell — & what can I do — if my child is having a serious problem? Other publications for parents are found at http://www.ed.gov/pubs/parents/.

❑ **Parent Power!**
http://edreform.com/parentpower/

Parent Power! is an electronic newsletter for parents who want to know more about the issues that affect their children's education.

❑ **ParenTalk Newsletter**
http://www.tnpc.com/parentalk

This online newsletter from the National Parenting Center includes articles from physicians and psychologists that deal with subjects from pregnancy to adolescence. Site search engine, forums and membership information are also listed.

Peer Helper Programs

❏ **(PDF Report) Conflict Resolution Education: A Guide to Implementing Programs**
http://www.ncjrs.org/pdffiles/conflic.pdf
A comprehensive and valuable resource. 144 pages.

❏ **California Association of Peer Programs**
http://www.cappeer.org/
The California Association of Peer Programs is dedicated to the initiation, enhancement, and promotion of youth service through quality peer programs.

❏ **Conflict and Peace studies**
http://www.synapse.net/~acdi20/links/conflict.htm
Tons of resources!

❏ **Conflict Resolution/Peer Mediation**
http://www.coe.ufl.edu/CRPM/CRPMhome.html
A research project from the University of Florida.

❏ **Emergency Support Network**
http://www.tunnecliffe.com.au/articles.html
Articles on this site are largely about peer helping issues taken from the Emergency Support Newsletter. With acknowledgment, you are free to reproduce these for other publications.

❏ **Fujifilm Photopals**
http://www.scholastic.com/photopals/
For kids and adults.

❏ **Health Education/Peer Counseling**
http://healthcenter.ucdavis.edu/healthed.html
This Health Education Program at the Cowell Student Health Center promotes wellness and disease/injury prevention through confidential peer counseling services, small- or large-group education, and a variety of publications. Trained peer counselors, workshop seminars, and printed materials (pamphlets and resource library) are available.

❏ **Healthy Oakland Teens**
http://www.caps.ucsf.edu/hotindex.html
Read about the Healthy Oakland Teens Project (HOT) which began in the fall of 1992 at an urban, ethnically diverse junior high school. The project's goal is to reduce adolescents' risk for HIV infection by using peer role models to advocate for responsible decision making, healthy values and norms, and improved communication skills. You can view and download their entire curriculum.

❏ **JALMC's Peer Mediation Program**
http://www.jalmc.org/peer/
JALMC's Peer Mediation Program in Chautauqua County, N.Y. Includes links to peer mediation / conflict resolution resources on the Internet and "Peer Mediation Program Reduces Student Conflict in Chautauqua County, N.Y. Schools" — an article from the National Labor Management Association newsletter.

❏ **Justice Information Center (NCJRS): Peer Justice and Youth Empowerment**
http://ojjdp.ncjrs.org/PUBS/peerhome.htm
An implementation guide for teen court programs in PDF format.

❏ **National Mentoring Partnership**
http://www.mentoring.org/
This partnership advocates for the expansion of mentoring; a resource for mentors and mentoring initiatives nationwide.

❑ **National Service-Learning Cooperative Clearinghouse**
http://www.servicelearning.org/

The Learn & Serve America National Service-Learning Clearinghouse collects and disseminates information for the service-learning field.

❑ **One World, Our World**
http://www.1wow.org/

A comprehensive site with resources for building peer mediation/conflict resolution programs and integrating them into school curricula.

❑ **Peer Assistance and Leadership (PAL)**
http://www.palusa.org/

Peer Assistance and Leadership is an award winning, non-profit program providing effective training in "resiliency" strategies. The PAL peer helping program combats problems such as violence in schools, drug abuse, teen pregnancy, gang participation and school dropouts by providing a critical line of defense both at school and in the home through building peer helping programs all over Texas.

❑ **Peer Helping**
http://www.sentex.net/~casaa/peer-helping

Brought to us from the Canadian Association of Student Activity Advisors, this site has many articles and tutoring tips.

❑ **Peer Mediation Links**
http://www.jalmc.org/peer/pm-links.htm

A neat program from the Citizenship Law-Related Education Program of the Maryland State Bar Association and the Maryland State Department of Education.

❑ **Peer Resources**
http://www.peer.ca/peer.html

Their mission is to provide high quality training, superior educational resources, and practical consultation to persons who wish to establish or strengthen peer helping, peer support, peer mediation, peer referral, peer education, peer coaching, and mentor programs in schools, universities, communities, and corporations.

❑ **Peer Resources Documents**
www.peer.ca

Peer Resources is Canada's leading producer of contemporary literature on peer helping, mentoring and coaching. Research reports, project summaries, annotated bibliographies, and background papers are a few of the documents available from Peer Resources.

❑ **Peer Web Site — U of Guelph**
http://www.peer.uoguelph.ca/

Largest peer helper program in Canada.

❑ **Placer County Peer Court**
http://www.peercourt.com/

Placer Peer Court is a partnership that challenges the entire community to take an active role in solving juvenile crime.

❑ **Sweet Briar College Academic Resource Center Peer Mentoring**
http://www.arc.sbc.edu/mentoring.html

Also a link to peer tutoring and other helpful resources.

❑ **The PALS Peer Mentoring Program**
http://www.calstatela.edu/academic/pals/

PALS, the Partnership for Academic Learning and Success program is a Peer Mentoring program designed specifically to help targeted first-time Freshmen meet educational, financial and other challenges associated with beginning college life.

❏ **The Peer Power Centre**
http://www.peerpower.on.ca

The Peer Power Centre was established in 1991, in London, Ontario, Canada in response to gaps in services for local youth. Peer support initiatives, specifically Peer Helping and Peer Mediation, are the cornerstone skills training programs of the Centre. The goal of the Peer Power Centre is to empower youth with the knowledge, skills, and access to resources they need, to better help themselves and their peers. This site contains useful info and especially resources for your peer program.

❏ **The Peer Support Foundation**
http://www.peersupport.com.au/

The Peer Support Foundation is an educational organisation committed to improving the quality of life for Victorian school students through peer group influence. Their intention is to help students resist peer pressure to behave anti-socially, adjust easily to a new grade or school, contribute to the spirit of community, and promote responsibility, self-confidence and leadership qualities. This site may help facilitate ideas in structuring your own program.

❏ **THE PEOPLE FOR PEACE CONFLICT RESOLUTION CENTER**
http://members.aol.com/pforpeace/cr

Includes resource links, articles, and papers.

❏ **The Well Woman Peer Education Program**
http://www.barnard.columbia.edu/health/well_woman/peered.htm

Well-Woman was established in 1994 to bring together all of the small, topical peer educator groups to form one comprehensive group for the Barnard and Columbia communities.

❏ **Yes You Can!**
http://www.ed.gov/pubs/YesYouCan/

The publication, Yes, You Can A Guide for Establishing Mentoring Programs to Prepare Youth for College. Also available for PDF download.

❏ **YLGB Peer Support Project**
http://www.peer-support.org.uk/

this peer support project provides peer support services for young lesbians, gays & bisexuals in Greater Manchester.

Reference

❏ **A Web of On-line Dictionaries**
http://www.bucknell.edu/%7Erbeard/
diction.html

Linked to more than 500 dictionaries of over 140 different languages.

❏ **Acronym Finder**
http://www.acronymfinder.com/

Look up one or more of 269, 000 acronyms/abbreviations & their meanings. A searchable database containing common acronyms and abbreviations about all subjects, with a focus on computers, technology, telecommunications, and the military.

❏ **All About Counseling**
http://www.allaboutcounseling.com

❏ **APA Style Resources**
http://www.psychwww.com/resource/
apacrib.htm

❏ **APA Style | Electronic References**
http://www.apastyle.org/elecref.html

❏ **Ask Jeeves: Search Results for "Leadership Quotes"**
http://webster.directhit.com/webster/
search.aspx?qry=Leadership+Qoutes&meta=rs

❏ **Cable in the Classroom Online**
http://www.ciconline.com/

Video and online content can help you and your students make meaningful connections to new information, reinforce previous learning, interact with other learners, and create original content.

❏ **Consumer World**
http://www.consumerworld.org/

Consumer World is a public service site which has gathered over 1700 of the most useful consumer resources on the Internet, and categorized them here for easy access.

❏ **Corbis Experience The Place for Pictures on the Internet**
http://www.corbis.com/

Send an electronic postcard with one of millions of photos.

❏ **David Allen & Company Productivity Newsletter**
http://www.davidco.com/
productivity_principles.php

Subscribe to "David Allen's Productivity Principles." A free monthly newsletter to keep you tuned in and on track for high performance living (in English and Spanish).

❏ **DSM-IV — Diagnostic and Statistical Manual of Mental Disorders — Fourth Edition**
http://www.psychologynet.org/dsm.html

❏ **epocrates**
http://www.epocrates.com/

A free clinical database with lots of features. Especially helpful is a section about pediatric dosages.

❏ **ERIC Clearinghouse on Assessment**
http://www.ericae.net/pare/

an online journal published by the ERIC Clearinghouse on Assessment and Evaluation (ERIC/AE) and the Department of Measurement, Statistics, and Evaluation at the University of Maryland, College Park. Its purpose is to provide education professionals access to refereed articles that can have a positive impact on assessment, research, evaluation, and teaching practice, especially at the local education agency (LEA) level.

❏ **familydoctor.org**
http://www.familydoctor.org/

Health information for the whole family from the American Academy of Family Physicians.

❑ **Federal Resources for Educational Excellence**
http://www.ed.gov/free/

Federal Resources for Educational Excellence (FREE) makes hundreds of Internet-based education resources supported by agencies across the U.S. Federal government easier to find.

❑ **FindArticles.com**
http://www.findarticles.com

The Web's first FREE article search.

❑ **Full-text state statutes and legislation on the Internet**
http://www.prairienet.org/~scruffy/f.htm

This page seeks to link to sites containing full-text state constitutions, statutes (called codes or compiled laws in some states), legislation (bills, amendments and similar documents), session laws (bills that have become laws), and administrative rules.

❑ **How to Cite Sources APA Style**
http://www.nova.edu/library/dils/lessons/apa/apa07.htm

Great examples from Nova Southeastern University.

❑ **How to Report Internet-Related Crime**
http://www.usdoj.gov/criminal/cybercrime/reporting.htm

❑ **Internet Citation Guides**
http://www.library.wisc.edu/libraries/Memorial/citing.htm

Help for citing electronic sources in research papers and bibliographies.

❑ **Joint Committee on Testing Practices**
http://www.apa.org/science/jctpweb.html

Resources and information from JCTP a group of professional organizations and test publishers that work together to improve the quality of testing practices.

❑ **Journal of Technology in Counseling**
http://jtc.colstate.edu/

The Journal of Technology in Counseling publishes articles on all aspects of practice, theory, research and professionalism related to the use of technology in counselor training and counseling practice.

❑ **Learn2**
http://www.tutorials.com/

Dubbed as the ability utility, this site can help you learn the things that "make life easier and/or more interesting: everything from the essentials of life to the esoteric, from practical to just plain fun. Happy learning!"

❑ **Legal Information Institute**
http://supct.law.cornell.edu/supct/

The Legal Information Institute offers Supreme Court opinions under the auspices of Project Hermes, the court's electronic-dissemination project. This archive contains (or will soon contain) all opinions of the court issued since May of 1990.

❑ **Microsoft in K-12 Education HOME**
http://www.microsoft.com/education/default.asp?ID=schools

❑ **MLA Style**
http://www.mla.org/main_stl.htm

The only MLA documentation style are the only ones available on the Internet that are authorized by the Modern Language Association of America.

❏ **MY HERO**

http://myhero.com

An interactive educational website, visitors may read about great figures like Rosa Parks, Martin Luther King, Jr., Mark Twain, and others, including many local heroes. They suggest their own heroes and write short biographies about them. Children honor inspiring parents, parents honor brave children. >From peacemakers such as Nelson Mandela to scientific visionaries like Albert Einstein, the My Hero web page has allowed thousands of children and their parents a chance to tell the world about the people who they most respect and admire. In honoring others, visitors, especially children, begin to realize their own power and potential.

❏ **National Study of School Evaluation Useful Links**

http://www.nsse.org/useful.html

Searchable and resourceful site!

❏ **NetHistory**

http://nethistory.urldir.com/

The most comprehensive directory of links (350+ and counting) to information about the history of the Internet, World Wide Web, Usenet, as well as related concepts such as e-mail, browsers, online games and BBSs.

❏ **Online Computer Library Center**

http://www.oclc.org/home/

Online Computer Library Center (OCLC) is a nonprofit, membership, library computer service and research organization dedicated to the public purposes of furthering access to the world's information and reducing information costs

❏ **Practitioner Developed Educational-Counseling Resources video driven conflict re**

http://www.worldviewpub.com/

The source for educator and counselor-developed, ready-to-use video-driven conflict resolution, social skills and discipline training programs for preteens, teenagers and parents.

❏ **Psychwatch.Com**

http://psychwatch.com/

The RECORD is an online journal and news periodical with articles published, written, and submitted by Psychwatch.com readers and website visitors whose credentials follow their articles. Some articles have been published in professional journals, and thus have been peer-reviewed. Others are not peer reviewed, and are submitted for by persons whose credentials follow the article, and are posted by Psychwatch for the interest of their readers.

❏ **Sample Assessment Instruments**

http://www.eed.state.ak.us/tls/frameworks/wrldlang/wlinstr3.html

From the Alaska Department of Education & Early Development & Early Development.

❏ **SuperKids Educational Software Review**

http://www.superkids.com/

SuperKids reviews and rates educational software based on a carefully developed set of criteria. Reviews are written by teams that include educators, parents, and children from across the United States.

❏ **Talbot's Student Planning**

http://www.talbotsbook.com/

A selection of colleges, schools, and other assists for after high school.

❏ **The Counseling Zone**

www.counselingzone.com/

Transcripts of counseling related Internet chats.

❏ **The Merrow Report on PBS & NPR**

http://www.pbs.org/merrow/

The Merrow Report, an engaging documentary series, is about learning; about stretching your mind; about television that educates. Full text of many transcripts are available for download.

❏ **The State of the World's Children 2002**

http://www.unicef.org/sowc02/

Also available in PDF.

❏ **The Virtual Reference Desk**
http://www.vrd.org/

A Project of the ERIC Clearinghouse on Information & Technology and the National Library of Education with support from the Office of Science and Technology Policy.

❏ **This to That**
http://thistothat.com/

When you are not sure which type of glue to use :)

❏ **Virtual Harassment: Women and Online Education by Julia K. Ferganchick-Neufang**
http://www.firstmonday.dk/issues/issue3_2/fergan/

The authors analyze conditions of cyberspace that may prove problematic for female instructors and offer suggestions for dealing with such issues.

❏ **Vocabulary**
http://www.vocabulary.com/

Participate in FREE vocabulary puzzles to enhance vocabulary mastery

❏ **Volunteering By Youth Under 18**
http://www.serviceleader.org/advice/youth.html

❏ **Welcome to KidsCampaigns!**
http://www.kidscampaigns.org/home.html

Learn more about this nationwide campaign. Includes a great link to children's mental health.

❏ **Welcome to the Oxford Text Archive**
http://ota.ahds.ac.uk/

Recently appointed as a Service Provider for the UK-based Arts and Humanities Data Service, the Oxford Text Archive forms part of a national network of centers dedicated to the dissemination of quality, scholarly electronic resources, and to the support of UK-based academics involved with the creation of such materials.

❏ **WLH — Psychology**
http://www.iatp.md/aspm/resurse/World%20Lecture%20Hall.htm

The Psychology part of the World Lecture Hall which contains pages created by faculty worldwide who are using the Web to deliver class materials. See also distance education courses offered by The University of Texas System.

❏ **Yellow Pages for Kids with Disabilities**
http://www.fetaweb.com/help/states.htm

❏ **Zines on the Net**
http://fromnowon.org/zines.html

This is a partial listing of the hundreds of ZINES (electronic magazines) which can be found on the Internet. Many of these are lists of ZINES. Others are individual electronic publications. Because this list was meant to engage teachers in thinking about how to use such resources with older students, there has been no attempt to remove or screen controversial or offensive ZINES.

Research

❏ **APlus Research & Writing for High School and College Students**
http://www.ipl.org/teen/aplus/

Includes a guide to researching and writing a paper, help for finding information in cyberspace and in your library, and links to online resources for research and writing.

❏ **Bill Trochim's Center for Social Research Methods**
http://trochim.human.cornell.edu

According to the author, this website is for people involved in applied social research and evaluation. In addition to his own work, you'll find lots of links to other locations on the Web that deal in applied social research methods. You'll also find comprehensive course resource centers for this instructor's courses at Cornell, previously published and unpublished papers, detailed examples of current research projects, useful tools for researchers (like a guide to selecting a statistical analysis), an extensive online textbook, a bulletin board for discussions, and more.

❏ **BUBL Information Service Home Page**
http://bubl.ac.uk/

Billed as a national information service for the higher education community, this site aims to provide a pathway to guide librarians, information professionals, academics and researchers through the maze of resources on the Internet by offering a structured and user-friendly gateway, mainly in the form of the BUBL subject tree.

❏ **Encyclopedia.com from Electric Library**
http://www.encyclopedia.com/

This site conveniently places an extraordinary amount of information at your fingertips.

❏ **ERIC Clearinghouse on Elementary and Early Childhood Education**
http://ericeece.org/

The Educational Resources Information Center (ERIC) is a national information system designed to provide users with ready access to an extensive body of education-related literature. Established in 1966, ERIC is supported by the U.S. Department of Education, Office of Educational Research and Improvement (OERI), and is administered by the National Library of Education.

❏ **Guide to U.S. Department of Education Programs and Resources**
http://web99.ed.gov/GTEP/Program2.nsf

Excellent resource and easy to search.

❏ **Library of Congress Home Page**
http://www.loc.gov/

The Big Kahuna of references and resources.

❏ **Library Research Guides — UC Berkeley Libraries**
http://library.berkeley.edu/TeachingLib/Guides/

Including many services to individuals outside of the institution, this page is a collection of all of the Research Guides created by the UCB libraries.

❏ **National Center for Education Statistics**
http://nces.ed.gov/

The Purpose of the Center is to collect and report "...statistics and information showing the condition and progress of education in the United States and other nations in order to promote and accelerate the improvement of American education."

❏ **Skills Package How to Put Questionnaires on the Internet Part 1**
http://salmon.psy.plym.ac.uk/mscprm/forms.htm

According to the site, the purpose of this web page is to describe how to go about putting a questionnaire on the Internet. Although this is a relatively straightforward process it may be worth answering the question "Why bother?".

❏ **The Internet Public Library Education Reference**
http://www.ipl.org/ref/RR/static/edu0000.html

Information about schooling and instruction and the provision of knowledge or training in a particular area or for a particular purpose.

❏ **The Internet Writing Journal**
http://www.writerswrite.com/journal/

Known as the a one-stop resource for professional writers.

❏ **The Psychology of Cyberspace**
http://www.rider.edu/users/suler/psycyber/psycyber.html

According to the owner, the purpose of this web site or "online hypertext book" is to explore the psychological dimensions of the environments created by computers and online networks. It is intended as an evolving conceptual framework for understanding the various psychological components of cyberspace and how people react to and behave within it.

❏ **UMich Documents Center**
http://www.lib.umich.edu/govdocs/

The Documents Center is a central reference and referral point for government information, whether local, state, federal, foreign or international. Its web pages are a reference and instructional tool for government, political science, statistical data, and news.

❏ **AACTE Education Policy Resource and Information Clearinghouse**
http://www.edpolicy.org/

This clearinghouse is designed to help people access information on education policy at the national, regional, or state level. To access information, click on the region or state in which you are interested.

❏ **Adolescence Directory on line**
http://education.indiana.edu/cas/adol/adol.html

Adolescence Directory On-Line (ADOL) is an electronic guide to information on adolescent issues. It is a service of the Center for Adolescent Studies at Indiana University. Educators, counselors, parents, researchers, health practitioners, and teens can use ADOL to find Web resources for these topics:

❏ **Animation Factory's MediaBuilder**
http://www.mediabuilder.com/

Enhance your e-mail, web pages, and PowerPoint presentations by adding free backgrounds, animations, and clipart. You can receive a free newsletter with a new sample every day.

❏ **Apple Learning Interchange**
http://henson.austin.apple.com/edres/curric.shtml

Resources for integrating technology into the classroom, complete with curriculum and lesson plans.

❏ **Awesome Clipart for Kids**
http://www.awesomeclipartforkids.com/

❏ **Basic Guide to Program Evaluation**
http://www.mapnp.org/library/evaluatn/fnl_eval.htm

❏ **BrainPlay.com: Smart Choices for Growing Kids.**
http://www.brainplay.com/

Many reviews for children's software and opportunity to purchase online.

❑ **Cancer.gov — Cancer Information**
http://cancer.gov/cancerinformation

❑ **Center for Adolescent Studies**
http://education.indiana.edu/cas/

❑ **ChildLine UK Web Site**
http://www.childline.org.uk/

ChildLine is the UK's free national helpline for children and young people in trouble or danger. A host of fact sheets on many topics!

❑ **CIT Infobits**
http://www.unc.edu/cit/infobits/

CIT Infobits is an electronic service of the University of North Carolina at Chapel Hill Academic & Technology Networks' Center for Instructional Technology. Each month the CIT's Information Resources Consultant monitors and selects from a number of information technology and instruction technology sources that come to her attention and provides brief notes for electronic dissemination to educators.

❑ **Classroom Management Ideas from the First Grade Team Members!**
http://hometown.aol.com/BiblioCat4/manage.htm

❑ **ClinicalTrials.gov**
http://clinicaltrials.gov/

The U.S. National Institutes of Health, through its National Library of Medicine, has developed ClinicalTrials.gov to provide patients, family members and members of the public current information about clinical research studies.

❑ **CLN WWW Home Page**
http://www.cln.org/cln.html

This page is designed to help K-12 teachers integrate technology into their classrooms. The site boasts over 220 menu pages with more than 3,900 annotated links to educational WWW sites, as well as over 100 WWW resources of our own — all organized within an intuitive structure.

❑ **Coolsig — Find Great E-mail Signature Files!**
http://www.coolsig.com/

Want a new e-mail signature file? Something fun? You've come to the right place. Coolsig is now the biggest signature collection on the Internet!

❑ **Cooperative Learning Center**
http://www.clcrc.com

The Cooperative Learning Center is a Research and Training Center focusing on how students should interact with each other as they learn and the skills needed to interact effectively.

❑ **Counseling Books**
http://www.counsellingbooks.com/

❑ **Counselor Connection**
http://ericcass.uncg.edu/counselorconnection.html

Internet resources for professional counselors from ERIC/CASS.

❑ **Current Codes**
http://www.currentcodes.com/

Hundreds of well-known online stores like Barnes and Noble, Staples, and Amazon.com have a place within their shopping cart for a "coupon code" that gives a percent or dollar amount off your purchase. If you don't know the code, you can't take advantage of the discount. You can find these secret discount codes listed on many sites across the Internet but the problem with these sites is that they're usually personal homepages and they don't maintain their lists! Currentcodes.com has a full-time staff of trained individuals whose only job is to find new codes and verify the accuracy of the existing database.

❑ **e.thePeople**
http://www.e-thepeople.org/

Welcome to e.thePeople, the digital town hall for the nation. In cooperation with over 1,000 sites around the Internet, e.thePeople promotes intelligent and diverse discussion and political action.

❏ **EdPub On-Line Ordering System**
http://www.ed.gov/pubs/edpubs.html

This system is intended to help you identify and order U.S. Department of Education products. You can use searching options to identify the specific products you are seeking. During the initial stage of this system, individuals will be able to only request 1 product per order. After a few weeks, you will be able to order up to 5 different products per order.

❏ **Education World: Personal & Social Development**
http://www.educationworld.com/counseling/personal/index.shtml

Resources to help you work with both the general student population, and with students that need individualized attention.

❏ **Educator's Guide to Free Speech vs. Censorship on the Internet**
http://lrs.ed.uiuc.edu/wp/original/censorship

A collection of essays and resources on the ethical issues of free speech vs. censorship and how they impact three specific situations in K-12 education: acceptable use policies, student web pages, and filtering/blocking software

❏ **Electronic Catalog of NCES Products and On-Line Library**
http://nces.ed.gov/pubsearch

Find information about publications and data products that the National Center for Education Statistics has released. In most cases you may also browse the content of the publication or download files that you can work with on your own computer.

❏ **Electronic School**
http://www.electronic-school.com/

Electronic School chronicles technological change in the classroom, interprets education issues in a digital world, and offers readers — some 80,000 school board members, school administrators, school technology specialists, and other educators — practical advice on a broad range of topics pertinent to the implementation of technology in elementary and secondary schools throughout North America.

❏ **FindingStone Counseling, Consulting, Education & Training**
http://www.findingstone.com/

Some online tests, lots of info, and useful links.

❏ **Florida State Fire College Coloring Book (PDF)**
http://www.fsfckids.ufl.edu/assets/pdf/ColoringBook2.pdf

❏ **Free Art Ideas For Kids, Parents, and Teachers**
http://members.tripod.com/~artworkinparis/index-3.html

This site should be useful for ideas and activities when conducting play counseling with children or making art a part of other guidance and counseling interventions.

❏ **FrontPage tips**
http://www.frontpagetips.com/

Free Microsoft FrontPage tips delivered weekly to your e-mail box.

❏ **Functional Behavioral Assessment**
http://cecp.air.org/fba

❏ **Graphics Library Index**
http://www.jsmagic.net/free/

Direct links to free graphics of all sorts. In return for providing a link back to the site, you may use any of these graphics.

❑ **Great Sites!**
http://www.ala.org/parentspage/
greatsites/

A directory of "amazing, spectacular, mysterious, wonderful web sites for kids and the adults who care about them." Compiled by the Children and Technology Committee of the Association for Library Service to Children, a division of the American Library Association.

❑ **Guidance & Counseling Curriculum Guide**
http://www.republic.k12.mo.us/guide/
guide_co.htm

Well created document divided by guidance & counseling goals by grade level.

❑ **High School Survival Kit**
http://cuip.uchicago.edu/www4teach/98/
teams/Peerpals/home.htm

Includes communication, note taking, time management, homework, reading strategies, testing, peer relations, and teacher resources.

❑ **Homeschool.com — Your Virtual Homeschool**
http://homeschool.com/

❑ **Homeschooling Resource Catalogs**
http://www.home-ed-magazine.com/
HSRSC/hsrsc_03cts.html

Short but sweet.

❑ **Honor Level System**
http://www.honorlevel.com

All about discipline.

❑ **Houghton Mifflin Education Place**
http://eduplace.com/

K-8 resources for teachers, students, and parents. Includes Reading/Language Arts, Math, Science, Social Studies, Intervention, Professional Development, activities, games, and textbook support.

❑ **How Do You Feel Today?**
http://www.howdoyoufeeltoday.com/

Universally enjoyed by teachers, school nurses, doctors, psychologists, counselors, therapists, social workers, cat lovers, children, and your Aunt Helen and Uncle Roger.

❑ **Ice Breakers**
http://www.littlefalls.co.za/icebreakers.cfm

❑ **Icon Collections — Images for Your Web Page**
http://www.monroe.lib.in.us/~lchampel/
imgarch.html

You can find collections of images on the WWW that you can use to decorate your own Web page. Generally, the images in these archives are in the "public domain," which means they don't have any copyright restrictions on them. Or, the creators of the images have given their permission for others to use the images for free.

❑ **In and Out of the Classroom with Microsoft PowerPoint 97**
http://www.microsoft.com/education/
?ID=Tutorials

On online guidebook for using MS PowerPoint.

❑ **Internet Resources for Nonprofits — Online sites, links and directories.**
http://www.ucp-utica.org/uwlinks/
directory.html

❑ **Kelly Bear**
http://www.kellybear.com/

The Kelly Bear materials were created to provide easy-to-use resources that would strengthen communication and positive relationships between adults (parents, grandparents, teachers, counselors) and children ages 3-9. They help children understand their feelings, become socially competent, learn to be responsible, and develop healthy living habits.

❑ **KIM'S KORNER for TEACHER TALK**
http://www.kimskorner4teachertalk.com/

❏ **LEARN CPR — CPR information and training resource.**
http://www.learncpr.org
An extensive guide and informational resource for CPR training (to supplement the real thing).

❏ **LifeMatters: Well-Being & Health Forums, Courses, and Products**
http://www.lifematters.com/
LifeMatters is a synthesis of our professional experience as counselors and educators and personal life experiences. Our contribution is promoting the point of view that taking charge of one's health and well-being; physically, mentally, emotionally and spiritually, is a possibility for everyone.

❏ **Make Stuff — The 'You Can Make It' site for crafts, hobbies, entrepreneurs and p**
http://www.make-stuff.com/
All kinds of recipes, formulas, craft projects and ideas that you can make yourself.

❏ **Microsoft's Homepage**
http://www.microsoft.com/
Tons of free and valuable resources!

❏ **MidLink Magazine Home**
http://www.ncsu.edu/midlink/
This electronic magazine for kids in middle school was recognized as an official site of the 1998 Winter Olympics.

❏ **National Clearinghouse on Child Abuse and Neglect Information**
http://www.calib.com/nccanch/
The Clearinghouse is a national resource for professionals and others seeking information on child abuse and neglect and child welfare.

❏ **National Education Telecommunications Network: Guidance**
http://www.netn.net/20111.htm
Highly resourceful links and tools.

❏ **New Middle School Teacher Guide**
http://www.middleweb.com/
1stDResources.html
Includes sections and resources about the first days of school, new teachers, books for new and restless teachers, and general resources.

❏ **No Child Left Behind Resources**
http://www.surfline.ne.jp/janetm/IT4L/
nclb.html
OII compiled list of resources related to No Child Left Behind legislation, research in reading, writing and math, assessment and technology literacy.

❏ **Northwest Education Magazine**
http://www.nwrel.org/nwedu/
According to the site, the mission of the Northwest Regional Educational Laboratory (NWREL) is to improve educational results for children, youth, and adults by providing research and development assistance in delivering equitable, high quality educational programs. The site offers valuable information about programs and services such as training & technical assistance; research & development for educational improvement; and education & community services.

❏ **Online Psych**
http://www.onlinepsych.com
Many mental health forums and links to articles, games, issues, and databases.

❏ **Online Writing Center Home Page**
http://www.colostate.edu/Depts/
WritingCenter/
The Online Writing Center at Colorado State University is an ongoing project created by the Center for Research on Writing and Communication Technologies. A highly resourceful site with many useful links.

❏ **OWL.org**
http://www.owl.org

OWL.org is a FREE service of the National Education Association and its State and Local Affiliates. Devoted to "Educators Helping Educators," OWL.org is an online community where educators connect to share their knowledge and experience. OWL.org supports teachers and school staff with practical tips, strategies, and education materials.

❏ **PBS TeacherSource**
http://www.pbs.org/teachersource/

PBS TeacherSource makes it easy to locate and use the best television and Web resources available, as well as keep you on top of important community services provided by your PBS station.

❏ **PDFzone.COM**
http://www.pdfzone.com/

Your online hub to all things Acrobat & PDF.

❏ **PedagoNet — Learning Resources**
http://www.pedagonet.com/

An innovative search engine, PedagoNet facilitates the exchange of learning resources. Books, chat room, discussion forum, jobs, clipart, webpage creation, postcards, valuable links and free information are available.

❏ **Prevention Yellow Pages**
http://www.tyc.state.tx.us/prevention/

A worldwide directory of programs, research, references and resources dedicated to the prevention of youth problems and the promotion of nurturing children.

❏ **Promising Practices in School Counseling**
http://www.schoolnet.ca/vp-pv/quiz/LMI/PROMISNG.DOC

Short, but sweet. Contains several documents in PDF format.

❏ **Public Education Network Community Action Guide**
http://www.publiceducation.org/pubs/pubpreorder/orderform.asp

Public Education Network has developed an indispensable 80-page guide for community leaders, parents and educators on how to use NCLB to advocate for improved public education.

❏ **PubList.com**
http://www.publist.com/

PubList.com is a highly comprehensive directory of information about more than 150,000 publications and more than 8000 newspapers around the world. It's easy to use. And it's free.

❏ **Really Good Stuff Online!**
http://www.reallygoodstuff.org

Includes FREE downloadable activity guides.

❏ **Resiliency In Action**
http://www.resiliency.com/

Resiliency In Action is dedicated to the exciting, hopeful, and very real concept of resiliency. The purpose of RAI is to spread the news of resiliency through sharing research and facilitating the practical application and evaluation of the resiliency paradigm. The site also contains an opportunity to subscribe to a newsletter ($30 for individuals), sample articles, calendar of events, and a speaker list.

❏ **Ripple Effects**
http://www.rippleeffects.com/

Ripple Effects, Inc. is a San Francisco-based company that provides people with software tools to help with the social-emotional elements that affect productivity, academic achievement and everyday happiness.

❏ **S.C.O.R.E. CyberGuides**
http://www.sdcoe.k12.ca.us/score/cyberguide.html

According to the site, CyberGuides are supplementary, web-based units of instruction centered on core works of literature. They are designed for the classroom with one online computer. Each CyberGuide contains a student and teacher edition, objectives, a task and a process by which it may be completed, teacher-selected web sites and a rubric. CyberGuides aligned with California's Academic Content Standards as indicated in the Teacher Guides.

❏ **Safe Kids**
http://www.safekids.com/

Tips, advice and suggestions to make your family's online experience fun and productive!

❏ **Sample Lesson Plan**
http://udel.edu/~kenlev/lessonplan.htm

A sample classroom guidance lesson plan written by Ken Levering about Being A Good Student. Includes an online pretest and related links.

❏ **School Counseling Resources**
http://www.libraries.wright.edu/libnet/subj/cou/cpmeta/sc.html

Tons of links!

❏ **Scout Report Homepage**
http://wwwscout.cs.wisc.edu/scout/report/

The Scout Report is the flagship publication of the Internet Scout Project. Published every Friday both on the web and by e-mail, it provides a fast, convenient way to stay informed of valuable resources on the Internet. The site is compiled by a team of professional librarians and subject matter experts who select, research, and annotate each resource. This site is The Internet Scout Project is located in the Department of Computer Sciences at the University of Wisconsin-Madison, and is funded by a grant from the National Science Foundation. Internet Scout is part of the InterNIC.

❏ **Somerset Media**
http://www.somersetmedia.com

Lots of neat inspirational posters for counselors.

❏ **Songs for Teaching: Educational Music to Promote Learning**
http://songsforteaching.homestead.com

❏ **STANDARDS: The International Journal of Multicultural Studies**
http://stripe.colorado.edu/~standard/

This resource is free!

❏ **State Mental Health Resources**
http://mentalhealth.about.com/library/us/blstate.htm

Easily find mental health resources in your state.

❏ **Student Leader Magazine Online**
http://www.studentleader.com/

This leadership magazine for college and college-bound students is a great resource for any who want to develop leadership skills. Each issue has stimulating articles that include leadership tips from students at schools all across the USA.

❏ **Study Guides for testing, reading, writing, and classroom participation**
http://www.iss.stthomas.edu/studyguides/

❏ **Symantec AntiVirus Research Center**
http://www.sarc.com/

THE place to go for virus and antivirus information.

❏ **T.H.E. Journal**
http://www.thejournal.com/

T.H.E. JOURNAL provides educators with a nationwide forum in which they can share their successful experiences in employing technology to improve learning and its administration. Each issue is equivalent to attending an educational technology seminar in the convenience of a subscriber's own home or office.

❏ **Technology in School Counseling — Electronic Discussion Groups**
http://cbweb1.collegeboard.org/cblist/html/techsch.html

This is the place for online exchanges among school counselors and counselor educators relating to the use of technology in school counseling.

❏ **Test Anxiety Scale- Learning Skills Publications**
http://www.learningskills.com/test.html

A printable test online.

❏ **The Center for Health and Health Care in Schools — Homepage**
http://www.healthinschools.org

The Center for Health and Health Care in Schools (CHHCS) is a nonpartisan policy and program resource center located at The George Washington University School of Public Health and Health Services.

❏ **The Ethics Connection**
http://www.scu.edu/Ethics/

From the opening homepage, the user is presented with opportunities to interact: links to other sections of the site, areas of dialogue and practicing ethics, and the latest news and publications in the field of ethics and the site itself. A powerful, site-specific internal search engine enables users to pinpoint the data which they might need among hundreds of constantly refined libraries of ethical information and decision-making tools.

❏ **The Guidance Channel!**
http://guidancechannel.com

The Guidance Channel is an educational publishing and media company whose mission is to provide children, students, parents, adults and professionals with timely and effective tools that help them or their clients make critical life choices.

❏ **The Scout Report**
http://scout.cs.wisc.edu/scout/report

The Scout Report is the flagship publication of the Internet Scout Project. Published every Friday both on the web and by e-mail, it provides a fast, convenient way to stay informed of valuable resources on the Internet. This site is a must.

❏ **Webtime Stories**
http://www.kn.pacbell.com/wired/webtime/

An annotated collection of web sites for people who love children's literature.

Search Engines

❏ **100hot**
http://www.100hot.com/
A tracking of the 100 most frequented websites in various areas from business to health and fitness.

❏ **Academic Info**
http://www.academicinfo.net/
Academic Info is a subject directory of Internet resources tailored to a college and university audience. Each subject guide is an annotated listing of the best general Internet sites in the field, as well as a gateway to specialized and advanced research tools. On each page you may find links to online publications, language and study aids, reference materials, databases, archives, virtual libraries, tutorials or other educational materials.

❏ **Alexa**
http://www.alexa.com/
Alexa is a free advertising-supported Web navigation service. It works with your browser and accompanies you as you surf, providing useful information about the sites you are viewing and suggesting related sites.

❏ **AlltheWeb.com**
http://www.alltheweb.com/
"AlltheWeb indexes over 2.1 billion web pages, 118 million multimedia files, 132 million FTP files, two million MP3s, 15 million PDF files and supports 49 languages, making it one of the largest search engines available to search enthusiasts. AlltheWeb provides the freshest information because we update our index every 7 to 11 days and index up to 800 news stories per minute from 3,000 news sources."

❏ **Alta Vista Main Page**
http://www.altavista.digital.com/
According to the site, The evolving AltaVista search service is an invaluable tool for finding information on the Web. Recent successes in translation have made it possible for words, phrases, and even entire web sites to be translated into many different languages. Innovations like this have made our search service, the number one choice for millions of Internet users. Many utilities and other kinds of search capabilities are also available at this site.

❏ **Anzwers**
http://www.anzwers.com.au/cgi-bin/print_search.pl
Explore over 21,000 subjects.

❏ **APA PsychCrawler Search Engine**
http://www.psychcrawler.com/
PsychCrawler is a product of the American Psychological Association created to provide quick access to quality content in the field of psychology. This search engine currently indexes five organizational sites that have "substantial authoritative content in the area of psychology." PsychCrawler searches the Websites of the APA, the National Institute of Mental Health, the Substance Abuse and Mental Health Services Administration, the US Department of Health and Human Services, the Center for Mental Health Services, and the APA Help Center.

❏ **Ask Jeeves for Kids!**
http://www.ajkids.com/
Fun for adults too!

❏ **AT&T Toll-Free Internet Directory**
www.anywho.com

According to the site, this is a fast, FREE way to find sources for the products or services you need from Abdominal Supports to Zippers. . . Accountants to Zoos. . . Abrasives to Zinc anywhere in the country. There are more than 150,000 businesses and organizations listed here and ALL of them offer toll-free numbers for your convenience.

❏ **Beaucoup Search Engines**
http://www.beaucoup.com

❏ **collegeBOT**
http://www.collegenet.com/cbot/basic/index_html

Enter the keyword you're looking for and CollegeBOT will return links to education pages containing your keyword. Want to see Virtual Tours? Enter 'Virtual Tours' and click "Go".

❏ **Debriefing**
http://www.debriefing.com/

An effective metasearch engine.

❏ **Ditto.com — See the web**
http://ditto.com/

Ditto's visual search is easy, fun and fast.

❏ **Dogpile**
http://www.dogpile.com/

Results are a bit much to get through although worth exploring.

❏ **Ed-X: Online Education and Distance Learning Search Engine**
http://www.ed-x.com/

Ed-X.Com is a search engine and web resource for distance learning and online education with comprehensive information on over 20,000 online courses and degree programs from 700 online colleges worldwide. Use the Ed-X online education index below to locate online college courses or distance learning certificate and degree programs.

❏ **Education World(tm) — Education Topics**
http://db.education-world.com/perl/browse

Chock full of resources including lesson plans, educational site reviews, administrative issues, financial planning, and much more.

❏ **Electric Library Personal Edition**
http://www.elibrary.com/

Whether for work, school, or home, you'll have immediate and unlimited access to hundreds of full-text magazines and newspapers, along with newswires, books, transcripts and thousands of pictures and maps! Minimal cost for this service.

❏ **ERIC Digests**
http://www.ericfacility.net/ericdigests/index/

A search engine of full text ERIC digests.

❏ **Excite NetSearch**
http://www.excite.com/

❏ **Global Schoolhouse**
http://www.gsn.org/

The Global Schoolhouse Project was a technology demonstration project funded in part by the National Science Foundation. The project was designed to demonstrate the potential of high speed Internet connectivity in the public school classroom.

❏ **Google!**
http://www.google.com/
My personal favorite!

❏ **GoTo.com — Search Made Simple.**
http://www.goto.com/

GoTo.com, the new, simpler search engine which provides users with the fastest and easiest way to find the most relevant web sites on any topic.

❏ **Government search engine**
http://www.firstgov.gov/

Now called FirstGov, this site is the U.S. government's official web portal. Whatever you want or need from the U.S. government, it's here on FirstGov.gov. You'll find a rich treasure of online information, services and resources.

❏ **Graduate School Directories — Educational and School Counseling**
http://www.gradschools.com/listings/menus/edu_counsel_menu.html

A directory of graduate schools with a clickable map of the US.

❏ **HotBot**
http://www.hotbot.com/

❏ **InfoSeek**
http://www.infoseek.com/

Advanced search features allow you to search for a specific site, URL, title, or links to a page. No Boolean operators needed.

❏ **KidsClick! Web Search**
http://sunsite.berkeley.edu/KidsClick!/

KidsClick! was created by a group of librarians at the Ramapo Catskill Library System, as a logical step in addressing concerns about the role of public libraries in guiding their young users to valuable and age appropriate web sites.

❏ **Liszt**
http://www.liszt.com/

Find one or more of over 90,000 mailing lists.

❏ **LookSmart — exploring World**
http://www.looksmart.com/

Great directory with major categories and an easy to use design.

❏ **Lycos Pictures and Sounds**
http://multimedia.lycos.com/

A special search feature that lets you search for only sound files. This search engine allows you to use radio buttons to search for sound-related sites. You can also access the sound search engine via a drop-down box from Lycos main page.

❏ **Lycos: Your Personal Internet Guide**
http://www.lycos.com/

Currently the second most visited hub on the Internet, with more than 40 percent reach.

❏ **MapQuest!**
http://www.mapquest.com/

Find directions and print a map.

❏ **MetaCrawler**
http://www.metacrawler.com/

Great for searching multiple engines at once.

❏ **My Virtual Reference Desk**
http://www.refdesk.com/myency.html
Comprehensive!

❏ **ProFusion**
http://www.profusion.com/

For sophisticated researchers who know what they want.

❏ **Project Vote Smart — A Voter's Self-Defense System**
http://www.vote-smart.org/

Find the performance of over 13,000 political leaders.

❏ **Public Records from KnowX.com**
http://www.knowx.com/

KnowX.comTM provides comprehensive public records information at a consistently low price. KnowX.comTM public records databases contain millions of records, each compiled from official sources and updated regularly. Click here for KnowX.comTM standard prices. Most public records database searches are $0.50 during peak hours and FREE the rest of the day! (Peak Hours are from 11 a.m. to 6 p.m. EST, Monday through Friday.

❏ **Reference.COM Search**
http://www.reference.com/

Reference.COM makes it easy to find, browse, search, and participate in more than 150,000 newsgroups, mailing lists, and web forums.

❏ **Search Library of Congress Finding Aids**
http://lcweb2.loc.gov/faid/

For the Library of Congress.

❏ **SEARCH.COM**
http://search.com/

Also includes specialty searches in many categories.

❏ **Snap**
http://www.snap.com/

Brought to us by NBC.

❏ **Switchboard**
http://www.switchboard.com/

Anyone with a Web browser can look up the names, phone number and street addresses of friends, colleagues and businesses, typically in less than a second.

❏ **Symantec Security Response — Search and Expanded Threats Page**
http://www.symantec.com/avcenter/vinfodb.html

Search for viruses by keyword or category.

❏ **Teoma**
http://www.teoma.com/

Instead of ranking results based upon the sites with the most links leading to them, Teoma analyzes the Web as it is organically organized — in naturally-occurring communities that are about or related to the same subject — to determine which sites are most relevant.

❏ **The Argus Clearinghouse**
http://www.clearinghouse.net/

A selection of topical guides.

❏ **The List — The Definitive ISP Buyer's Guide**
http://thelist.internet.com/

Find Internet Service Providers virtually anywhere.

❏ **The Ultimate White Pages**
http://www.theultimates.com/white/

❏ **Tile.Net**
http://www.tile.net/

Comprehensive Internet reference site with free e-mail subscriptions.

❏ **TKM's EDUCATION WEB SEARCH**
http://alpha.tkm.mb.ca/education

Highly specific to educational sites.

❏ **VolunteerMatch**
http://www.volunteermatch.org/

Connecting volunteers with nearly 25,000 community service organizations around the U.S.

❏ **WhoWhere?!**
http://www.whowhere.lycos.com/

WhoWhere offers a variety of services that makes searching for people and businesses on the Internet a quick and easy process. Through a point-and-click interface, you simply type in a name, or portions of a name, and within seconds you will receive relevance-ranked responses to your queries. As a global communications directory, WhoWhere enables you to find, communicate and collaborate.

❏ **WWWomen.com! The Premier Search Directory for Women Online!**
http://www.wwwomen.com/

❏ **Yahoo**
http://www.yahoo.com/

A premier search engine uniquely categorized by humans.

❏ **Yahoo! People Search**
http://people.yahoo.com/

Search for e-mails and telephone numbers.

❏ **Yahooligans!**
http://www.yahooligans.com/

Kids only version of Yahoo.

❏ **Zip Code Lookup and Address Information**
http://www.usps.gov/ncsc/

Your letter carrier will love you.

Software

❏ **Citation Bibliographic and Research Note Data**
http://www.citationonline.net/

Citation is a bibliographic database system which installs on the Tools menu of MSWord 6.0c, 7, and now 97, as well as WordPerfect for Windows 6.0a, 6.1, 7, and 8 — so it is always available to you as you are writing. The program reports to support over 1000 publishing styles for footnotes/ endnotes, numbered references, and bibliographies, and provide you with one of the most powerful and easy to use custom report writers available. A free demonstration copy is available for download.

❏ **Cog & Psy Sci: Software**
http://www-psych.stanford.edu/cogsci/software.html

Brought to us from the good people at Stanford's psychology department.

❏ **Computers In Mental Health**
http://www.ex.ac.uk/cimh/welcome.htm

These pages list software items applicable to mental health. Using a frame-capable browser, topics can be selected from the list of keywords on the left to give links to descriptions of specific products.

❏ **Copernic Agent 6.0**
http://www.copernic.com/desktop/products/agent/download.html

Copernic Agent 6.0 is one of the more user-friendly and powerful ones available. Copernic Agent 6.0 Basic is a free Web-search engine that has the capability to query over 90 search engines grouped into categories.

❏ **Ebase**
http://www.ebase.org/

ebase 2.0 is powerful and affordable (free) database software created by TechRocks, a 501(c)(3) nonprofit organization, for other nonprofits.

❏ **Educast: The Education News Service for Teachers & Administrators**
http://www.educast.com/

Unlike conventional screen savers, Educast displays valuable news and information, and connects you to first-rate Internet sites with the click of a mouse. Click on the Key Features button to learn about our quality content and providers.

❏ **ELIZA**
http://www-ai.ijs.si/eliza/eliza.html

ELIZA — a friend you could never have before. Use the original attempt at virtual counseling.

❏ **FerretSoft**
http://www.ferretsoft.com/netferret

Excellent web search software, one of which is free (WebFerret) and highly useful.

❏ **File Mine**
http://www.filemine.com/

Another shareware and freeware warehouse.

❏ **Freeware Arena — The best and most useful freeware for Windows**
http://www.freewarearena.com

Free, free, free!

❏ **Incredimail**
http://www.incredimail.com

IncrediMail is an advanced, feature-rich FREE e-mail program that offers you an unprecedented interactive experience. Unique multimedia features will enable you to tailor your e-mail experience so that it fits your mood and personality. Visual effects will entertain your every sense.

❏ **inResonance Advocate**
http://www.inresonance.com/iRsolutions/info_advocate.htm

A digital cumulative folder for college guidance counselors. It is an easy-to-use, powerful tool that replaces thick, paper files and dramatically reduces paper shuffling. Advocate is built using FileMaker Pro and is multi-user, cross platform and network capable. A must see!

❏ **Jans Freeware Collection**
http://jansfreeware.com/

❏ **Jumbo!**
http://www.jumbo.com/

Another great software site.

❏ **Melms e-mail list management**
http://www.mywebattack.com/gnomeapp.php?id=105759

MELMS is a basic e-mail list management program to manage an unlimited number of e-mail lists with up to 30,000 e-mail addresses each. The program can automatically add e-mail addresses to the list by checking your POP3 account. You can also import from the clipboard or add individual e-mails manually. Additional features include duplicate checking, signature support and logging.

❏ **Microsoft Office 3rd Party Downloads**
http://office.microsoft.com/downloads/ouvp.aspx

❏ **Microsoft: Works 6.0 Converter**
http://office.microsoft.com/downloads/2002/wp6rtf.aspx

The Works 6.0 Converter converts word processor documents created in Microsoft Works 6.0 to Microsoft Word and other versions of Works. Specifically, this converter works with Works 2000, 4.5, and 4.x, and Word 2002, 2000, and 97 on machines running Microsoft Windows 98, 2000 Professional, Millennium Edition, and XP.

❏ **NetMeeting**
http://www.microsoft.com/windows/
netmeeting/

NetMeeting is a FREE product that provides a conferencing solution for the Internet and corporate intranet. Powerful features let you communicate with both audio and video, collaborate on virtually any Windows-based application, exchange graphics on an electronic whiteboard, transfer files, use the text-based chat program, and much more. Using your PC and the Internet, you can now hold face-to-face conversations with friends and family around the world, and it won't cost a fortune to do so! Because NetMeeting works with any video capture card or camera that supports Video for Windows, you can choose from a wide range of video equipment.

❏ **NewFreeware.com: Software archive**
http://www.newfreeware.com/

Another very good freeware collection — this one is very big.

❏ **NoBuck$ Freeware Connection**
http://www.nobucksfreeware.com/
home.htm

Pretty good collection of freeware.

❏ **Opera**
http://www.opera.com

The Opera Web browser application features several novel features, such as keyboard shortcuts, zooming ability, integrated searches, and mouse gestures.

❏ **PC Educational**
http://www.sharewarejunkies.com/
winedu.htm

❏ **PictureStories**
http://www.instituteofthefuture.org/
picturestories

PictureStories lets you make little webpages of stories you write where some of the words are replaced with images (called a "rebus"). What makes PictureStories cool is that the images are dynamically pulled from popular web-based image search engines (like Yahoo).

❏ **Power Searcher**
http://www.mywebattack.com/
gnomeapp.php?id=105858

Power Searcher is an advanced file search and print utility that can find files by full or partial name, size, date, attributes, or contents. You can specify whether you want to find just files, just folders, or both.

❏ **PowerPoint Templates**
http://www.soniacoleman.com/
Templates.htm

FREE — 208 PowerPoint template kits.

❏ **Qmail**
http://www.mywebattack.com/
gnomeapp.php?id=105695

QMailer is a tool for sending personalized e-mail to subscribers. It can automatically process subscription requests and unsubscribe requests that are sent from a web site form or by e-mail. The program comes with an Internet plugin (POP3) and an Outlook plugin that interacts with MS Outlook.

❏ **Schoolhouse Technologies — Worksheet Factory**
http://www.schoolhousetech.com/
dlwordsearch.html

A free program designed to help you quickly and easily create professional looking word search puzzles to provide your students with the extra vocabulary and spelling practice they need in a format that they find very enjoyable.

❏ **Shareware Psychological Consultation**
http://www.netpsych.com/share/

An example of psychological consultation over the Net.

❏ **SHAREWARE.COM**
http://www.shareware.com/

Another contender.

❏ **Software for Schools and Nonprofits.**
http://www.npsoft.org/

Store focusing on discounted software for schools and non-profits.

❏ **SourceForge.net: Project Info — Elephant Memory**
http://sourceforge.net/projects/reminder/

System tray-based event reminder, with configuration panel. Create quick and simple events and when the time comes, a reminder window will pop-up, giving you the ability to snooze or delete the event.

❏ **Superior Search — The Advanced Search Tool for PCs and Networks**
http://www.superiorsearch.com/

Superior Search is a tool that makes it much easier for Windows users to handle archived files. Superior Search offers a variety of format- and language-independent document search functions that help you find the desired information as quickly as possible. This tool allows high-speed text searches in large numbers of files.

❏ **The Freebie Zone's Main menu page**
http://www.wizardry-design.com/souvenir.shtml

Free animation and background design.

❏ **Therascribe**
http://www.wiley.com/legacy/products/subject/psychology/therascribe/

A software program called Therascribe assist a counselor in developing Individual Educational Programs (IEPs) and conducting functional assessments. The treatment planning program helps you choose from thousands of pre-written treatment statements to help you create comprehensive treatment plans and detailed progress notes. The program recommends appropriate combinations of behavioral definitions, long-term goals, short-term objectives, and therapeutic interventions for all major DSM-IV diagnoses. It tracks client demographic data, mental status and prognosis, treatment modality, discharge criteria, and provider credentials; it also provides treatment outcome tracking with 3-D graphing

❏ **ThinkWave: Education Software for Teachers**
http://www.thinkwave.com/

A gradebook program.

❏ **TimeGen Time Tracking Software**
http://www.brianhansen.net/timegen/

TimeGen is a time tracking utility that is designed to help you keep track of the time you've spent on various tasks and projects throughout the day. You add projects or tasks to TimeGen and click between them as you work on different things. TimeGen keeps a running total of all time spent on specific projects and displays accumulated time in the format you specify.

❏ **Totwise**
http://www.totwise.com/

Totwise is an easy to use, full-featured management and billing program specially designed for programs such as preschools, day care centers, sports leagues, scouting programs, and other youth oriented programs. It is fully networkable among up to 250 users and runs on Windows 98 through XP and Macintosh 8.6 through 10.2 computers, even in a mixed environment. This is a free program for 100 or less number of children.

❏ **TUCOWS**
http://www.tucows.com/

TUCOWS is your place on the Web to access the latest and greatest Windows 95/ 98, Windows NT, Windows 3.1 and Macintosh Internet Software, performance rated and checked for viruses.

❏ **Walsh's Classroom Sociometrics**
http://www.classroomsociometrics.com/

Sociometry employs sociograms, scatter charts, and bar graphs to depict the social climate of a classroom.

❏ **WinSite**
http://www.winsite.com/

Billed as the planet's largest software archive for Windows shareware and trialware on the Internet.

❏ **ZDNet Software Library**
http://www.zdnet.com/swlib/

My all-time favorite!

Special Education

❏ **ADDHELP — Attention Deficit Disorder**
http://www.addhelp.com/home.html

A site for parents and teachers.

❏ **Deaf World Web**
http://dww.deafworldweb.org/

News, an ASL dictionary, e-mail directory, and much, much, more...

❏ **Gifted Children Monthly**
http://www.gifted-children.com/

Gifted-Children.com is a networking and information medium dedicated to making a difference in the pursuit of educational excellence for children of special talents and abilities.

❏ **Hoagies' Gifted Education Page**
http://www.hoagiesgifted.org/

A comprehensive resource guide for education of gifted children. It's full of great information, with links to the most complete, easiest to use, resources on nearly every aspect of gifted education available on the Internet, plus lots of annotations and first hand information provided by parents facing the same challenges that you are facing.

❏ **National Center to Improve Practice in Special Education**
http://www2.edc.org/NCIP/

NCIPnet houses a series of facilitated discussion conferences focusing on technology and special education. NCIPnet enables you to communicate with other members of NCIPnet—technology coordinators, staff developers, teachers, specialists, clinicians, administrators, university faculty, parents, advocates, and consumers—who share a common desire to improve the use of technology with students who have disabilities.

❏ **National Information Center for Children and Youth with Disabilities**
http://www.nichcy.org/

NICHCY is the national information and referral center that provides information on disabilities and disability-related issues for families, educators, and other professionals. Our special focus is children and youth (birth to age 22).

❏ **NCWD/Youth**
http://www.ncwd-youth.info/

NCWD/Youth is one of two technical assistance centers funded by the US Department of Labor to assist the workforce development community address issues affecting the employment of people with disabilities.

❏ **SERI — Special Education Resources on the Internet**
http://seriweb.com/

Special Education Resources on the Internet (SERI) is a collection of Internet accessible information resources of interest to those involved in the fields related to Special Education. This collection exists in order to make on-line Special Education resources more easily and readily available in one location.

❏ **Special Education, Learning Disabilities Resources, Services, Professionals**
http://www.iser.com/

ISER helps parents find local special education professionals to help with learning disabilities and attention deficit disorder assessment, therapy, advocacy, and other special needs.

❏ **The Federal Resource Center for Special Education**
http://www.dssc.org/frc/

The FRC is a special education technical assistance project funded by the U.S. Department of Education's Office of Special Education and Rehabilitative Services, and is part of the Regional Resource and Federal Centers Network.

❏ **The LD OnLine Home Page**
http://www.ldonline.org/

As described by the site, an interactive guide to learning disabilities for parents, teachers, and children.

❏ **UVa Special Education Web Site**
http://curry.edschool.virginia.edu/go/specialed/

Special Education Resources from the Curry School of Education at the University of Virginia.

Special Issues

- **11 Ways to Keep Your New Year's Resolution to Quit Smoking**
  http://www.quitsmoking.com/tips.htm

- **A Place for Us...Oppositional Defiant Disorder Support Group**
  http://www.conductdisorders.com/
  Related articles, books, treatment programs and more.

- **depressedteens.com**
  http://www.depressedteens.com/indexfl.html
  An educational site dedicated to help teenagers and their parents and educators understand the signs and symptoms of teenage depression and provide resources for those ready to reach out and get the help they need.

- **Dr. Kimberly Young — The Center for On-line Addiction**
  http://netaddiction.com/
  Much about Net addiction from a leader in the field.

- **Eating Disorder Referral and Information Website**
  http://www.edreferral.com/
  This site provides information and treatment resources for all forms of eating disorders.

- **Guide to Gay and Lesbian Resources**
  http://www.lib.uchicago.edu/e/su/gaylesb/glguide.html
  Compiled by Frank Conaway, Sebastian Hierl, and Sem C. Sutter at the University of Chicago Library, this thorough bibliography offers an excellent guide to the voluminous amount of scholarly work on gay and lesbian themes.

- **Harassment-Free Hallways: How to Stop Sexual Harassment in Schools**
  http://www.aauw.org/7000/ef/harass
  This FREE guide reflects dozens of collective years of work that experts have conducted on the issue. AAUW hopes this informative, concise, and action-oriented resource will help you create harassment-free schools.

- **Internet Addiction — Dr. GROHOL's Mental Health Page — Online Addiction**
  http://psychcentral.com/netaddiction/
  A nice article by Dr. John M. Grohol.

- **Let Their Voices Be Heard**
  http://wbgu.org/grief/sidey.html
  Helping children with grief.

- **Lightning Strike Pet-Loss Support Page**
  http://www.lightning-strike.com/
  Offering a "cybershoulder" for grieving pet owners.

- **Maine Project Against Bullying**
  http://lincoln.midcoast.com/~wps/against/bullying.html
  Information about the project and valuable resources.

- **National Association of Anorexia Nervosa and Associated Disorders**
  http://www.anad.org/
  The oldest national non-profit organization helping eating disorder victims and their families. In addition to its free hotline counseling, ANAD operates an international network of support groups for sufferers and families, and offers referrals to health care professionals, who treat eating disorders.

- **Poverty, AIDS and Children's Schooling: A Targeting Dilemma**
  http://econ.worldbank.org/files/18719_wps2885.pdf
  Written by Martha Ainsworth and Deon Filmer of the World Bank, this 44-page working paper examines the relationship between orphan status, household wealth, and child school enrollment.

❏ **Southeastern Connecticut Gang Activities Group**
http://www.segag.org/

❏ **The Bipolar Child — A book about Early-Onset Bipolar Disorder**
http://www.bipolarchild.com/
Supports the book although includes lots of helpful tools too.

❏ **The Compassionate Friends — Grief support after the death of a child**
http://www.compassionatefriends.org/
The Compassionate Friends is a national nonprofit, self-help support organization which offers friendship and understanding to families who are grieving the death of a child of any age, from any cause. There is no religious affiliation. There are no membership fees or dues, and all bereaved family members are welcome.

❏ **Youth Suicide Prevention Programs (full text)**
http://aepo-xdv-www.epo.cdc.gov/wonder/prevguid/p0000024/p0000024.asp
Highly comprehensive.

Special Topics

❏ **Anxiety Disorders Education Program**
http://www.nimh.nih.gov/anxiety/
A national education campaign developed by the National Institute of Mental Health (NIMH) to increase awareness among the public and health care professionals that anxiety disorders are real medical illnesses that can be effectively diagnosed and treated.

❏ **BIPOLAR DISORDER**
http://www.nimh.nih.gov/publicat/bipolar.htm
Information about Bipolar disorder from the National Institute of Mental Health.

❏ **CDC National AIDS Clearinghouse**
http://www.cdcnac.org/
Operated by the CDC National Prevention Information Network, AIDS Clearinghouse's (NAC) services are designed to facilitate the sharing of HIV/AIDS, STD and TB resources and information. This site contains many publications and helpful links (e.g., informational bout HIV/AIDS, STD, TB, Databases, Ordering Procedures for Free Publications, a Poster Gallery, PSA's for Youth, and Online Tutorials, and).

❏ **Counseling and Supervision Via the WWW/Internet**
http://osu.orst.edu/instruct/coun510/ethics/coun.htm
The information presented is adapted from both the American Counseling Association (ACA), American Psychological Association (APA), and Oregon State University ethical standards of practice.

❏ **Dr. Ivan's Depression Central**
http://www.psycom.net/depression.central.html
This site is a clearing house for information on all types of depressive disorders and on the most effective treatments for individuals suffering from Major Depression, Manic-Depression (Bipolar Disorder), Cyclothymia, Dysthymia and other mood disorders.

❏ **Emotional Intelligence (EQ)**
http://eqi.org/

This site contains lots of practical information on Emotional Intelligence (EQ), among other things.

❏ **Exploratorium- ExploraNet**
http://www.exploratorium.edu/

The Exploratorium is a museum of science, art, and human perception with over 500 interactive "hands on" exhibits.

❏ **Fast Food Facts — Interactive Food Finder**
http://www.olen.com/food

Includes nutritional information for more than 1,000 fast-food items.

❏ **FMF — 911 For Women**
http://www.feminist.org/911/
1_supprt.html

Created by the Feminist Majority Foundation, this site offers feminist and women related resources.

❏ **Get Your ANGRIES Out**
http://members.aol.com/AngriesOut/

Lessons in conflict resolution designed for children, adults and families.

❏ **Girl Power!**
http://www.health.org/gpower

The national public education campaign sponsored by the Department of the Health and Human Services to help encourage and empower 9- to 14- year old girls to make the most of their lives.

❏ **GriefNet**
http://www.griefnet.org/

GriefNet.org is an Internet community of persons dealing with grief, death, and major loss.

❏ **Helping Children Cope with Disaster**
http://www.sarbc.org/ciskid1.html
Helpful info and links.

❏ **HIV InSite**
http://hivinsite.ucsf.edu/

HIV InSite is a project of the University of California San Francisco AIDS Program at San Francisco General Hospital, and the UCSF Center for AIDS Prevention Studies, projects of the UCSF AIDS Research Institute. This site provides a great deal of information about prevention, social issues, news, and medical info. Also available is a biweekly (free) newsletter and an interactive expert advice feature.

❏ **It Takes All Kinds Discussions**
http://www.pbs.org/cgi-bin/pov/
learn_discuss/public/discuss.cgi

❏ **Library — Internet Reference Collection — Loss, Death & Grief**
http://www.santarosa.edu/library/Refs/
death.shtml

A site of "The best places to visit to learn about coping with grief, and grief counseling resources."

❏ **Lisa Taylor Austin's Web Page on Gangs**
http://www.gangcolors.com/

Links include Professional Biography , Interviews, Letter from a Gang Banger, Gang Graffiti, Lecture & Presentation Offerings, Related Links , Manual and Tapes for Purchase, Bookstore, and Attorney Assistance.

❏ **National Center for Bilingual Education**
http://www.ncbe.gwu.edu/

The National Clearinghouse for Bilingual Education (NCBE) is funded by the U.S. Department of Education's Office of Bilingual Education and Minority Languages Affairs (OBEMLA) to collect, analyze, and disseminate information relating to the effective education of linguistically and culturally diverse learners in the U.S. NCBE provides information through its World Wide Web server and produces a weekly news bulletin, Newsline, and manages a topical electronic discussion group, NCBE Roundtable.

❏ **Pat McClendon's Clinical Social Work Page**

http://www.ClinicalSocialWork.com/

Highly informative and resourceful.

❏ **Positive Discipline**

http://www.empoweringpeople.com/

Articles, a free newsletter, books, training, and site search engine.

❏ **Radiance: The Magazine For Large Women**

http://www.radiancemagazine.com/

An upbeat, positive magazine about body acceptance with a kids section.

❏ **Rape- Let's Stop It**

http://katesfeminist.info/rape/

These pages are an index of resources on the Web about rape.

❏ **RealAudio about Dealing with Death from NPR**

http://www.npr.org/programs/death/971103.death.html

Roundtable Discussion on End of Life Issues taped on Monday November 3rd on All Things Considered.

❏ **Resources and Information on Alcohol, Tobacco and Other Drugs**

http://www.arf.org/isd/info.html

Links to a library catalogue, bibliographies, audio-visuals, public information materials, statistics, publications, frequently asked questions, and other links.

❏ **School Psychology Resources Online — Sandra Steingart, Ph.D.**

http://www.bcpl.net/~sandyste/school_psych.html

This site contains information about learning disabilities, ADHD, gifted, autism, adolescence, parenting, psychological assessment, classroom management, special education, k-12, mental health, reading, research, and more. Users can reprint valuable handouts for parents and teachers.

❏ **Sexual harassment case profiles**

http://www.inform.umd.edu/EdRes/Topic/WomensStudies/GenderIssues/SexualHarassment/

This is a high quality women's studies database.

❏ **Sexual Harassment Guidance [OCR]**

http://www.ed.gov/legislation/FedRegister/announcements/1997-1/031397b.html

Office of Civil Rights document titled Sexual Harassment Guidance: Harassment of Students by School Employees, Other Students, or Third Parties

❏ **Shape Up America!**

http://www.shapeup.org/

This website is designed to provide you with the latest information about safe weight management, healthy eating, and physical fitness.

❏ **Suggestions for Teachers and School Counselors**

http://www.compassionatefriends.com/teachers.htm

Dealing with grief and bereavement.

❏ **Suicide Information & Education Center (SIEC)**

http://www.siec.ca/

This simple, but resourceful page is searchable and contains links to information resources, a library, Frequently Asked Questions (FAQ), Training, and Helpful Crisis Support.

❏ **The Body: AIDS Treatment News**

http://www.thebody.com/atn/atnpage.html

Information about "reports on experimental and standard treatments, especially those available now."

❏ **The WholeFamily Center — Kid-Teen Center**
http://www.wholefamily.com

Winner of many awards, this highly decorated site is dedicated to healthy living among parents, couples, and teens. Users may "hang out" in the teen center and join the on-line family drama, "talk" with teens from next door to around the world. The site also has on-line teen advisor; a "raising" your parents section, Family Workout Room; Evaluation Center to identify the problems areas and strengths in your relationships with friends and family; reference center, chat rooms, free newsletter, and much more.

❏ **Trauma Info Pages**
http://www.trauma-pages.com/

The Trauma Info Pages focus primarily on emotional trauma and traumatic stress, including PTSD (Post-traumatic Stress Disorder), whether following individual traumatic experience(s) or a large-scale disaster.

❏ **US Department of Education Technology Initiatives**
http://www.ed.gov/Technology/

Links to resources, publications, and more.

❏ **Violence in Schools Initiative**
http://europa.eu.int/en/comm/dg22/violence/home.html

This initiative aims at reinforcing European co-operation on issues related to safety at school and violence. Since this initiative is envisaged for an initial two year period, the extent of cooperation will be limited and will address in particular the exchange of information and experiences through participation in joint actions.

❏ **Virtual Presentation Assistant**
http://www.ukans.edu/cwis/units/coms2/vpa/vpa.htm

The Virtual Presentation Assistant is an online tutorial for improving your public speaking skills.

❏ **Youth Violence**
http://eric-web.tc.columbia.edu/pathways/youth_violence/

Within this guide, there are research studies, program and project overviews, and links to agencies addressing youth violence. This site is part of the ERIC Clearinghouse on Urban Education.

Tools

❏ **101 Web Templates**
http://www.101templates.com/

101Templates.com offers 700+ professional web design templates, web templates, web page templates, website templates Photoshop and frontpage templates with royalty free web template graphics.

❏ **AlcoholEdu**
http://www.alcoholedu.com/

Has a link to a tool which calculates one's blood alcohol level.

❏ **All Bookstores**
http://www.allbookstores.com/

At AllBookstores.com, we help you find the lowest book prices on new and used books by comparing prices at more than 2 dozen online bookstores.

❏ **Behavior Rubric Maker**
http://teachers.teach-nology.com/web_tools/rubrics/behavior/

❏ **Bloglet**
http://www.bloglet.com/

Bloglet is a service that allows your readers to subscribe to your site via e-mail. Once your readers sign up, they will receive a daily e-mail with a summary of your posts from that day.

❏ **BrainPOP**
http://www.brainpop.com/

BrainPOP is a producer of educational animated movies for K-12. The company creates original animated movies to explain concepts in a voice and visual style that is accessible, educational and entertaining for both children and adults. Check out the ones already available online.

❏ **Bravenet.com Webmaster Resources Website**
http://www.bravenet.com/

Tons of free tools and resources to help you build your web page.

❏ **Classroom Materials Makers**
http://teachers.teach-nology.com/web_tools/materials/

Make classroom materials by filling out a simple form. The materials are made instantly and can be printed directly from your computer.

❏ **Click-N-Type**
http://members.ac.net/lakerat/cnt/

Click-N-Type is an on-screen full featured virtual keyboard designed for anyone who needs help using a physical keyboard with special consideration for the severely handicapped.

❏ **Create Adobe PDF Online**
http://createpdf.adobe.com/

Adobe's PDF file format is still the best way to share files exactly the way you intended them to appear. But if you need to make only the occasional PDF, don't spend $250 for Adobe Acrobat. Instead, upload your documents and images and try the online PDF creator. Your first five conversions are free.

❏ **Create Mailto URLs**
http://developer.netscape.com/viewsource/husted_mailto/mailtoApp.html

Very useful tool for creating links which generate sophisticated e-mails.

❏ **Digital Literacy Checklist**
http://courses.washington.edu/hs590a/modules/69/diglit/diglit.htm

Digital literacy is "the ability to understand and use information in multiple formats from a wide range of sources when it is presented via computers" This page helps you evaluate your level of digital literacy.

❏ **ePALS Classroom Exchange**
http://www.epals.com

ePALS has thousands of classroom profiles bringing people in hundreds of countries together as cross-cultural learning partners and friends.

❏ **Evite**
http://www.evite.com

Make sure everybody knows about your next get-together by sending an electronic invitation. Simply log on to Evite, personalize an invitation with details and directions, and broadcast the message to all your friends or co-workers. Best of all, Evite lets you track who has accepted or declined and who's bringing the desert.

❏ **Extra javascript add ins for Frontpage 2000,2002**
http://www.extrafrontpage.com/extrajs.htm

❏ **Fandango: Buy movie tickets online**
http://www.fandango.com

❏ **FlamingText.com: Free online tool for generating custom webpage graphics and ani**
http://www.flamingtext.com

See your name in flames and more!

❏ **Fontscape**
http://www.fontscape.com/

The Fontscape font directory is designed to help you find the ideal typeface for your application, whether it's a publishing project, graphic design, logo, or simply a font for your document. It includes fonts from over a hundred publishers, including Adobe, Agfa-Monotype, Berthold, Bitstream, Elsner+Flake, FontFont, ITC, Letraset, Linotype, P22, URW++, and many smaller foundries.

❏ **Free, printable, greeting cards, calendars, pictures**
http://www.printfree.com/

❏ **FreeLists — Free, No-hassle Mailing Lists**
http://www.freelists.org

"FreeLists provides the Internet community with Free, no-hassle, high-quality mailing lists. We don't use advertisements and we don't charge for higher-than-a-certain-volume lists. That means you don't have to worry about too many people signing up, nor the amount of traffic on your list(s). FreeLists is about just getting the message across to your subscribers."

❏ **Get Involved — Media Campaign**
http://www.mediacampaign.org/getinvolved

Message Maker enables users to create stickers, magnets, iron-on transfers, transparencies, notecards, and other media to craft unique messages identifying influences acting against drug use, i.e., "anti-drugs." Examples of anti-drug messages involving pets, clubs (activities), and sports are provided. Also available on the same site — downloadable media kits.

❏ **Group Work Checklist**
http://pblchecklist.4teachers.org/view.php3?id=47472

A short but useful checklist for evaluating how effectively kids work together in groups.

❏ **HorizonLive**
http://www.horizonlive.com

HorizonLive enables educational institutions, government agencies, and corporations to conduct effective, real-time, interactive web-based communications over intranets or the Internet, regardless of geographic location, bandwidth, operating system, or physical disability.

❏ **Html Gear**
http://htmlgear.lycos.com/

Enhance your website with these free interactive tools.

❏ **Hypnosoft**
http://www.hypnosoft.com

The world's first custom, talking computer hypnosis. Now, you can easily create the perfect hypnosis to fit your exact needs and preferences — any topic, any imagery! Then, have it sent to any e-mail address, your own or some else's (for a fabulous gift).

❏ **Mollyguard Events**
http://www.mollyguard.com/events2/

Collect event registration fees online with Mollyguard.

❏ **MyBookmarks.com**
http://mybookmarks.com/

MyBookmarks is a free Internet service that allows you to keep your browser bookmarks and favorites online so you can access them from anywhere.

❏ **myImager.com**
http://myimager.com/

Upload or call images from anywhere on the web and edit them freely with the dozens of tools and filters.

❏ **PayPal**
https://www.paypal.com/

Accept credit cards online.

❏ **PiNet — The Landmark Project**
http://pinetlibrary.com/

At the base of PiNet is a powerful bookmark managing system that is totally web based, which means that when you add a bookmark to your PiNet Library at school, it will be waiting for you at home.

❏ **PPTools — Power tools for PowerPoint**
http://www.rdpslides.com/pptools/

PowerTools for PowerPoint power users.

❏ **ProTeacher! Classroom management ideas for elementary school teachers in grades**
http://www.proteacher.com

Lots of links and resources.

❏ **Random.org — True Random Number Service**
http://www.random.org/

Random.org offers true random numbers to anyone on the Internet. If you want to know how the numbers are made and what it is that makes them true, read the introduction to randomness and random numbers.

❏ **RhymeZone**
http://rhymezone.com/

Type in a word below to find its rhymes, synonyms, definitions, and more.

❏ **School District Finance Peer Search**
http://nces.ed.gov/edfin/search/search_intro.asp

This search tool on the NCES website lets you compare the finances of one school district with its peers. Peer districts are districts which share similarities among these characteristics: total students; student/teacher ratio; Percent Children in Poverty; District Type; and Locale Code.

❏ **Smart Translator**
http://igspot.ig.com.br/lucianosiqueira/smart/

Small, fast and simple Internet based translation software. And it's FREEWARE! Smart Translator stays at the system tray and with a simple mouse click you can translate to/from English and French, German, Italian, Spanish, Portuguese or Russian.

❏ **Teacher Tools — by Teachers for Teachers**
http://www.teachertools.org

This is a large collection of forms, information, packets and letters needed by teachers. They are available to download for your convenience. Save yourself some time with these

❏ **Test Junkie**
http://www.queendom.com

All kinds of tests!

❏ **The International Salary Calculator**
http://www2.homefair.com/calc/
salcalc.html

You never know ... Use this calculator to compare the cost of living in hundreds of U.S. and international cities. On this page, you select origin and destination countries. If you select USA, then also select states—otherwise ignore the state selection. On the next page, you select specific cities. The third page returns your answer.

❏ **The Mail Archive**
http://www.mail-archive.com/lists.html

The Mail Archive automatically detects when it receives mail from a new list. During normal operation, e-mail is archived shortly after it is received. In many cases, the new list will show up within a few hours. Sometimes, if there are enormous amounts of mail flying about, it can take much longer (over a day!) for messages to appear on the site. The new list will become searchable within one week.

❏ **The Official U.S. Time**
http://www.time.gov/

This site displays the official time for all zones in the U. S. Using a Java-enabled browser, it continuously updates the time and claims to be accurate to within several tenths of a second (depending on your connection). It also offers a file download that synchronizes your PC's clock to that of the National Institute of Standards and Technology (NIST).

❏ **Timer StopWatch**
http://clte.asu.edu/active/StopWatch.swf

Set the minutes and seconds and click go! (requires flash plugin at www.macromedia.com)

❏ **Toolbox: Technology for Mild Disabilities**
http://www.ed.sc.edu/caw/
toolboxvendors.html

❏ **votations**
http://www.votations.com/

FREE professional web and e-mail based polls, surveys and targeted newsletter tools and hosting solutions.

❏ **WebEnalysis**
http://www.webenalysis.com/

WebEnalysis offers free web site tools such as free online polls and free online greeting cards.

❏ **Webmaster Web Site Tools**
http://www.webmastersites.com/tools/
tools.shtml

Lots of them too!

❏ **Your Mailinglist Provider**
http://www.yourmailinglistprovider.com/

YourMailinglistProvider offers you a free, professional yet easy-to-use mailinglist to set up a newsletter for your site!

CHAPTER EIGHT

Internet Glossary

The prolification of computer and network technology has made a ubiquitous impact on our culture and way of life to the extent that those involved with technology might see themselves as part of a subculture. As with any culture, the technology subculture, or technoculture, uses distinctive terminology or language that must be learned to effectively conceptualize, communicate, and practice rituals and norms of the culture. Similar to a beginning counseling student who must first learn the language of various theoretical constructs to more successfully apply them, counseling students must also learn and understand the language of technology. "Geekspeak," as such a language is affectionately called, allows counselors to apply knowledge of technological processes towards developing requisite skills.

Geekspeak encompasses distinctive words, and especially acronyms, (e.g., FTP, FAQ, DNS, MPEG, HTML, URL, PPP, POP3, and ASCII to name a very few) which represent certain computer and network objects and procedures. Speaking fluent Geekspeak means that a counselor must also learn and understand the jargon of the technoculture. For instance, consider the following Geekspeak excerpts and their translations:

Geekspeak: Because the file is 22 megs and won't get past his firewall, I'll have to use the sneakernet.

Translation: Because a computer file is too large (22 megabytes) and will not travel past a recipient's security measures, the sender of the file will have to resort to transporting the data by carrying physical media such as diskettes from one computer to another, instead of transferring the data over a computer network.

Geekspeak: The counseling theories channel had a flame war after a newbie lurker posted without first reading the FAQ.

Translation: The user in this case is a chat room newcomer who is seen as someone who regularly reads the group's postings although either never or infrequently contributes. During an Internet chat discussion dedicated to counseling theories, he/she posted a question or request for information that has already been frequently addressed over the group's communication history. The information is considered common knowledge and disruptive to the group's current focus. If the user would have first consulted the group's frequently asked questions (FAQ) file as common Internet etiquette calls for, he/she would have been a more highly informed and constructive participant. Consequently, the post began an acrimonious dispute among members of the group.

So as to make this glossary useful and comprehensive, I augmented this list which the best and most laconic definitions from several sources which included Education World Internet Glossary (www.education-world.com), Squareonetech (www.Squareonetech.com), Microsoft (www.microsoft.com), Webopedia (www.webopedia.com) and (http://www.icactive.com/_internetglossary.html):

Acceptable Use Policy. A statement of the procedures, rights and responsibilities of a user of a technology solution and any disciplinary procedures that will be enforced for misuse of the technology.

Bandwidth. A measurement of a network's transmission speed, how much data a network can transfer in a given amount of time.

Baud rate. The number of transitions per second made by a modem.

Bitnet. An education and research network that makes up part of the Internet, mainly used for e-mail & listservs.

Bits per second (BPS). Measurement of the data transmission for a modem or network.

Bookmark. The process of saving a URL in your Web browser. Allows the user to return to a particular site or entry by making a record of it.

Bounced. When an e-mail message is returned to sender due to a failure to deliver, the message has been "bounced".

Browser. Software that lets you locate, view, and retrieve information on the World Wide Web using a graphical user interface or GUI.

BTW. Abbreviation for "By the Way" used in e-mail, newsgroup, and chat communication.

Bug. A glitch that keeps a software program from being able to perform all of its capabilities or that affects its ability to function.

Bulletin board system. A service dedicated to a specific topic where users post messages that are read by others. It is a computer or computers that offer dial-in communication which offers users the ability to send e-mail, use news-groups, and sometimes access the Internet. For example, see www.schoolcounselor.com/bbs

Byte. The amount of memory space needed to store one number, letter, or symbol in a computer.

CD-ROM (compact disc-read only memory). A round silver colored plastic disk that comes with massive amounts of information embedded and ready to be used. Unlike diskettes, CD-ROM disks can be read by any type of computer with a CD-ROM drive.

Chat. To communicate in real-time through the Internet. When you chat with someone, the typed words appear on a "shared" screen.

Client-server. Two computer systems linked by a network or modem connection where the client computer uses resources by sending requests to the server computer.

Compressed files. Most Internet files are reduced in size to make transfer easier and faster. Programs may be uncompressed by simply launching them or may require other software such as PKUNZIP (www.winzip.com) after they are transferred.

Connect time. The duration of time a computer is connected to a telecommunications service.

Database. A collection of information stored oftentimes in a computerized format. Examples: library catalogs, school records, search engines, and financial data.

Dial-up connection. Connecting to an Internet service provider through a modem and telephone line, typically a Point-to-Point Protocol (PPP) connection.

Disk. A round plastic magnetic device on which computer programs and data are saved. there are three main types of disks: hard disks (maintained inside the computer usually indicated by c:), diskettes (a.k.a. floppy disks usually indicated by a:), and compact disks (see CD-ROM, usually indicated by d: or e:).

DNS. Abbreviation for Domain Name System. A distributed client-server database system which links domain names with their numerical IP addresses.

Domain name. The name of a computer or server on the Internet in the form of a string of names or numbers, separated by periods.

Download. The transfer a file or files from a remote computer to the user's computer.

Electronic mail (E-mail). A letter or memo sent to a person or group electronically on the Internet; messages are stored on a computer until the receiver accesses the system and reads the message.

E-mail address. A user's electronic mailbox name or address, needed for linking the sender of e-mail and the recipient.

Ethical standards. Guidelines for the appropriate use of technology solutions and the maintenance of privacy of the contents of the system. These are generally specified in an Acceptable Use Policy, particularly where there is concern about the security of the system or the availability of objectionable materials obtained throughout the system. Counselors should also refer to their designated professional ethical documents (e.g., American School Counselor Association, www.schoolcounselor.org) for other ethical guidelines related to the use of technology.

FAQ. Abbreviation for Frequently Asked Questions. A document (often a hypertext document) containing common questions and answers for a particular website or topic. This list is especially prepared to help novice users to more quickly adapt to new standards of practice, especially in a chat room or listserv discussion.

File. Information stored on a magnetic media such as a disk which may contain a computer program, a document, or a collection of data.

Finger. Internet service that provides information about the users on a particular computer.

Freeware. Software that is available free of charge for personal use.

Flame. Personal verbal attacks on other Internet users, via e-mail, USENET, or mailing lists. Flame wars occur when a series of flames are sent back and forth between two or more people.

FTP. Short for "file transfer protocol." It's a system of rules for communicating over the Internet, and it allows you to transfer files to and download files from other computers. A browser such as Microsoft« Internet Explorer contains the tools you need to handle FTPs. So with Internet Explorer, you can download any file available on the Internet. Anonymous FTP allows you to connect to remote computers and to transfer publicly available computer files or programs.

Gateway. A computer system that connects two incompatible services such as a commercial online service and the Internet.

GIF. Graphical Interchange Format is a commonly used graphics file format for image files on the Internet.

Gopher. A play on the words "go for." A text menu-based browsing service on the Internet. The user selects an item on the menu and is led to either a file or another menu.

Hardware. Physical parts of a computer and its peripherals that you can touch (e.g., monitor, keyboard, hard disk, floppy drive).

Home page. The main page of hypertext-based information for an individual or organization on the World Wide Web (WWW).

HTML (Hypertext Markup Language). A programming language used to build Web sites. It contains standard codes, or tags, that determine how a Web page looks when your browser displays it. HTML tags also make possible the hyperlinks that connect information on the World Wide Web.

HTTP. Abbreviation for Hyper Text Transfer Protocol. Often this is the initial sequence of letters in a web address.

Interface. The connection between a computer and the person trying to use it. It can also be the connections required between computer systems so that communication and exchanges of data can take place.

Internaut. Slang for someone who is an experienced Internet user.

Internet address (a.k.a. IP address). An assigned series of numbers unique to each computer on the Internet which is used to identify it for data exchanges.

Intranet. Network internal to an organization that uses Internet protocols and browsers.

Internet. The worldwide, interconnected system of computer networks.

Internet Protocol (IP). A protocol that ensures data goes where it is supposed to go on the Internet.

Internet Relay Chat (IRC). An Internet service accessed through software programs that features real-time communication on channels devoted to specific topics.

ISP. Abbreviation for Internet Service Provider. A company that provides access to the Internet, such as a phone company or other commercial enterprises.

JAVA. An object-oriented programming language developed by Sun Microsystems to create applets, or programs that can be distributed as attachments to Web documents. An applet can be included in an HTML page, much as an image can be included. When you use a Java-capable browser to view a page containing a Java applet, the applet's code is transferred to your system and executed by the browser.

JPEG (Joint Photographic Experts Group). An image file format that is common to the Internet.

LAN. Abbreviation for Local Area Network. Used to connect computers over a short distance such as computers within the same organization, company, or office.

LISTSERV. An e-mail list server. A computer program that maintains lists of e-mail addresses in order that users can participate in an electronic discussion or conference. There are thousands of listserv on all imaginable topics.

Login/Logon. The process entering in information related to an account name and its password in order to access a time-sharing computer.

Logout/Logoff. A command that notifies the host computer that the user is ready to disconnect from the system.

Microsoft Internet Explorer. A graphical World Wide Web browser.

Modem. Acronym for modulator-demodulator. A modem is a device or program that enables a computer to transmit data over telephone lines. Modems may be internal or external to the computer case and are classified according to the speed (kps or kilobytes per second) with which they receive information (28.8kps, 36kps, 58.6kps).

Mosaic. A browser program developed by the National Center for Supercomputing Applications that provides the internet user with a point-and-click interface to WWW, Gopher, FTP, and other Internet services

Netiquette. The unwritten "rules" of etiquette used on the Internet.

Netscape. A graphical World Wide Web browser.

Network. A set of computers that all use the same protocol in order to exchange information among themselves.

Newbie. Slang for someone who is new to the Internet or a specific aspect of it.

Newsgroup. A discussion group that is related to one topic.

Password. Secret code of letters and numbers needed to gain access to a time-sharing computer or FTP system, or to protect Web pages.

Peripheral. A device that is attached to a computer, such as a monitor, keyboard, mouse, modem, printer, scanner, and speakers.

Posting. Can refer to a message or article that appears on a newsgroup or message board system, or the act of sending an electronic message to a newsgroup or message board.

PPP. Abbreviation for Point to Point Protocol. It is a protocol used for sending information via a modem which is connected to the Internet.

Protocol. The rules make possible the exchange of messages between users on the Internet, or within any given network.

Plug-in. A software component required by an Internet browser to expand its abilities. For example, LiveAudio is a Netscape plug-in that enables it to play audio.

Resolution. The clarity of the images produced on a monitor screen or printout.

Scripting. A programming shortcut that gives nontechnical users a way to create richer content on their computers and gives programmers a quick way to create simple applications. Scripting enables you to set and store variables, and work with data in your HTML code. Many Web sites now employ scripting to check the browser a user is running, validate input, work with applets or controls, and communicate to the user.

Search Engine. A tool or program which allows keyword searching for relevant sites or information on the Internet.

Shareware. Software distributed on the basis of an honor system. Most shareware is delivered free of charge, but the author usually requests that you pay a small fee if you like the program and use it regularly. By sending the small fee, you become registered with the producer so that you can receive service assistance and updates. You can copy shareware and pass it along to friends and colleagues, but they too are expected to pay a fee if they use the product.

SLIP. Stands for Serial Line Internet Protocol. Similar to PPP, this is another protocol that is used with a modem to establish an internet connection.

Smiley. A sideways happy face, made using text characters. It is generally used in e-mail to signify that the statement preceding it is a joke, or sarcasm, in an effort to prevent anyone from becoming offended. It is usually made with a colon, followed by a dash, and then a parentheses, e.g. :-) but there are endless variations.

Snail mail. Slang for regular, paper mail sent through the postal services (also surface mail).

Streaming Audio/Video. Media files on the Internet that play as they are being downloaded.

Suite. A collection of software programs (e.g., word processor, spreadsheet, presentation, database, and voice recognition) that are sold together and are supposed to work together efficiently and use similar commands.

TCP/IP. Short for Transmission Control Protocol/Internet Protocol. A group of protocols that specify how computers communicate over the Internet. All computers on the Internet need TCP/IP software.

Telnet. An Internet command that allows your computer to directly connect and interact with remote computers, often through a text-based 'terminal' environment. Often involves the need for passwords and access information.

Unix. A computer operating system developed by AT&T Bell Labs and used to develop the Internet. It is no longer the sole operating system used to run servers.

Upgrade. To install a higher version or release of software on a computer system, or too add memory or newer types of equipment to a computer system.

Upload. Transferring a file or files from the user's computer to a remote computer.

URL. Short for Uniform Resource Locator. A string of characters used to uniquely identify a page of information on the Web.

Usenet. A group of computers that exchange network news information.

Users. The people who use technology as a tool to do their jobs.

WAIS. Short for Wide Area Information Server. An Internet search service that locates documents containing a keyword or phrase.

WAN. Stands for Wide Area Network. A network of computers that covers a large geographical distance such as a state.

Whois. An Internet database that provides information on a person or an organization.

WWW. Stands for World Wide Web. A very popular Internet service that organizes information using a hypertext and hypermedia system of linking documents, FTP sites, gopher sites, WAIS, and telnet.

Other Terms That Have Circulated the Net And Have Become Part of the Net Culture Include:

404. Someone who's clueless. From the World Wide Web message "404, URL Not Found," meaning that the document you've tried to access can't be located. "Don't bother asking him...he's 404."

Alpha Geek. The most knowledgeable, technically proficient person in an office or work group. "Ask Russ, he's the alpha geek around here."

Cobweb Site. A World Wide Web Site that hasn't been updated for a long time. A dead web page.

Egosurfing. Scanning the net, databases, print media, or research papers looking for the mention of your name.

Elvis Year. The peak year of something's popularity. "Barney the dinosaur's Elvis year was 1993."

Keyboard Plaque. The disgusting buildup of dirt and crud found on computer keyboards. "Are there any other terminals I can use? This one has a bad case of keyboard plaque."

Tourists. People who are taking training classes just to get a vacation from their jobs. "We had about three serious students in the class; the rest were tourists."

World Wide Wait. The real meaning of WWW.

References

American Corporate Council Association. (1999). Available online: http://www.acca.com.

Arnold, A.M. (1998). Rape in cyberspace: Not just a fantasy. *Off Our Backs, 28(2)*, p. 12-13.

Associated Press. (May 31, 1998). *Study: Internet 'addicts' often show other disorders.*

Baggerly, J. (2002). Practical technological applications to promote pedagogical principles and active learning in counselor education. *Journal of Technology in Counseling, Vol 2(2)*, Available online: http://jtc.colstate.edu/vol2_2/baggerly/baggerly.htm.

Bevilacqua, A. (1997). *Computers and the law.* Available online: http://wings.buffalo.edu/Complaw/CompLawPapers/bevilacq.htm.

Bialo, E. R., & Sivin-Kachala, J. (1996). *The effectiveness of technology in schools: A summary of recent research.* Washington, DC: Software Publishers Association.

Bloom, J.W. (November, 1997). *NBCC WebCounseling Standards.* Alexandria, VA: Counseling Today. Available online: http://www.counseling.org/ctonline/archives/ct1197/webcounseling.htm.

Cairo, P. C., & Kanner, M. S. (1984). Investigating the effects of computerized approaches to counselor training. *Counselor Education and Supervision, 24*, p. 212-221.

Caplan, S. E. (2002). Problematic Internet use and psychosocial well-being: Development of a theory-based cognitive-behavioral measurement instrument. *Computers in Human Behavior, Vol. 18(5)*, p. 553-575.

Casey, J. A., Bloom, J. W., & Moan, E. R. (1994). Use of technology in counselor supervision. In L. D. Borders (Ed.), *Counseling supervision*. Greensboro: University of North Carolina, ERIC Clearinghouse on Counseling and Student Services. (ERIC Document Reproduction Service No. ED 372 357)

Casey, J. A. (1999). Computer assisted simulation for counselor training of basic skills. *Journal of Technology in Counseling, Vol 1(1)*, Available online: http://jtc.colstate.edu/vol1_1/simulation.htm.

Center for Applied Special Technology. (1996). *The role of online communications in schools: A national study.* Peabody, MA: CAST. Available online: http://www.cast.org/udl/OnlineExec.RTF.

Chapman, W., & Katz, M. R. (1983). Career information systems in the secondary schools: A survey and assessment. *Vocational Guidance Quarterly, 32*, p. 165-177.

Childress, C. (1998). *The risks and benefits of online therapeutic interventions.* Online symposia for the 1998 APA.

Christie, B.S. (Retrieved June 21, 2002). *Counseling supervisees experiences of distance clinical supervision.* Available online: http://cybercounsel.uncg.edu/book/manuscripts/tenets.htm.

Clark, Gr. (2000). Interactive career counseling on the Internet. *Journal of Career Assessment, Vol 8(1)*, p. 85-93.

Cohen, L. (1998). *Conducting research on the Internet.* Available online: http://www.albany.edu/cetl/resources/gradstud/research.html

Coursol, D., & Lewis, J. (Retrieved June 21, 2002). *Cybersupervision: Close encounters in the new millennium.* Available online http://cybercounsel.uncg.edu/book/manuscripts/cybersupervision.htm.

D'Andrea, M. (1995). Using computer technology to promote multicultural awareness among elementary school-age students. *Elementary School Guidance & Counseling, 30(1)*, p. 45-55.

Delmonico, D.L., Daninhirsch, C., Page, B., Walsh, J., L'Amoreaux, N.A., & Thompson, R.S. (2000). The Palace: Participant responses to a virtual support group. *Journal of Technology in Counseling, Vol. 1(2),* Available online: http://jtc.colstate.edu/vol1_2/palace.htm.

Fargen, T. (1996). Surfing the Internet in gym class: Physical education E-mail KeyPals. *Teaching & Change, 3(3)*, p. 272-281.

Federal Trade Commission. (2003). *ID Theft.* Available online http://www.consumer.gov/idtheft/.

Finn, J. (1995). Computer-based self-help groups: A new resource to supplement support groups. *Social Work with Groups, 18(1)*, p. 109-117.

Fox, R. & Straw, J. (1998). Student cyberaddiction ... *Communications of the ACM, Vol. 41(3)*, p. 11-14.

Freeman-Longo, R. E. (2000). Children, teens, and sex on the Internet. *Sexual Addiction & Compulsivity, Vol. 7(1-2)*, p. 75-90.

Froehle, T. C. (1984). Computer-assisted feedback in counseling supervision. *Counselor Education and Supervision, 24*, p. 168-175.

Fulton, D. (August, 1998). E-rate: A resource guide for educators. ERIC Clearinghouse on Information & Technology, Available online: http://ericir.syr.edu.

Gary, J.M. (2001). *Impact of cultural and global issues on online support groups.* ERIC Digest CG-01-01. Available online: http://ericcass.uncg.edu/digest/2001-01.html.

Gerler, E. (1995). Advancing elementary and middle school counseling through computer technology. *Elementary School Guidance & Counseling, 30(1)*. p. 8-15.

Gilster, P. (1997). *Digital literacy.* New York: Wiley.

Glover, B. L. (1995). DINOS (drinking is not our solution): Using computer programs in middle school drug education. Elementary School *Guidance & Counseling, 30(1)*, p. 55-62.

Grassian, E. (1998). *Thinking critically about world wide web resources.* UCLA College Library. Available online: http://www.library.ucla.edu/libraries/college/help/critical.

Grumman, C. (June 26, 1996). *HTTP: www.help logged on, tuned in and hooked on the Internet: There are those who just can't stop surfing.* Chicago Tribune, p. 1.

Hansen, S. (2002). Excessive Internet usage or Internet addiction?: The implications of diagnostic categories for student users. *Journal of Computer Assisted Learning, Vol. 18(2)*, p. 232-236.

Haring-Hidore, M. (1984). In pursuit of students who do not use computers for career guidance. *Journal of Counseling and Development, 63*, p. 139-140.

Harris-Bowlsbey, J. (2001). Computer-based career planning systems: Dreams and realities. *Career Development Quarterly, Vol 49(3)*, p. 250-260.

Harris, J. (1972). *Computer-assisted guidance systems.* Washington, DC: National Vocational Guidance Association.

Howard, S., & Hall, M.N. (2000). Computer addiction: A critical consideration. *American Journal of Orthopsychiatry, Vol. 70(2)*, p. 162-168.

Indiana's fourth grade project: Model applications of technology. Second Year, 1989-90. (1990). Indiana State Department of Education. Indianapolis: Advanced Technology, Inc. Available online: http://www.buddynet.net/ (version current as of April 1998).

Jedlicka, D. & Jennings, G. (2001). Marital therapy on the Internet. *Journal of Technology in Counseling, Vol. 2(1)*, Available online: http://jtc.colstate.edu/vol2_1/Marital.htm.

Jencius, M. & Sager, D. E. (2001). The practice of marriage and family counseling in cyberspace. *Family Journal, Vol. 9(3)*, p. 295-301.

Jones, K. D. & Karper, C. (2000) How to develop an online course in counseling techniques. *Journal of Technology in Counseling, Vol 1(2)*, Available online: http://jtc.colstate.edu/vol1_2/online.htm.

Kulik, J.A. (1994). Meta-analytic studies of findings on computer-based instruction. In E.L. Baker and H.F. O'Neil, Jr. (Eds.), *Technology assessment in education and training.* Hillsdale, NJ: Lawrence Erlbaum.

Lago, C. (1996). Computer therapeutics. *Counselling, 7*, p. 287-289.

Guangzhou, J. (2002). *Outlining proper uses going online.* Available online: http://www1.chinadaily.com.cn/cndy/2002-05-20/70278.html.

Lamb, G. M. (2003). Online gambling: Where it stops, nobody knows. *Christian Science Monitor.* Available online: http://newsobserver.com/24hour/technology/story/727138p-5316450c.html.

LaQuey, T. (1994). *The Internet companion: A beginner's guide to global networking (2nd edition)* Available online: http://www.obs-us.com/obs/english/books/editinc/top.htm.

Lumsden, J. A., Garis, J. W., Reardon, R. C., Unger, M. P., & Arkin, S. (2001). A blueprint for building an online career portfolio. *Journal of Career Planning & Employment, Vol. 62(1)*, p. 33-40.

Magid, L. (1996). *Yahooligans Rules for Online Safety.* Available online: http://www.yahooligans.com.

McFadden, J. (2000). Computer-mediated technology and transcultural counselor education. *Journal of Technology in Counseling, Vol 1(2)*, Available online: http://jtc.colstate.edu/vol1_2/transcult.html.

Myrick, R. D., & Sabella, R. A. (1995). Cyberspace: New place for counselor supervision. *Elementary School Guidance & Counseling, 30(1)*, p. 35-44.

National Center for Education Statistics. (2002). *Internet access in U.S. public schools and classrooms: 1994–2001.* Available online: http://nces.ed.gov/pubs2002/2002018.pdf.

National Telecommunications and Information Administration. (2002). *A nation online: How Americans are expanding their use of the Internet.* Washington, D.C.: Author.

Neukrug, E. S. (1991). Computer-assisted live supervision in counselor skills training. *Counselor Education and Supervision, 31*, p. 132-138.

Offer, M., & Sampson, J. P., Jr. (1999). Quality in the content and use of information and communications technology in guidance. *British Journal of Guidance and Counseling, 27*, p. 501-516.

Pacienza, A. (November 14, 2002). *Online shoppers battle addiction; People can't control their compulsions.* Toronto: The Edmonton Sun.

President's information technology advisory committee interim report to the president (August, 1998). National Coordination Office for computing, Information, and Communications, 4201 Wilson Blvd., Suite 690, Arlington, VA 22230, 703-306-4722.

Pyle, K. R. (1984). Career counseling and computers: Where is the creativity? *Journal of Counseling and Development, 63*, p. 141-144.

Robson, D. (2000). Ethical issues in Internet counselling. *Counselling Psychology Quarterly, Vol. 13(3)*, p. 249-257.

Katz, M. R., & Shatkin, L. (1983). Characteristics of computer-assisted guidance. *The Counseling Psychologist, 11(4)*, p. 15-31.

Kivlighan, D. M., Jr., Johnston, J. A., Hogan, R. S., & Mauer, E. (1994). Who benefits from computerized career counseling? *Journal of Counseling & Development, 72*, p. 289-292.

Rogers, C.R., (1957). The necessary and sufficient conditions of therapeutic personality change. *Journal of Consulting Psychology, 21,* p. 95-103.

Rust, E. B. (1995). Applications of the International Counselor Network for elementary and middle school counseling. *Elementary School Guidance & Counseling, 30(1),* p. 16-25.

Sabella, R.A. (2000). School counseling and technology. In Wittmer, J. *Managing your school counseling program: K-12 developmental strategies (second edition).* Minneapolis, MN: Educational Media Corporation.

Sabella, R.A. (September/October, 2001). *E-learning.* ASCA School Counselor. Alexandria, VA: ASCA School Counselor.

Sabella, R.A. & Halverson, B. (In press). *Building virtual communities in school counseling.* ERIC digest.

Sabella, R.A. & Booker, B. (in review). *Using technology to promote your guidance and counseling program among stake holders.*

Sampson, J. P., Jr., & Krumboltz, J. D. (1991). Computer-assisted instruction: A missing link in counseling. *Journal of Counseling & Development, 69,* p. 395-397.

Sampson, J.P., Kolodinsky, R.W., & Greeno, B.P. (1997). Counseling on the information highway: Future possibilities and potential problems. *Journal of Counseling and Development, 75(3),* p. 203-212.

Sampson, J.P., Norris, D.S., Wilde, C.K., Slatten, M.L., and Reardon, R.C. (1998). *Computer-assisted career guidance: Disability issues bibliography.* Available online http://icdl.uncg.edu/ft/060100-04.html.

Sampson, J. P., Jr. (1990). Computer-assisted testing and the goals of counseling psychology. *The Counseling Psychologist, 18,* p. 227-239.

Sampson, J. P., Jr. (1999a). *Effective design and use of Internet-based career resources and services.* IAEVG (International Association for Educational and Vocational Guidance) Bulletin, 63, p. 4-12.

Sampson, J.P. (Retrieved October 14, 2002). *Intelligent Access and Use of Assessment and Information Resources to Promote Career Development.* Available online: http://www.pt3.org/VQ/html/sampson.html.

Sanders, P., & Rosenfield, M. (1998). Counselling at a distance: Challenges and new initiatives. *British Journal of Guidance & Counselling, 26(1),* p. 5-10.

Schnieders, H.L. (Retrieved June 21, 2002). *From a bug in the ear to a byte in the eye: Implications for Internet-delivered, live counselor supervision.* Available online: http://cybercounsel.uncg.edu/book/manuscripts/Schnieders.htm.

Schrock, K. (1998). *Evaluation of world wide web Sites: An annotated bibliography.* ERIC Clearinghouse on Information & Technology. Available online: http://ericit.org.

Sharf, R. S., & Lucas, M. (1993). An assessment of a computerized simulation of counseling skills. *Counselor Education and Supervision, 32,* p. 254-266.

Shulman, H. A., Sweeney, B., & Gerler, E. R. (1995). A computer-assisted approach to preventing alcohol abuse: Implications for the middle school. *Elementary School Guidance & Counseling, 30(1),* p. 63-77.

Solomon, D. J. (2001). Conducting web-based surveys. *Practical Assessment, Research & Evaluation, 7(19).* Available online: http://ericae.net/pare/getvn.asp?v=7&n=19.

Stone, C. B, & Turba, R. (1999). School counselors using technology for advocacy. *Journal of Technology in Counseling, Vol. 1(1).* Available online: http://jtc.colstate.edu/vol1_1/advocacy.htm.

Suler, J. (1999). *The psychology of cyberspace.* Available online: http://www.rider.edu/users/suler/psycyber/psycyber.html.

Suler, J.R. (1999). To get what you need: Healthy and pathological Internet use. *CyberPsychology and Behavior, 2,* p. 385-394.

Sullivan, D. (1998). *Search engine watch.* Available online: http://searchenginewatch.com

Russell A. Sabella, Ph.D.

Sullivan, D. (2002). *How search engines work.* Available online: http://searchenginewatch.com/webmasters/work.html.

Templeton, B. (Retrieved January 22, 2003). *10 big myths about copyright explained.* Available online: http://www.templetons.com/brad/copymyths.html.

Thomas, L.G., & Knezek, D.G. (1998). *Technology literacy for the nation and for its citizens.* International Society for Technology in Education. Available online: http://www.iste.org.

Thompson, S. H. (November 3, 2002). *Clicking the habit.* Tampa, FL: The Tampa Tribune.

Tsai, C. L., & Sunny, S. J. (2001). Analysis of attitudes toward computer networks and Internet addiction of Taiwanese adolescents. *CyberPsychology & Behavior, Vol. 4(3)*, p. 373-376.

Tyler, J.M. (January, 2000). *Computer-mediated group counseling: A demonstration.* Program presented at the annual meting of the Association for Specialists in Group Work, Deerfield Beach, FL.

U.S. Department of Commerce. (2000). *Falling through the net: Toward digital inclusion.* Available online: http://search.ntia.doc.gov/pdf/fttn00.pdf.

United States Internet Council (USIC) & International Technology and Trade Associates (ITTA) Inc. (2000). *State of the Internet.* Washington, D.C.: Authors. Available online: http://www.usinternetcouncil.org/papers/stateoftheinternet2000/intro.html.

Using the Internet, for teachers, schools, students; an introduction. (1997). Available on-line http://www.geocities.com/Athens/4610/.

Walz, G. R. (1996). Using the I-Way for career development. In R. Feller & G. Walz (Eds.), *Optimizing life transitions in turbulent times: Exploring work, learning and careers.* Greensboro: University of North Carolina, ERIC Clearinghouse on Counseling and Student Services. p. 415-427.

Webopedia. (1999). *Online encyclopedia.* Available online: http://webopedia.internet.com.

Webopedia. (2003). *Online encyclopedia.* Available online: http://webopedia.internet.com.

WebsiteJournal. (November 10,1998) Vol. 1(9). Available online: http://www.WebSiteJournal.com.

WebReference. (1998). *What makes a great website?* Available online: http://www.webreference.com/greatsite.html.

Weinberg, N., Uken, J.S., Schmale, J., & Adamek, M. (1995). Therapeutic factors: Their presence in a computer-mediated support group. *Social Work with Groups, 18(4)*, p. 57-69.

Weinraub, M. (April 16, 1998). *Online divide exists between blacks, whites — study.* Reuters International. Available online: http://www.reuters.com.

Willard, N. (1996). *A legal and educational analysis of k-12 internet acceptable use policies.* Available online: http://www.erehwon.com/k12aup/legal_analysis.html.

Wong, Y, & Law, C. (Retrieved June 21, 2002). *Online counseling for the youth in Hong Kong: A synchronized approach.* Available online http://www2.uta.edu/cussn/husita/proposals/wong.htm.

Woodford, M. S., Rokutani, L., Gressard, C., & Berg, L. B. (2001). Sharing the course: An experience with collaborative distance learning in counseling education. *Journal of Technology in Counseling, Vol. 2(1)*, Available online: http://jtc.colstate.edu/vol2_1/Sharing.htm.

Young, K.S. (1998). *Caught in the net: How to recognize the signs of Internet addiction—and a winning strategy for recovery.* New York: John Wiley & Sons.

Virginia Department of Education Division of Technology. *Acceptable use policies: A handbook.* (Retrieved January 22, 2003). Available online: http://www.pen.k12.va.us/go/VDOE/Technology/AUP/home.shtml.

Russell A. Sabella, Ph.D.

Recommended Readings

ACES (Association for Counselor Education and Supervision) Technology Interest Network. (1999). *Technical competencies for counselor education students: Recommended guidelines for program development.* Available online: http://filebox.vt.edu/users/thohen/competencies.htm.

Ainsworth, M. (Retrieved June 21, 2002). *How to choose a competent counselor.* Available online: http://www.metanoia.org/.

Bleuer, J. C., & Walz, G. R. (1983). *Counselors and computers.* Ann Arbor: ERIC/CAPS. The University of Michigan.

Bloom, J.W. (November, 1997). *NBCC WebCounseling Standards.* Alexandria, VA: Counseling Today. Available online:: http://www.counseling.org/ctonline/archives/ct1197/webcounseling.htm.

Brent, E. E., & Anderson, R. E. (1990). *Computer applications in the social sciences.* Philadelphia: Temple University Press.

Cabannis, K. (2002). Computer-related technology use by counselors in the new millennium: A delphi study. *Journal of Technology in Counseling, Vol. 2(2).* Available online: http://jtc.colstate.edu/vol2_2/cabaniss/cabaniss.htm.

Campbell, T. (March/April, 1998). *The first e-mail message.* Pretext Magazine. Available online: http://www.pretext.com/mar98/.

Croft, V. (1991). *Technological literacy: Refined for the profession, applications for the classroom.* Unpublished paper presented at the 1991 annual conference of the International Technology Education Association.

Garcia, R.A. (April 02, 2002) *Writing e-mail about problems can improve health.* Texas A&M University. Available online: http://www.newswise.com/articles/2002/4/EXPRESS.TXM.html.

Getting America's Students Ready for the 21st Century: Meeting the Technology Literacy Challenge — June 1996 Available online: http://www.ed.gov/Technology/Plan/NatTechPlan/priority.html.

Greenwood, A. (2000). How the net can make a difference. *New Statesman, Vol. 129(4494),* p. 24-26.

Gross, N. (March 22, 1999). Building global communities. *Business Week, Issue 3621,* p. EB42.

Hayden, M. (1989). What is technological literacy? *Bulletin of Science, Technology and Society, 119,* p. 220-233.

Holden, G., Bearison, D.J., Rode, D.C., Rosenberg, G., & Fishman, M. (1999). Evaluating the effects of a virtual environment (STARBRIGHT World) with hospitalized children. *Research on Social Work Practice, Vol. 9(3),* p. 365-382.

Horrigan, J.B. (2001). *Online communities: Networks that nurture long-distance relationships and local ties.* Washington, D.C.: Pew Internet & American Life Project. Available online: http://www.pewinternet.org/reports/pdfs/PIP_Communities_Report.pdf.

Hughes, R.S. (2000). *Ethics and regulations of cybercounseling.* ERIC digest EDO-CG-00-3. Available online: http://ericcass.uncg.edu/digest/2000-03.html.

ICD. (September 20, 2001). *36 million e-mails per day by 2005*. Retrieved June 6, 2002 (http://www.e-gateway.net/infoarea/news/news.cfm?nid=1876)

Internet parental control frequently asked questions (FAQ). (May 22, 1998). Voters telecommunications watch. Available online:: http://www.vtw.org/ipcfaq

Isaacs, M. & Sabella, R.A. (September/October, 2002). *For better or for worse: Technology and the family.* ASCA School Counselor, p. 10-11.

ITEA, 2000. *Standards for technological literacy: Content for the study of technology.* International Technology Education Association. Available online: http://www.iteawww.org/TAA/PDF/xstnd.pdf.

Kahn, J. (February 7, 2000). Creating an online community — and a market — for the disabled. *Fortune, Vol. 141(3),* p. 188-190.

Kehus, M.J. (2000). Opportunities for teenagers to share their writing online. *Journal of Adolescent & Adult Literacy, Vol. 44(2),* p. 130-137.

Kommers, N., & Rainie, L. (2002). *Use of the internet at major life moments.* Washington, D.C.: Pew Internet & American Life Project. Available online: http://www.pewinternet.org/reports/pdfs/PIP_Major_Moments_Report.pdf.

Koufman-Frederick, A., Lillie, M., Pattison-Gordon, L., Watt, D.L., & Carter, R. (1999). *Electronic Collaboration: A Practical Guide for Educators.* Providence, RI: The LAB at Brown University. Available online: www.lab.brown.edu.

Leibowitz, W.R. (1999). Alumni offices use electronic media to forge closer ties with graduates. *Chronicle of Higher Education, Vol. 46(8),* pA45

Lindsay, G. (1988). Techniques and technology—Strengthening the counseling profession via computer use: Responding to the issues. *The School Counselor, 35,* 325-330.

Lucas, S. (October 18, 1999). CBS builds interactive web communities. *Brandweek, Vol. 40(39),* p. 61-64.

Lundberg, D.J., & Cobitz, C.I. (1999). Use of technology in counseling assessment: A survey of practices, views, and outlook. *Journal of Technology in Counseling, Vol. 1(1).* Available online: http://jtc.colstate.edu/vol1_1/assessment.htm.

Massy, W.F., & Zemsky, R. (1995). *Using information technology to enhance academic productivity.* EDUCOM: Wingspread Enhancing Academic Productivity Conference. Available online: http://www.educause.edu/nlii/keydocs/massy.html.

Microsoft in Education PowerPoint Tutorial. Retrieved June 5, 2001 from http://www.microsoft.com/education/tutorial/classroom/o2k/ppt.asp.

Mitchell, P. (2000). Internet addiction: Genuine diagnosis or not? *Lancet, Vol. 355(9204),* p. 632-633.

Moersch, C. (1995). *Levels of technology implementation (LoTi): A framework for measuring classroom technology use.* Available online: http://www.learning-quest.com/software/LoTiFrameworkNov95.pdf.

Murphy, L.J., & Mitchell, D.L. (1998). When writing helps to heal: E-mail as therapy. *British Journal of Guidance & Counselling, Vol. 26(1),* p. 21-32.

Ookita, S., & Tokuda, H. (2001). Virtual therapeutic environment with user projective agents. *CyberPsychology & Behavior, Vol. 4(1),* p. 155-167.

Oravec, J.A. (2000). Internet and computer technology hazards: Perspectives for family counselling. *British Journal of Guidance & Counselling, Vol. 28(3),* p. 309-414.

Pratarelli, M.E., & Browne, B.L. (1999). The bits and bytes of computer/Internet addiction: A factor analytic approach. *Behavior Research Methods, Instruments, & Computers, Vol. 31(2),* p. 305-314.

Robson, D., & Robson, M. (1998). Intimacy and computer communication. *British Journal of Guidance & Counselling, 26(1),* p. 33-41.